BBC

DOCTOR WHO

PRISONERS OF TIME

VOLUME 1

DOCTOR WHO
PRISONERS OF TIME
VOLUME 1

Cover by
FRANCESCO FRANCAVILLA
Collection Edits by
JUSTIN EISINGER and
ALONZO SIMON
Collection Design by
TOM B. LONG

1ST **DOCTOR**
1963 - 1966

2ND **DOCTO**
1966 -

ISBN: 978-1-61377-653-7   16 15 14 13   1 2 3 4

IDW founded by Ted Adams, Alex Garner, Kris Oprisko, and Robbie Robbins

IDW®

Ted Adams, CEO & Publisher
Greg Goldstein, President & COO
Robbie Robbins, EVP/Sr. Graphic Artist
Chris Ryall, Chief Creative Officer/Editor-in-Chief
Matthew Ruzicka, CPA, Chief Financial Officer
Alan Payne, VP of Sales
Dirk Wood, VP of Marketing
Lorelei Bunjes, VP of Digital Services

Special thanks to Kate Bush, Georgie Britton,
Caroline Skinner, Richard Cookson, and Ed Casey
at BBC Worldwide for their invaluable assistance.

DOCTOR WHO: PRISONERS OF TIME, VOLUME 1. MAY 2013. FIRST PRINTING. BBC, DOCTOR WHO (word marks, logos and devices) and TARDIS are trade marks of the British Broadcasting Corporation and are used under license. BBC logo © BBC 1996. Doctor Who logo © BBC 2009. TARDIS image © BBC 1963. Cybermen image © BBC/Kit Pedler/Gerry Davis 1966. IDW Publishing, a division of Idea and Design Works, LLC. Editorial offices: 5080 Santa Fe Street, San Diego CA 92109. Any similarities to persons living or dead are purely coincidental. With the exception of artwork used for review purposes, none of the contents of this publication may be reprinted without the permission of Idea and Design Works, LLC. Printed in Korea. IDW Publishing does not read or accept unsolicited submissions of ideas, stories, or artwork.

Originally published as DOCTOR WHO: PRISONERS OF TIME Issues #1–4.

Written by
SCOTT & DAVID TIPTON

Art by
SIMON FRASER, LEE SULLIVAN, MIKE COLLINS, and **GARY ERSKINE**

Colors by
GARY CALDWELL, PHIL ELLIOTT, and **CHARLIE KIRCHOFF**

Letters by
TOM B. LONG

Series Edits by
DENTON J. TIPTON

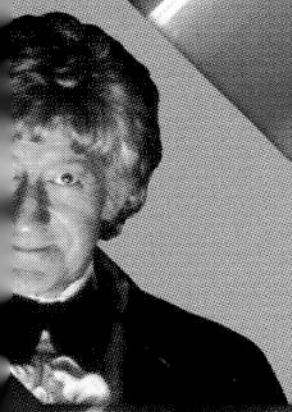

3RD DOCTOR
1970 - 1974

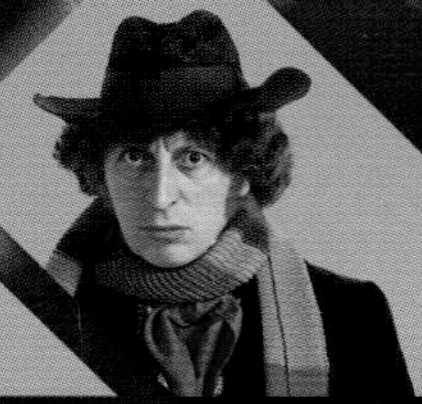

4TH DOCTOR
1974 - 1981

CHAPTER I
"Unnatural Selection"
Cover Art by Francesco Francavilla

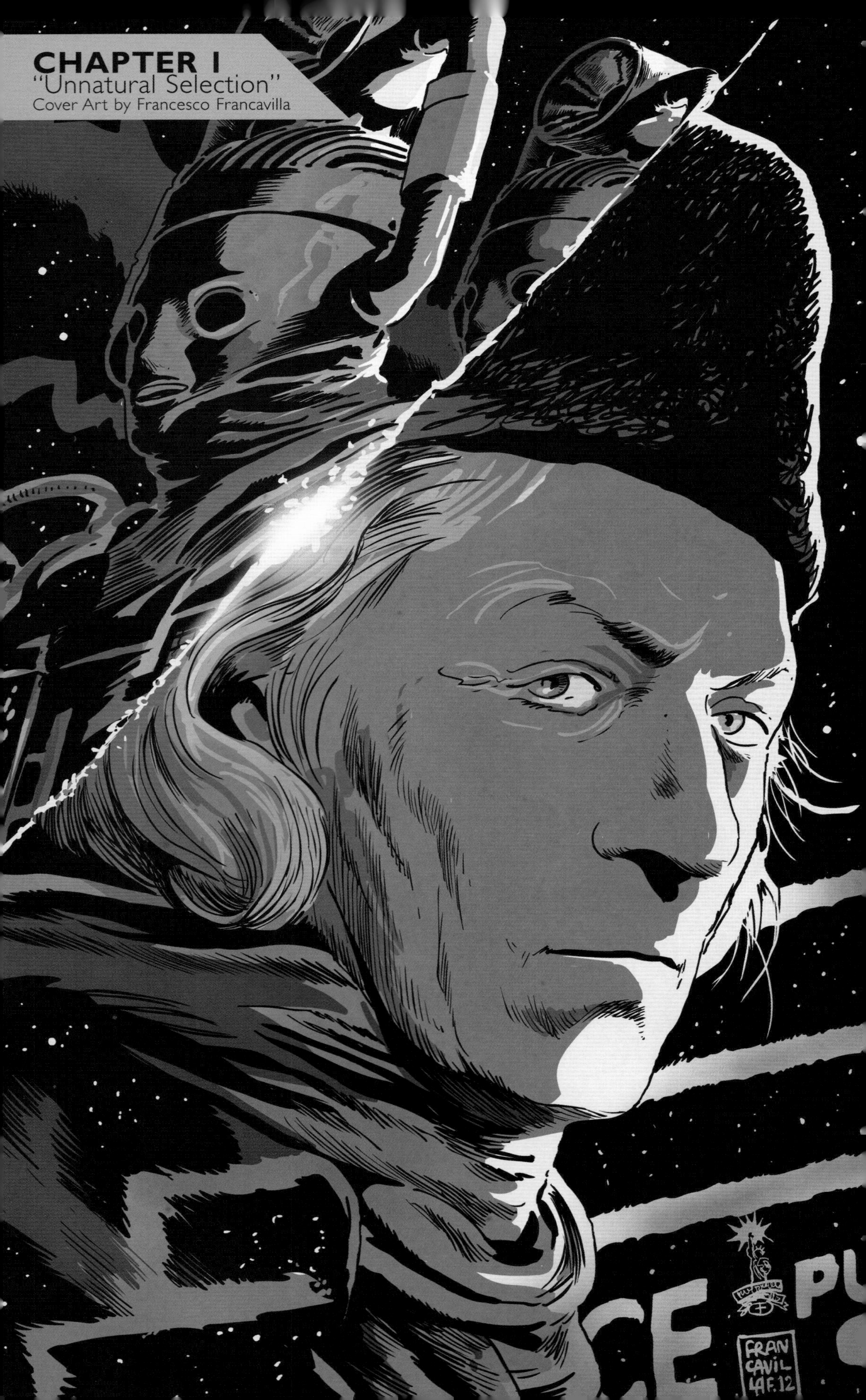
FRAN
CAVIL
LA F. 12

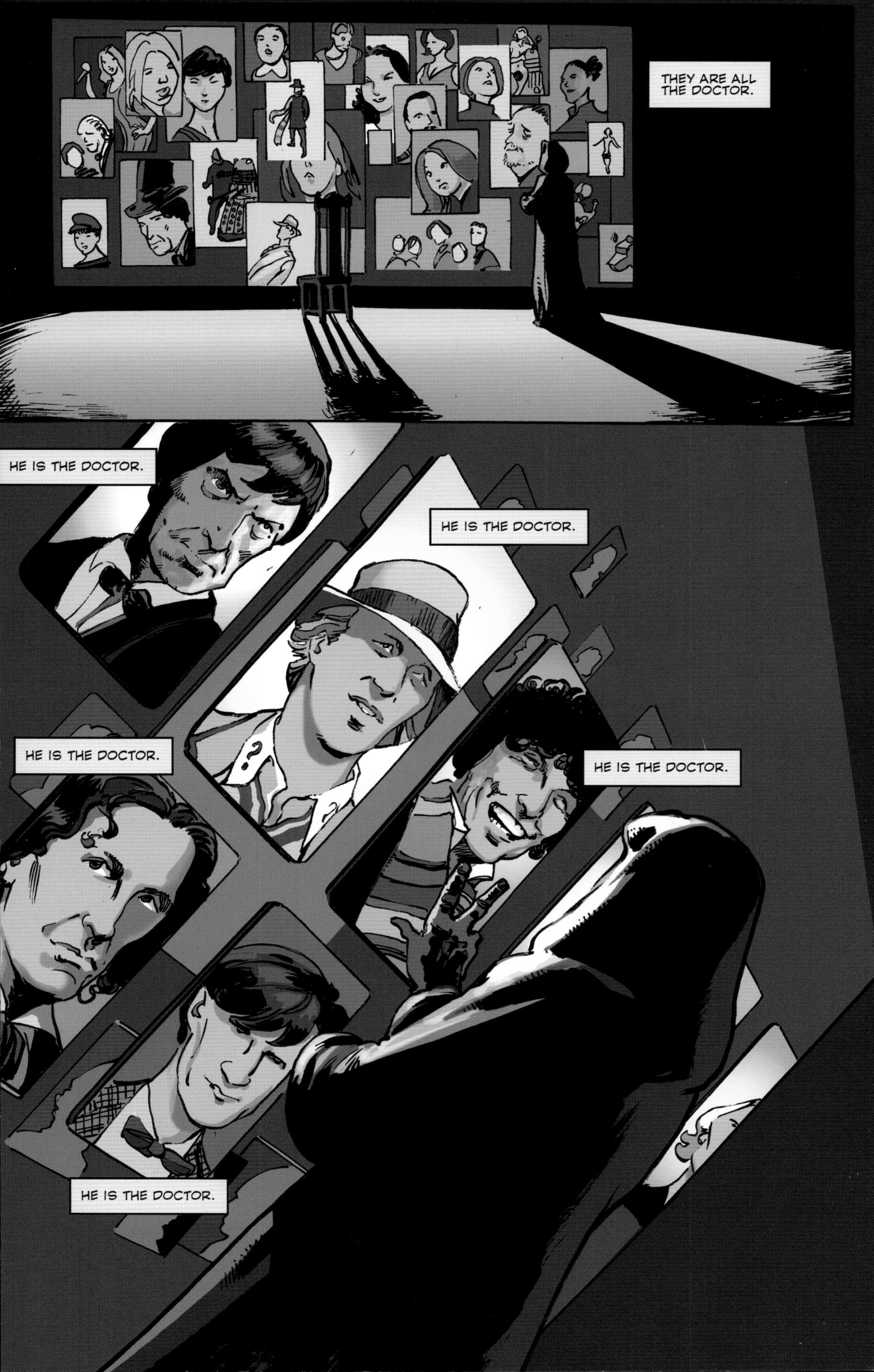
THEY ARE ALL THE DOCTOR.
HE IS THE DOCTOR.
HE IS THE DOCTOR.
HE IS THE DOCTOR.
HE IS THE DOCTOR.
HE IS THE DOCTOR.

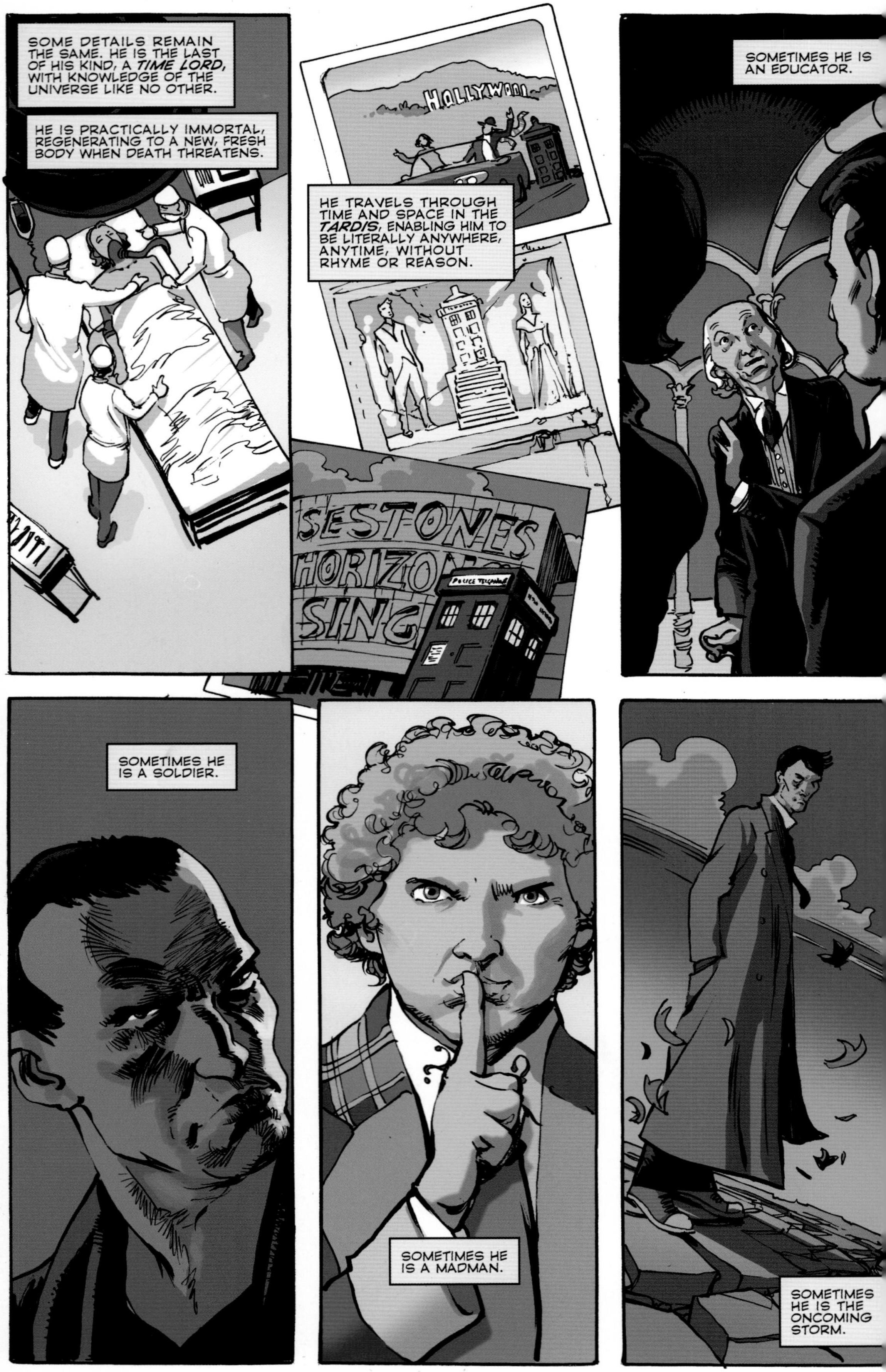

SOME DETAILS REMAIN THE SAME. HE IS THE LAST OF HIS KIND, A *TIME LORD*, WITH KNOWLEDGE OF THE UNIVERSE LIKE NO OTHER.
HE IS PRACTICALLY IMMORTAL, REGENERATING TO A NEW, FRESH BODY WHEN DEATH THREATENS.
HE TRAVELS THROUGH TIME AND SPACE IN THE *TARDIS*, ENABLING HIM TO BE LITERALLY ANYWHERE, ANYTIME, WITHOUT RHYME OR REASON.
SOMETIMES HE IS AN EDUCATOR.
SOMETIMES HE IS A SOLDIER.
SOMETIMES HE IS A MADMAN.
SOMETIMES HE IS THE ONCOMING STORM.

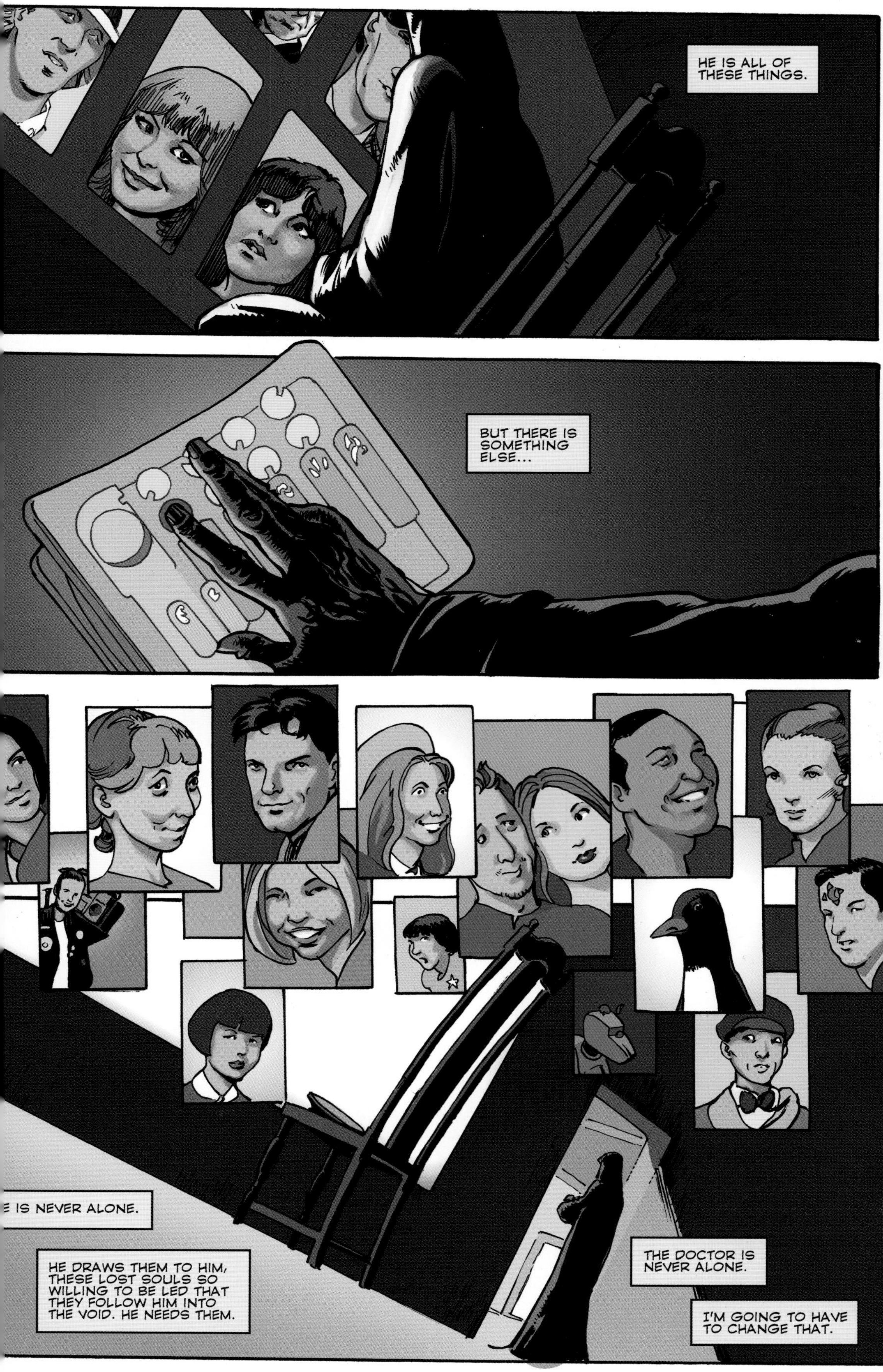
HE IS ALL OF THESE THINGS.
BUT THERE IS SOMETHING ELSE...
E IS NEVER ALONE.
HE DRAWS THEM TO HIM, THESE LOST SOULS SO WILLING TO BE LED THAT THEY FOLLOW HIM INTO THE VOID. HE NEEDS THEM.
THE DOCTOR IS NEVER ALONE.
I'M GOING TO HAVE TO CHANGE THAT.

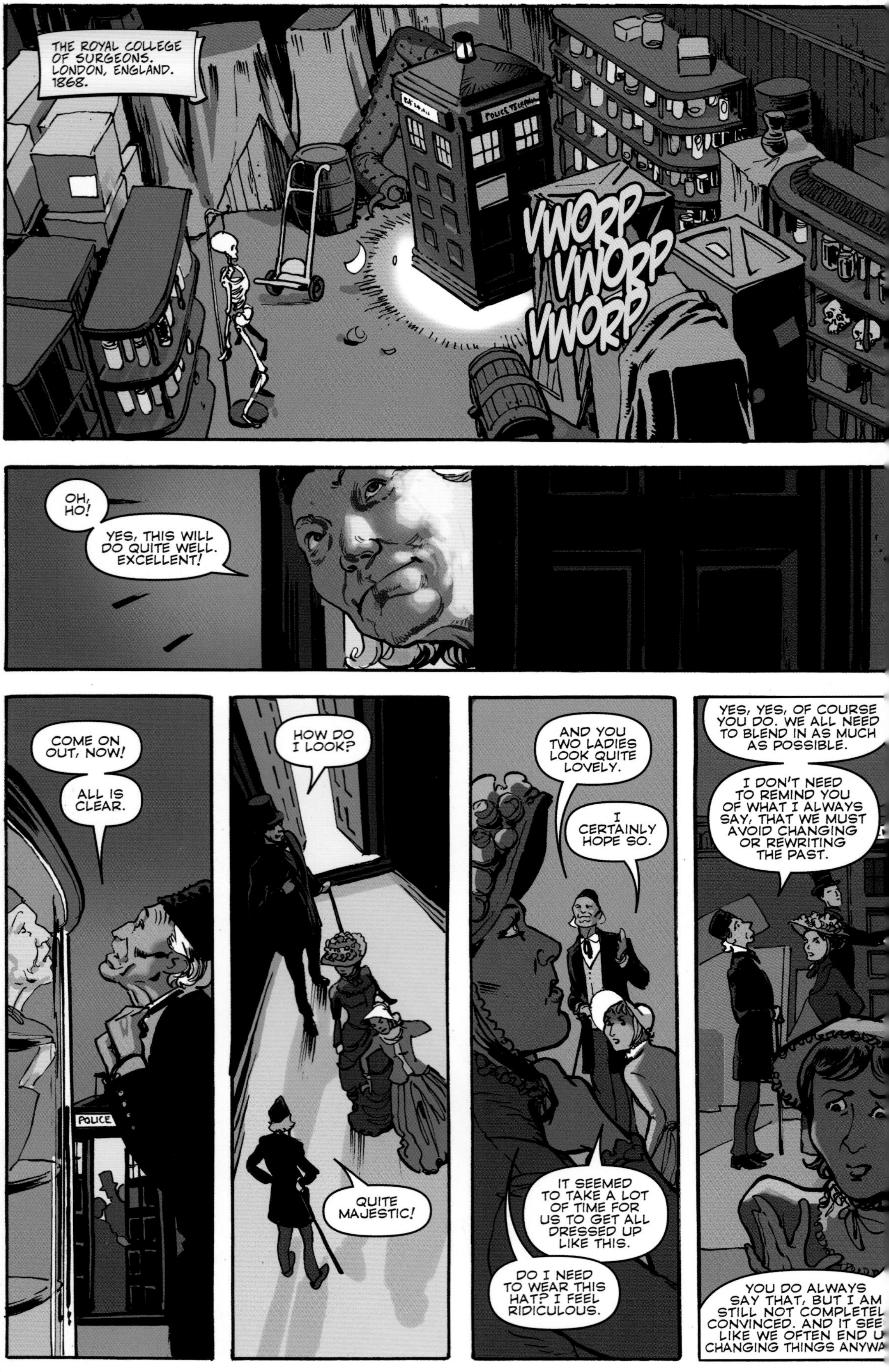
THE ROYAL COLLEGE OF SURGEONS. LONDON, ENGLAND. 1868.
VWORP VWORP VWORP
OH, HO!
YES, THIS WILL DO QUITE WELL. EXCELLENT!
COME ON OUT, NOW!
ALL IS CLEAR.
POLICE
HOW DO I LOOK?
QUITE MAJESTIC!
AND YOU TWO LADIES LOOK QUITE LOVELY.
I CERTAINLY HOPE SO.
IT SEEMED TO TAKE A LOT OF TIME FOR US TO GET ALL DRESSED UP LIKE THIS.
DO I NEED TO WEAR THIS HAT? I FEEL RIDICULOUS.
YES, YES, OF COURSE YOU DO. WE ALL NEED TO BLEND IN AS MUCH AS POSSIBLE.
I DON'T NEED TO REMIND YOU OF WHAT I ALWAYS SAY, THAT WE MUST AVOID CHANGING OR REWRITING THE PAST.
YOU DO ALWAYS SAY THAT, BUT I AM STILL NOT COMPLETEL CONVINCED. AND IT SEE LIKE WE OFTEN END U CHANGING THINGS ANYWA

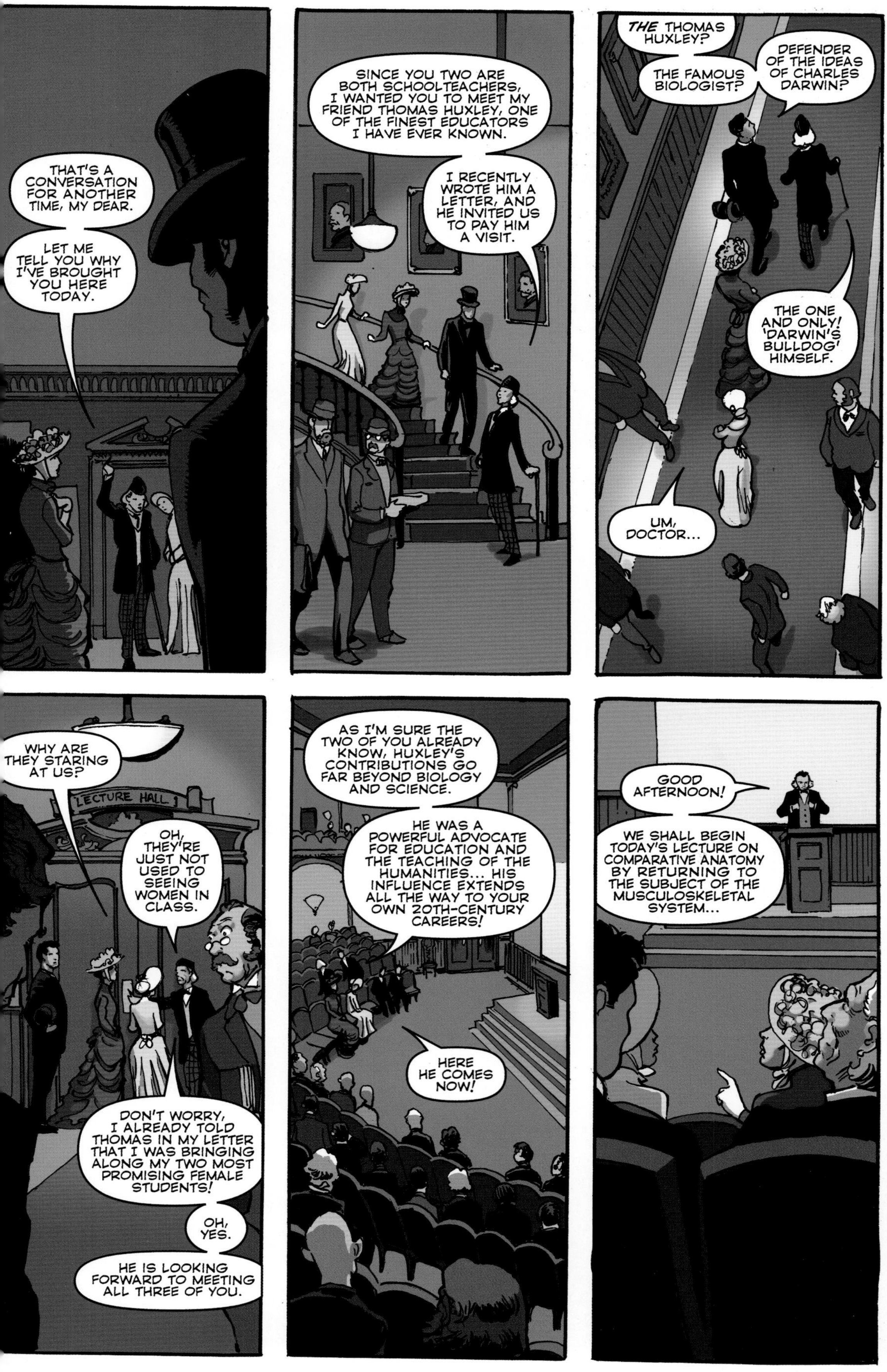
THAT'S A CONVERSATION FOR ANOTHER TIME, MY DEAR.
LET ME TELL YOU WHY I'VE BROUGHT YOU HERE TODAY.
SINCE YOU TWO ARE BOTH SCHOOLTEACHERS, I WANTED YOU TO MEET MY FRIEND THOMAS HUXLEY, ONE OF THE FINEST EDUCATORS I HAVE EVER KNOWN.
I RECENTLY WROTE HIM A LETTER, AND HE INVITED US TO PAY HIM A VISIT.
THE THOMAS HUXLEY?
THE FAMOUS BIOLOGIST?
DEFENDER OF THE IDEAS OF CHARLES DARWIN?
THE ONE AND ONLY! 'DARWIN'S BULLDOG' HIMSELF.
UM, DOCTOR...
WHY ARE THEY STARING AT US?
LECTURE HALL
OH, THEY'RE JUST NOT USED TO SEEING WOMEN IN CLASS.
DON'T WORRY, I ALREADY TOLD THOMAS IN MY LETTER THAT I WAS BRINGING ALONG MY TWO MOST PROMISING FEMALE STUDENTS!
OH, YES.
HE IS LOOKING FORWARD TO MEETING ALL THREE OF YOU.
AS I'M SURE THE TWO OF YOU ALREADY KNOW, HUXLEY'S CONTRIBUTIONS GO FAR BEYOND BIOLOGY AND SCIENCE.
HE WAS A POWERFUL ADVOCATE FOR EDUCATION AND THE TEACHING OF THE HUMANITIES... HIS INFLUENCE EXTENDS ALL THE WAY TO YOUR OWN 20TH-CENTURY CAREERS!
HERE HE COMES NOW!
GOOD AFTERNOON!
WE SHALL BEGIN TODAY'S LECTURE ON COMPARATIVE ANATOMY BY RETURNING TO THE SUBJECT OF THE MUSCULOSKELETAL SYSTEM...

THAT WAS FANTASTIC.

HE'S A BRILLIANT SPEAKER.

YES, IT WAS AN HONOR TO BE HERE FOR HIS LECTURE.

SOME OF HIS IDEAS SEEM VERY DATED AND INACCURATE TO ME.

THANK YOU, DOCTOR. I APOLOGISE FOR MY EARLIER LACK OF ENTHUSIASM ABOUT THIS VISIT.

NOT EVERYONE HAS YOUR 25TH-CENTURY EDUCATION, VICKI.

YOU HAVE TO KEEP THE CONTEXT IN MIND. THIS IS 1868.

YES, SOMETIMES I DO SEEM TO HAVE PROBLEMS WITH CONTEXT.

MY EDUCATION WAS SO MUCH BETTER AND MORE COMPREHENSIVE, THOUGH.

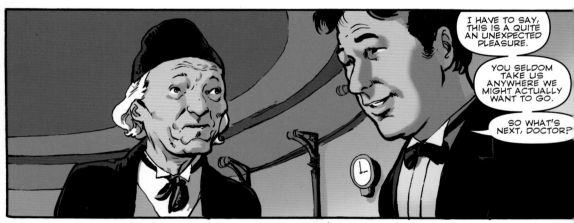

I HAVE TO SAY, THIS IS A QUITE AN UNEXPECTED PLEASURE.

YOU SELDOM TAKE US ANYWHERE WE MIGHT ACTUALLY WANT TO GO.

SO WHAT'S NEXT, DOCTOR?

I TOLD THOMAS THAT WE WOULD STOP BY AND CHAT WITH HIM BRIEFLY IN HIS OFFICE BEFORE WE GO.

BY ALL MEANS!

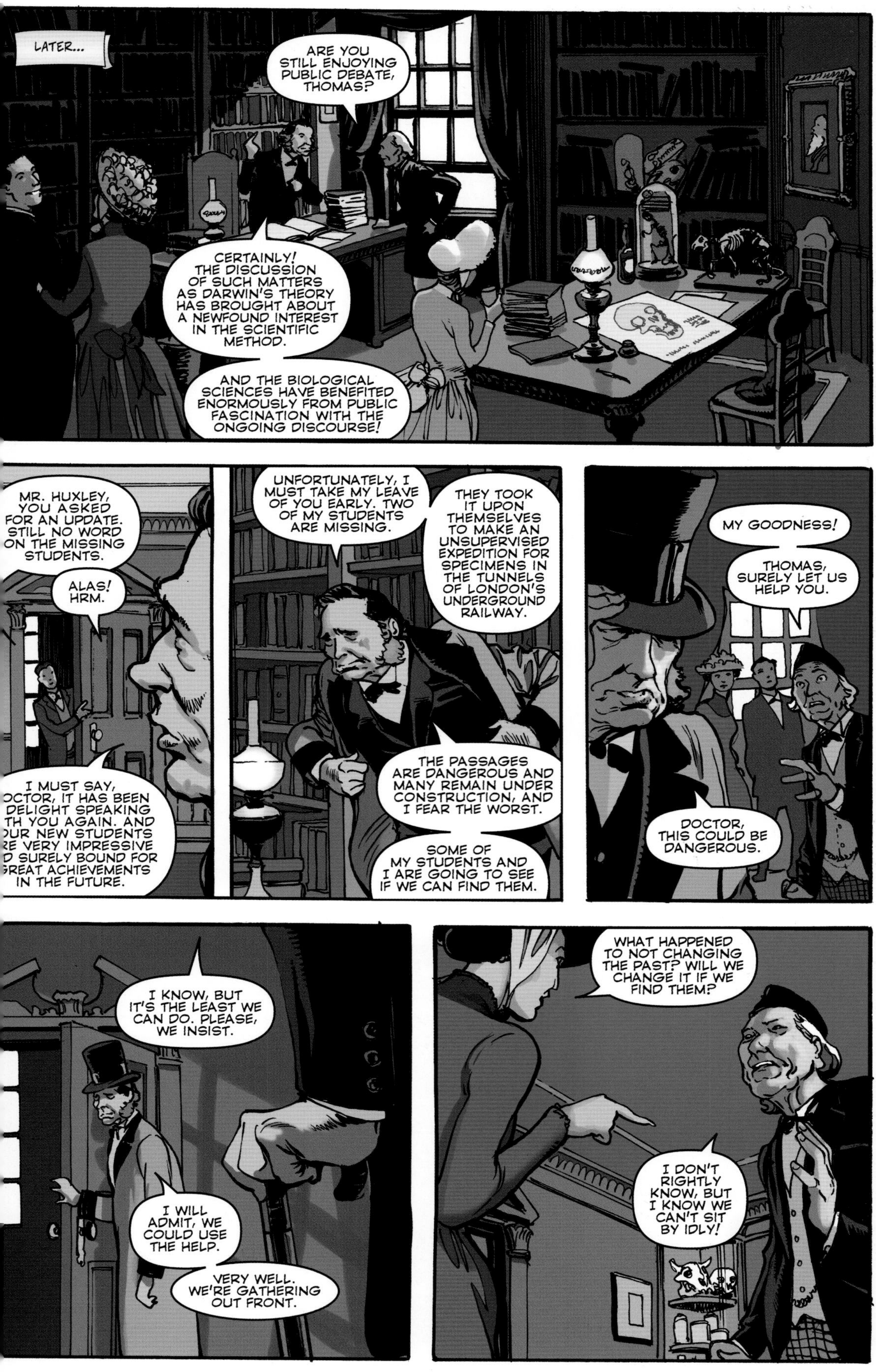
LATER...
ARE YOU STILL ENJOYING PUBLIC DEBATE, THOMAS?
CERTAINLY! THE DISCUSSION OF SUCH MATTERS AS DARWIN'S THEORY HAS BROUGHT ABOUT A NEWFOUND INTEREST IN THE SCIENTIFIC METHOD.
AND THE BIOLOGICAL SCIENCES HAVE BENEFITED ENORMOUSLY FROM PUBLIC FASCINATION WITH THE ONGOING DISCOURSE!
MR. HUXLEY, YOU ASKED FOR AN UPDATE. STILL NO WORD ON THE MISSING STUDENTS.
ALAS! HRM.
I MUST SAY, OCTOR, IT HAS BEEN DELIGHT SPEAKING TH YOU AGAIN. AND OUR NEW STUDENTS RE VERY IMPRESSIVE D SURELY BOUND FOR GREAT ACHIEVEMENTS IN THE FUTURE.
UNFORTUNATELY, I MUST TAKE MY LEAVE OF YOU EARLY. TWO OF MY STUDENTS ARE MISSING.
THEY TOOK IT UPON THEMSELVES TO MAKE AN UNSUPERVISED EXPEDITION FOR SPECIMENS IN THE TUNNELS OF LONDON'S UNDERGROUND RAILWAY.
THE PASSAGES ARE DANGEROUS AND MANY REMAIN UNDER CONSTRUCTION, AND I FEAR THE WORST.
SOME OF MY STUDENTS AND I ARE GOING TO SEE IF WE CAN FIND THEM.
MY GOODNESS!
THOMAS, SURELY LET US HELP YOU.
DOCTOR, THIS COULD BE DANGEROUS.
I KNOW, BUT IT'S THE LEAST WE CAN DO. PLEASE, WE INSIST.
I WILL ADMIT, WE COULD USE THE HELP.
VERY WELL. WE'RE GATHERING OUT FRONT.
WHAT HAPPENED TO NOT CHANGING THE PAST? WILL WE CHANGE IT IF WE FIND THEM?
I DON'T RIGHTLY KNOW, BUT I KNOW WE CAN'T SIT BY IDLY!

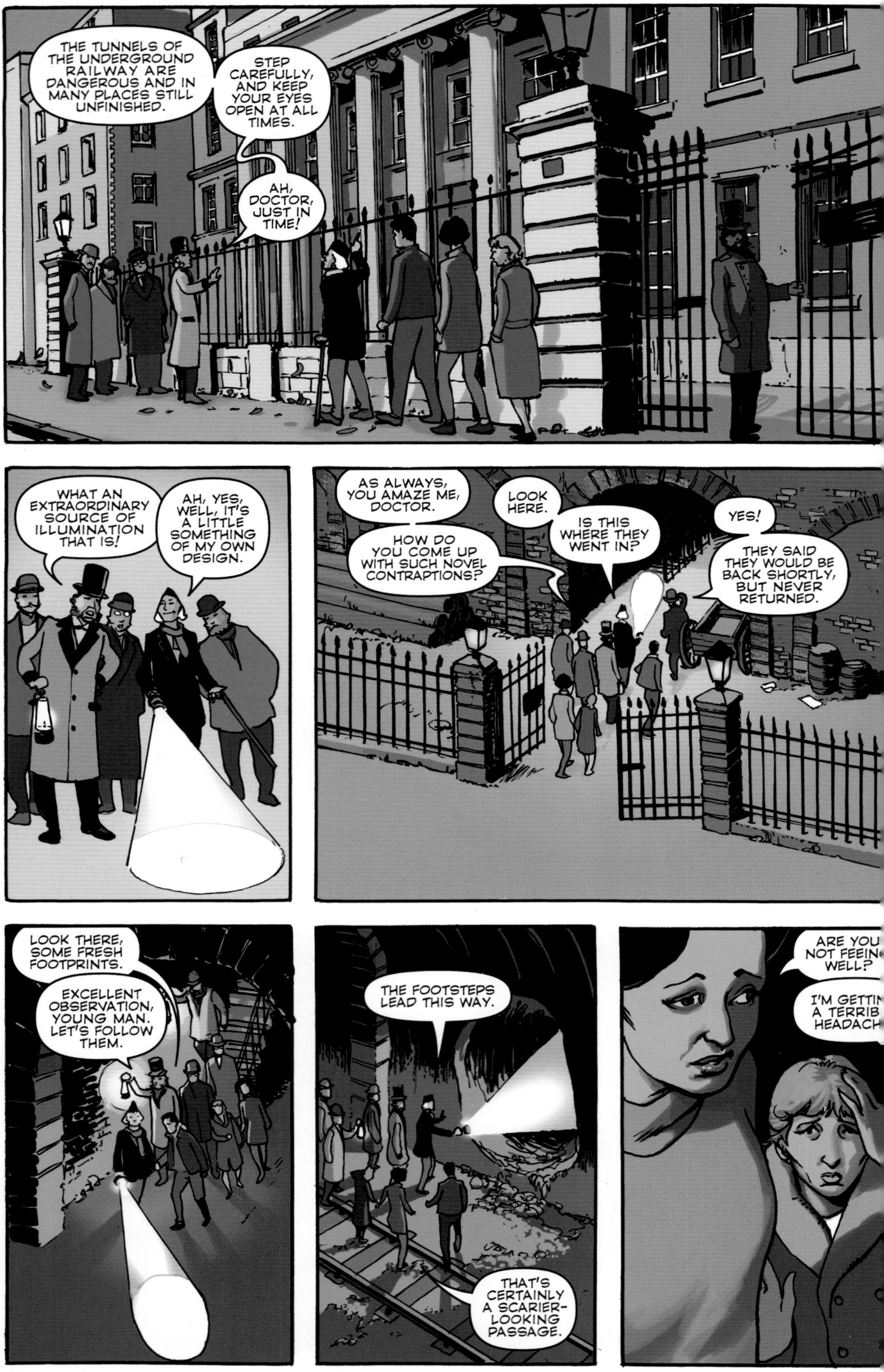
THE TUNNELS OF THE UNDERGROUND RAILWAY ARE DANGEROUS AND IN MANY PLACES STILL UNFINISHED.
STEP CAREFULLY, AND KEEP YOUR EYES OPEN AT ALL TIMES.
AH, DOCTOR, JUST IN TIME!
WHAT AN EXTRAORDINARY SOURCE OF ILLUMINATION THAT IS!
AH, YES, WELL, IT'S A LITTLE SOMETHING OF MY OWN DESIGN.
AS ALWAYS, YOU AMAZE ME, DOCTOR.
HOW DO YOU COME UP WITH SUCH NOVEL CONTRAPTIONS?
LOOK HERE.
IS THIS WHERE THEY WENT IN?
YES!
THEY SAID THEY WOULD BE BACK SHORTLY, BUT NEVER RETURNED.
LOOK THERE, SOME FRESH FOOTPRINTS.
EXCELLENT OBSERVATION, YOUNG MAN. LET'S FOLLOW THEM.
THE FOOTSTEPS LEAD THIS WAY.
THAT'S CERTAINLY A SCARIER-LOOKING PASSAGE.
ARE YOU NOT FEEIN WELL?
I'M GETTIN A TERRIB HEADACH

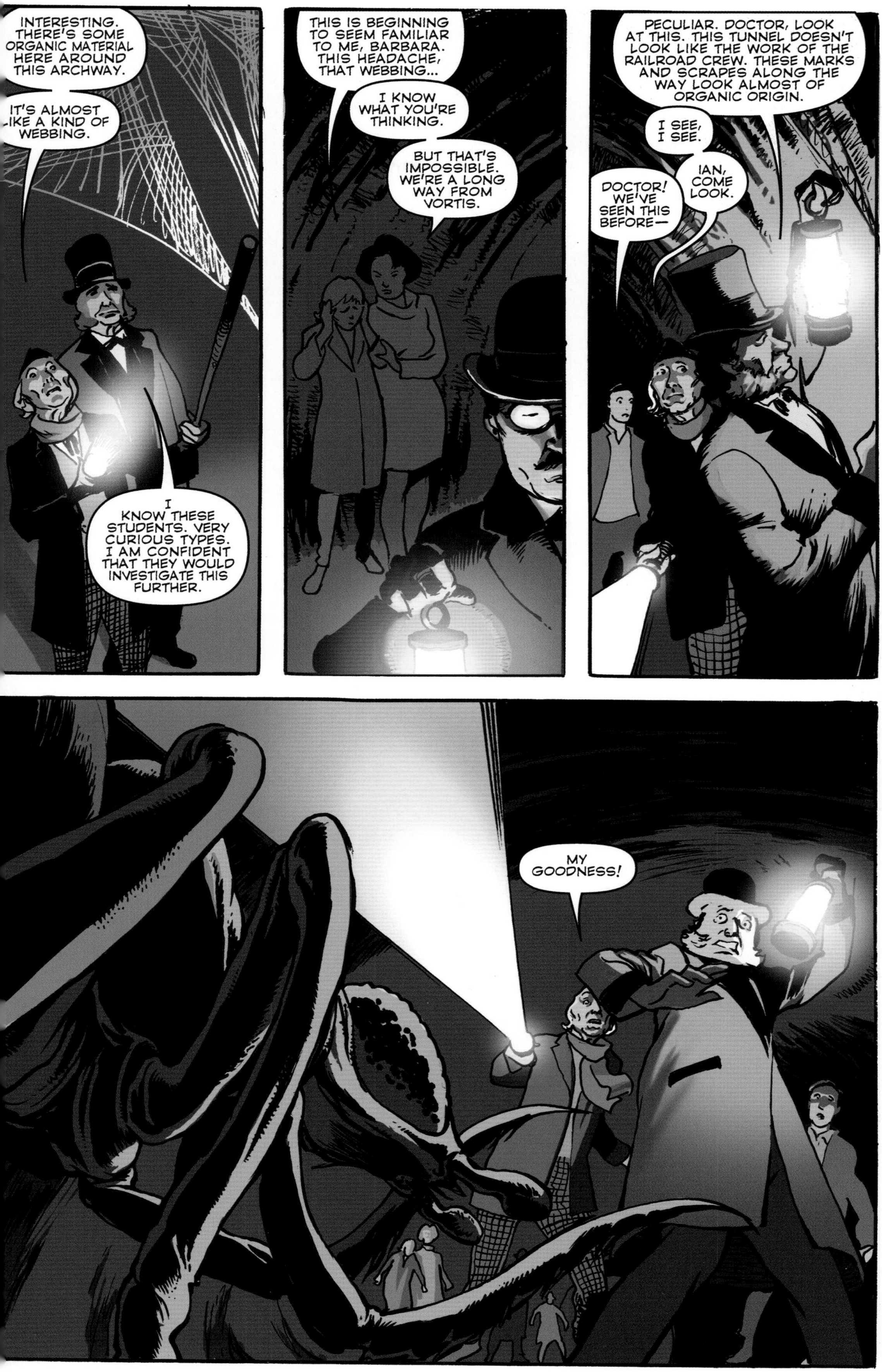
INTERESTING. THERE'S SOME ORGANIC MATERIAL HERE AROUND THIS ARCHWAY.
IT'S ALMOST LIKE A KIND OF WEBBING.
I KNOW THESE STUDENTS. VERY CURIOUS TYPES. I AM CONFIDENT THAT THEY WOULD INVESTIGATE THIS FURTHER.
THIS IS BEGINNING TO SEEM FAMILIAR TO ME, BARBARA. THIS HEADACHE, THAT WEBBING...
I KNOW WHAT YOU'RE THINKING.
BUT THAT'S IMPOSSIBLE. WE'RE A LONG WAY FROM VORTIS.
PECULIAR. DOCTOR, LOOK AT THIS. THIS TUNNEL DOESN'T LOOK LIKE THE WORK OF THE RAILROAD CREW. THESE MARKS AND SCRAPES ALONG THE WAY LOOK ALMOST OF ORGANIC ORIGIN.
I SEE, I SEE.
IAN, COME LOOK.
DOCTOR! WE'VE SEEN THIS BEFORE—
MY GOODNESS!

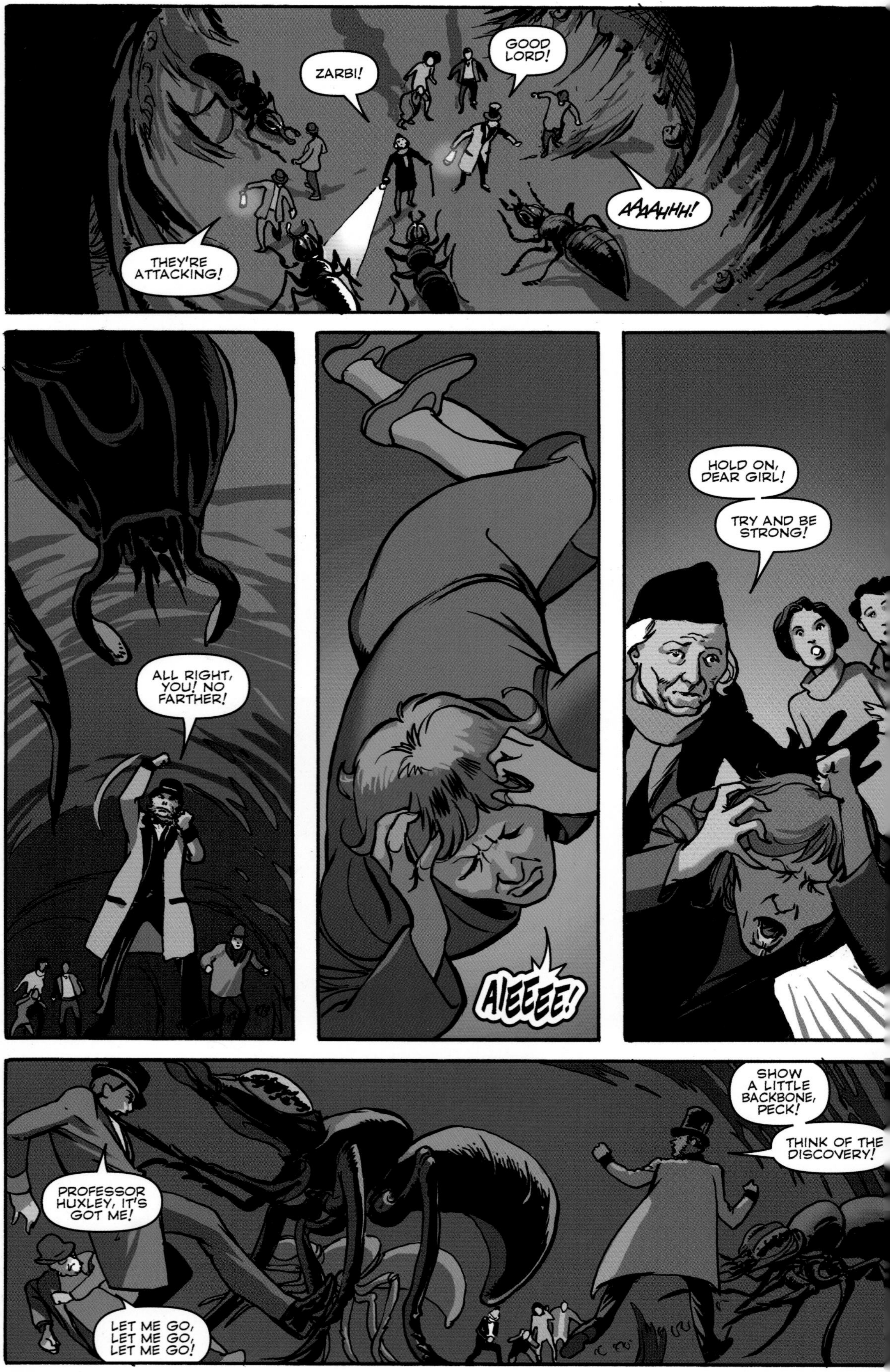
ZARBI!
GOOD LORD!
AAAAHHH!
THEY'RE ATTACKING!
ALL RIGHT, YOU! NO FARTHER!
AIEEEEE!
HOLD ON, DEAR GIRL!
TRY AND BE STRONG!
PROFESSOR HUXLEY, IT'S GOT ME!
LET ME GO, LET ME GO, LET ME GO!
SHOW A LITTLE BACKBONE, PECK!
THINK OF THE DISCOVERY!

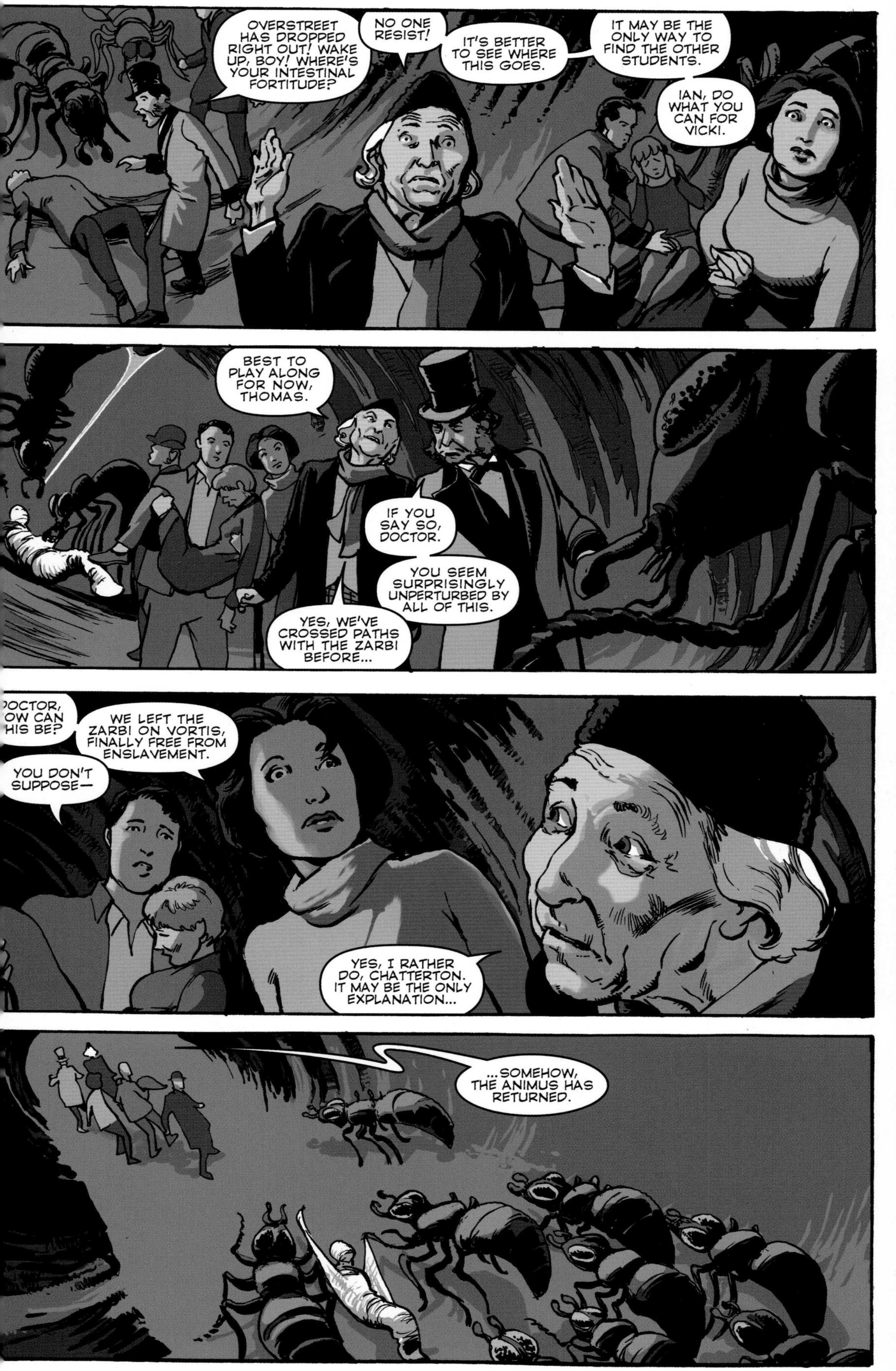
OVERSTREET HAS DROPPED RIGHT OUT! WAKE UP, BOY! WHERE'S YOUR INTESTINAL FORTITUDE?
NO ONE RESIST!
IT'S BETTER TO SEE WHERE THIS GOES.
IT MAY BE THE ONLY WAY TO FIND THE OTHER STUDENTS.
IAN, DO WHAT YOU CAN FOR VICKI.
BEST TO PLAY ALONG FOR NOW, THOMAS.
IF YOU SAY SO, DOCTOR.
YOU SEEM SURPRISINGLY UNPERTURBED BY ALL OF THIS.
YES, WE'VE CROSSED PATHS WITH THE ZARBI BEFORE...
OCTOR, OW CAN HIS BE?
WE LEFT THE ZARBI ON VORTIS, FINALLY FREE FROM ENSLAVEMENT.
YOU DON'T SUPPOSE—
YES, I RATHER DO, CHATTERTON. IT MAY BE THE ONLY EXPLANATION...
...SOMEHOW, THE ANIMUS HAS RETURNED.

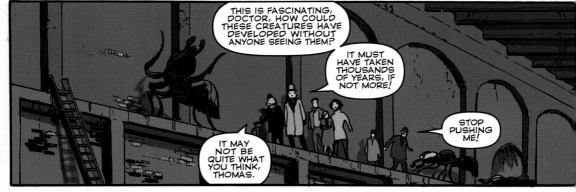

THIS IS FASCINATING, DOCTOR, HOW COULD THESE CREATURES HAVE DEVELOPED WITHOUT ANYONE SEEING THEM?

IT MUST HAVE TAKEN THOUSANDS OF YEARS, IF NOT MORE!

STOP PUSHING ME!

IT MAY NOT BE QUITE WHAT YOU THINK, THOMAS.

NOOOO!

AAARGGH!

MIND THE GAP

I'VE GOT YOU!

PUSH... AGAINST THE STONE... WITH YOUR FEET... TRY TO CLIMB!

DON'T LET GO!

ALL RIGHT, ALL RIGHT, WE'RE GOING!

DAMNED OVERGROWN INSECTS... DID I TELL YOU THAT I ONCE SAW A COLONY OF ANTS EAT THEIR WAY THROUGH AN ENTIRE HOUSE?

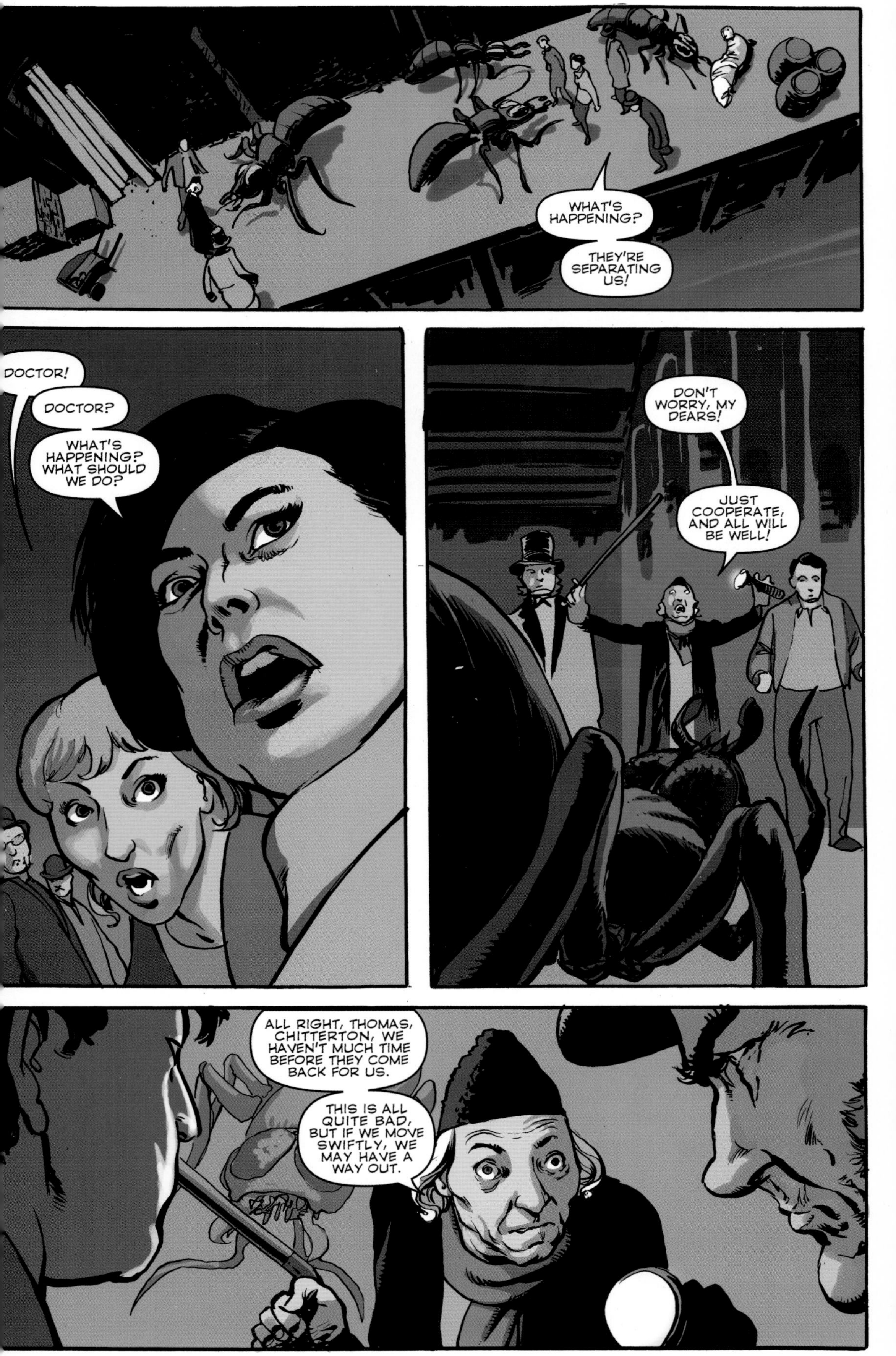
WHAT'S HAPPENING?
THEY'RE SEPARATING US!
DOCTOR!
DOCTOR?
WHAT'S HAPPENING? WHAT SHOULD WE DO?
DON'T WORRY, MY DEARS!
JUST COOPERATE, AND ALL WILL BE WELL!
ALL RIGHT, THOMAS, CHITTERTON, WE HAVEN'T MUCH TIME BEFORE THEY COME BACK FOR US.
THIS IS ALL QUITE BAD, BUT IF WE MOVE SWIFTLY, WE MAY HAVE A WAY OUT.

THOMAS, THIS IS WITHOUT QUESTION WHERE YOUR STUDENTS HAVE GONE.

AND OUR OWN EXPERIENCE WOULD INDICATE THAT THEY HAVE BEEN TAKEN. FOR PRECISELY WHAT FOUL PURPOSE, I'VE NOT YET BEEN ABLE TO ASCERTAIN.

I DON'T UNDERSTAND. THIS LOOKS LIKE LITTLE MORE THAN ANIMAL BEHAVIOUR. YOU CAN'T BE PROPOSING AN INTELLIGENT HAND BEHIND ALL THIS.

THIS IS NOT EVOLUTION IN ACTION, HUXLEY! THERE'S NOTHING NATURAL ABOUT IT! THESE CREATURES ARE NOT OF THIS WORLD!

OTHER WORLDS? PREPOSTEROUS! AND I THOUGHT YOU WERE A MAN OF SCIENCE, DOCTOR!

LOOK!

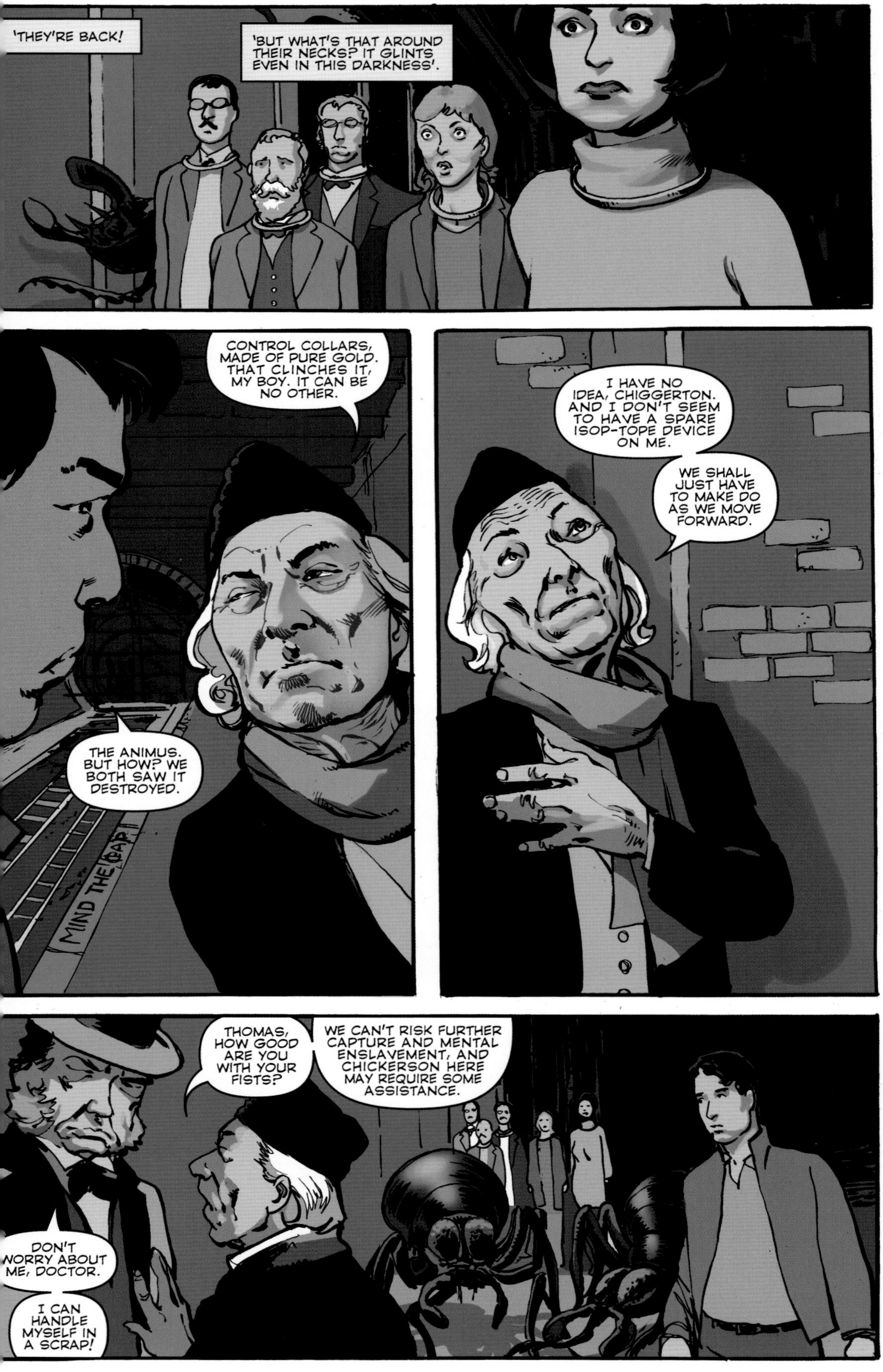
'THEY'RE BACK!
'BUT WHAT'S THAT AROUND THEIR NECKS? IT GLINTS EVEN IN THIS DARKNESS'.
CONTROL COLLARS, MADE OF PURE GOLD. THAT CLINCHES IT, MY BOY. IT CAN BE NO OTHER.
THE ANIMUS. BUT HOW? WE BOTH SAW IT DESTROYED.
MIND THE GAP
I HAVE NO IDEA, CHIGGERTON. AND I DON'T SEEM TO HAVE A SPARE ISOP-TOPE DEVICE ON ME.
WE SHALL JUST HAVE TO MAKE DO AS WE MOVE FORWARD.
THOMAS, HOW GOOD ARE YOU WITH YOUR FISTS?
WE CAN'T RISK FURTHER CAPTURE AND MENTAL ENSLAVEMENT, AND CHICKERSON HERE MAY REQUIRE SOME ASSISTANCE.
DON'T WORRY ABOUT ME, DOCTOR.
I CAN HANDLE MYSELF IN A SCRAP!

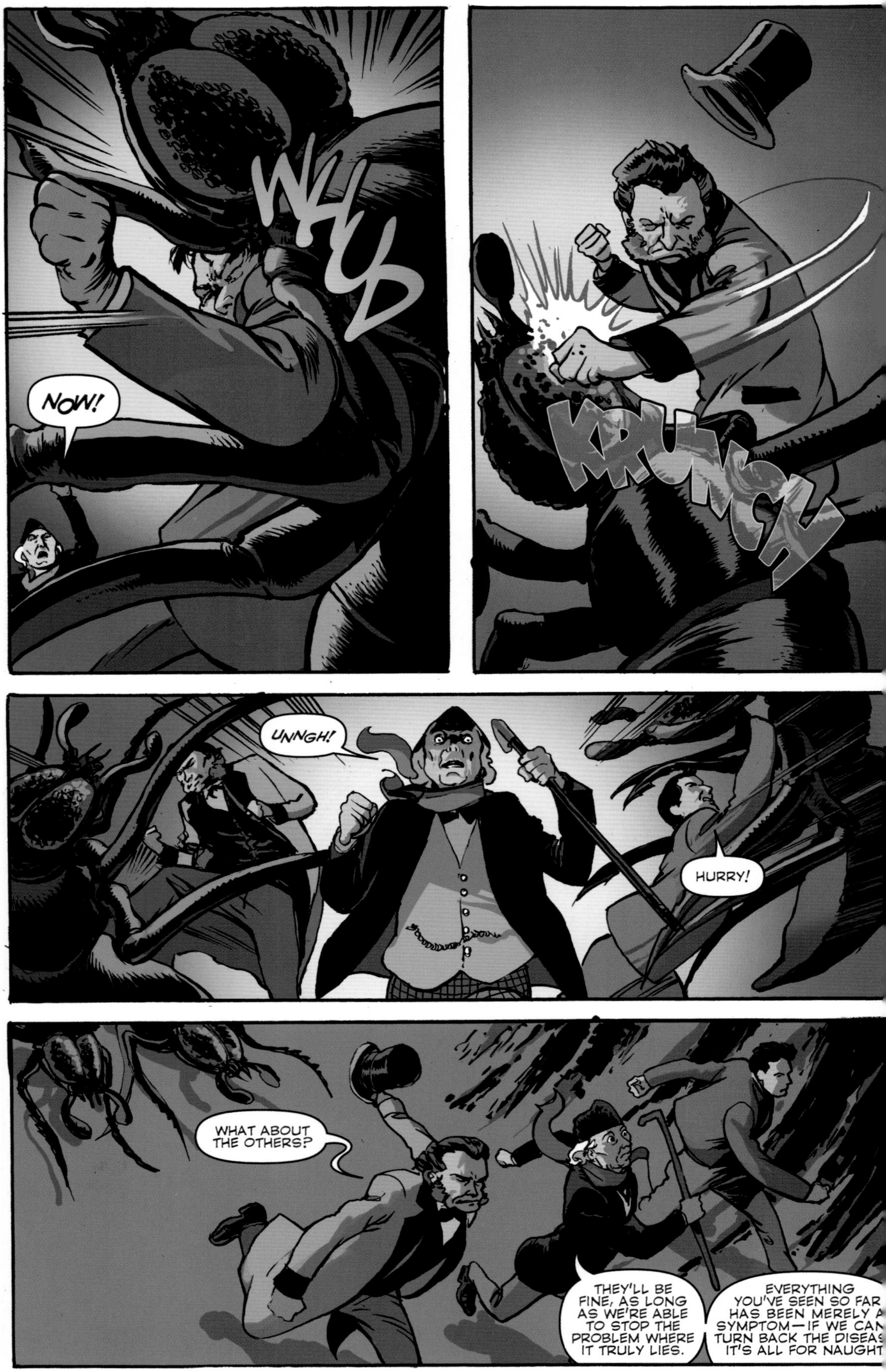
WHUD
NOW!
KRUNCH
UNNGH!
HURRY!
WHAT ABOUT THE OTHERS?
THEY'LL BE FINE, AS LONG AS WE'RE ABLE TO STOP THE PROBLEM WHERE IT TRULY LIES.
EVERYTHING YOU'VE SEEN SO FAR HAS BEEN MERELY A SYMPTOM—IF WE CAN TURN BACK THE DISEAS IT'S ALL FOR NAUGHT

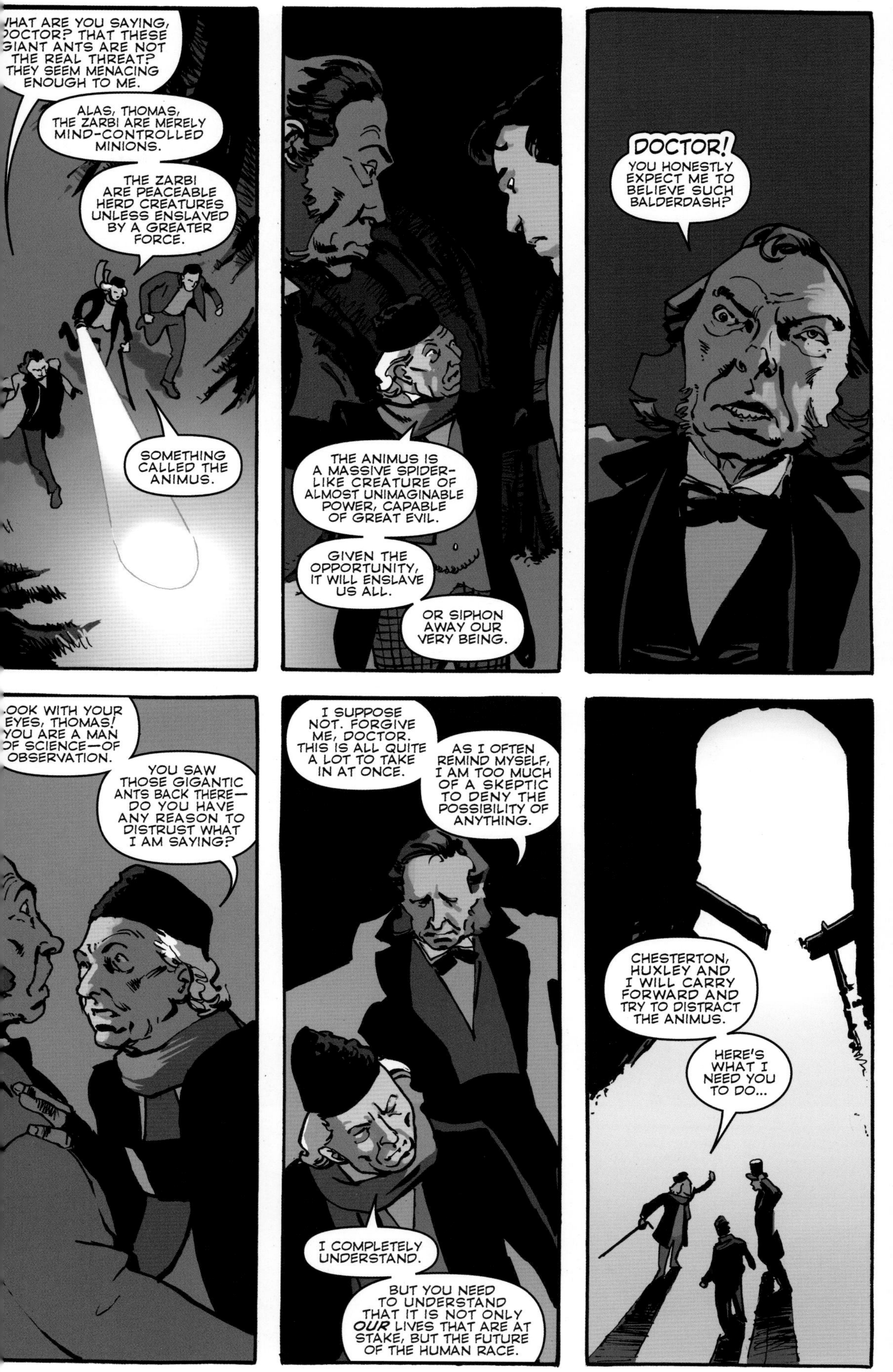
WHAT ARE YOU SAYING, DOCTOR? THAT THESE GIANT ANTS ARE NOT THE REAL THREAT? THEY SEEM MENACING ENOUGH TO ME.
ALAS, THOMAS, THE ZARBI ARE MERELY MIND-CONTROLLED MINIONS.
THE ZARBI ARE PEACEABLE HERD CREATURES UNLESS ENSLAVED BY A GREATER FORCE.
SOMETHING CALLED THE ANIMUS.
THE ANIMUS IS A MASSIVE SPIDER-LIKE CREATURE OF ALMOST UNIMAGINABLE POWER, CAPABLE OF GREAT EVIL.
GIVEN THE OPPORTUNITY, IT WILL ENSLAVE US ALL.
OR SIPHON AWAY OUR VERY BEING.
DOCTOR! YOU HONESTLY EXPECT ME TO BELIEVE SUCH BALDERDASH?
LOOK WITH YOUR EYES, THOMAS! YOU ARE A MAN OF SCIENCE—OF OBSERVATION.
YOU SAW THOSE GIGANTIC ANTS BACK THERE—DO YOU HAVE ANY REASON TO DISTRUST WHAT I AM SAYING?
I SUPPOSE NOT. FORGIVE ME, DOCTOR. THIS IS ALL QUITE A LOT TO TAKE IN AT ONCE.
AS I OFTEN REMIND MYSELF, I AM TOO MUCH OF A SKEPTIC TO DENY THE POSSIBILITY OF ANYTHING.
I COMPLETELY UNDERSTAND.
BUT YOU NEED TO UNDERSTAND THAT IT IS NOT ONLY OUR LIVES THAT ARE AT STAKE, BUT THE FUTURE OF THE HUMAN RACE.
CHESTERTON, HUXLEY AND I WILL CARRY FORWARD AND TRY TO DISTRACT THE ANIMUS.
HERE'S WHAT I NEED YOU TO DO...

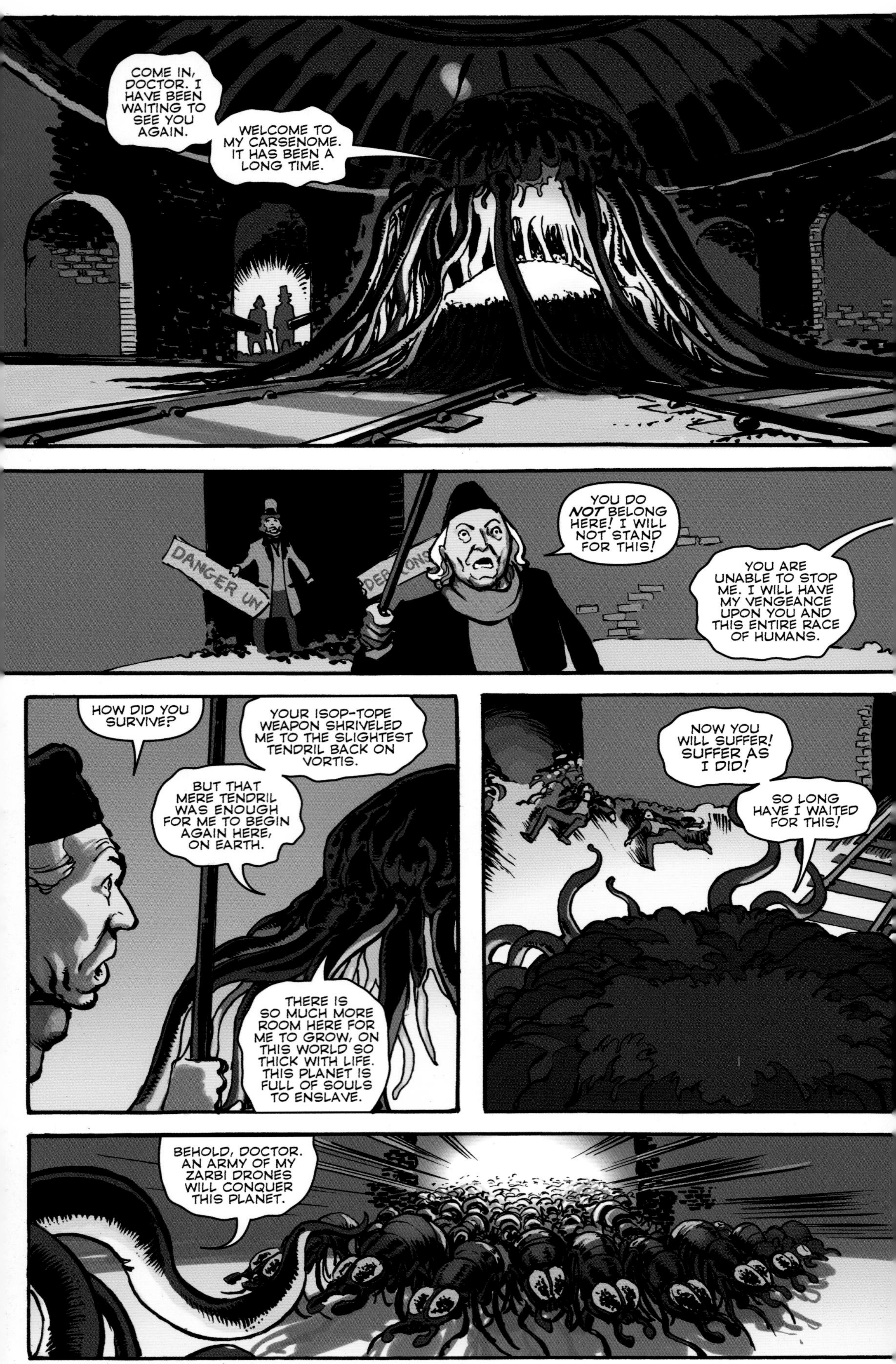
COME IN, DOCTOR. I HAVE BEEN WAITING TO SEE YOU AGAIN.
WELCOME TO MY CARSENOME. IT HAS BEEN A LONG TIME.
DANGER UN
YOU DO *NOT* BELONG HERE! I WILL NOT STAND FOR THIS!
YOU ARE UNABLE TO STOP ME. I WILL HAVE MY VENGEANCE UPON YOU AND THIS ENTIRE RACE OF HUMANS.
HOW DID YOU SURVIVE?
YOUR ISOP-TOPE WEAPON SHRIVELED ME TO THE SLIGHTEST TENDRIL BACK ON VORTIS.
BUT THAT MERE TENDRIL WAS ENOUGH FOR ME TO BEGIN AGAIN HERE, ON EARTH.
THERE IS SO MUCH MORE ROOM HERE FOR ME TO GROW, ON THIS WORLD SO THICK WITH LIFE. THIS PLANET IS FULL OF SOULS TO ENSLAVE.
NOW YOU WILL SUFFER! SUFFER AS I DID!
SO LONG HAVE I WAITED FOR THIS!
BEHOLD, DOCTOR. AN ARMY OF MY ZARBI DRONES WILL CONQUER THIS PLANET.

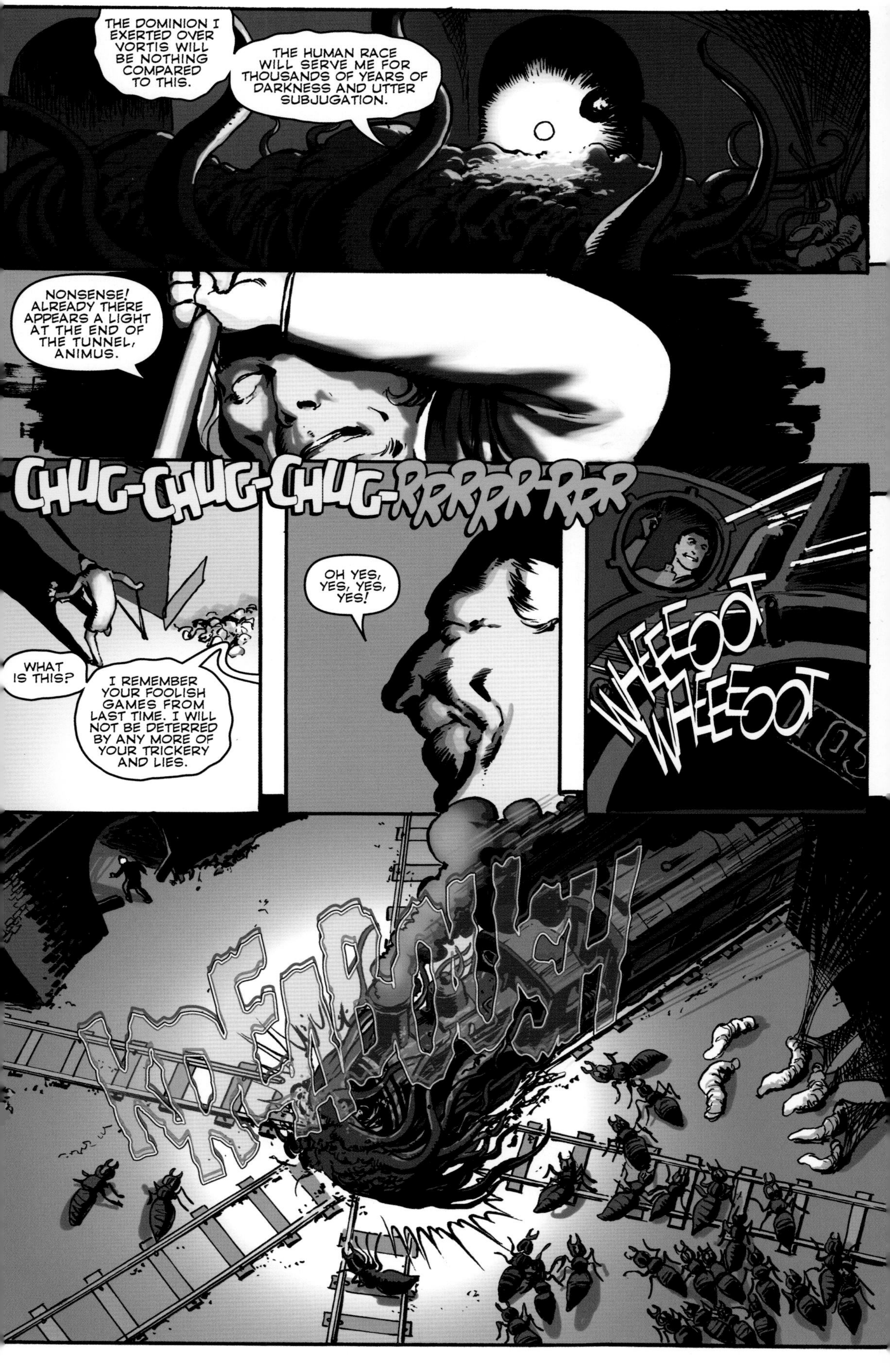
THE DOMINION I EXERTED OVER VORTIS WILL BE NOTHING COMPARED TO THIS.
THE HUMAN RACE WILL SERVE ME FOR THOUSANDS OF YEARS OF DARKNESS AND UTTER SUBJUGATION.
NONSENSE! ALREADY THERE APPEARS A LIGHT AT THE END OF THE TUNNEL, ANIMUS.
CHUG-CHUG-CHUG-RRRRR-RRR
WHAT IS THIS?
I REMEMBER YOUR FOOLISH GAMES FROM LAST TIME. I WILL NOT BE DETERRED BY ANY MORE OF YOUR TRICKERY AND LIES.
OH YES, YES, YES, YES!
WHEEEOOT WHEEEOOT

WELL DONE, CHESTERFIELD! GOOD GRACIOUS ME, THAT WAS CLOSE!

I'VE NEVER DRIVEN A TRAIN BEFORE.

CERTAINLY NEVER A 19TH-CENTURY ONE.

YOU DID A SPLENDID JOB. COME, COME, LET'S GATHER OURSELVES.

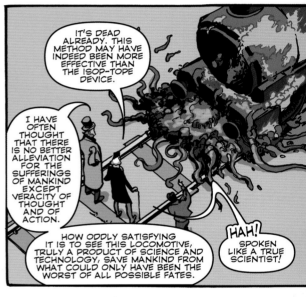

IT'S DEAD ALREADY. THIS METHOD MAY HAVE INDEED BEEN MORE EFFECTIVE THAN THE ISOP-TOPE DEVICE.

I HAVE OFTEN THOUGHT THAT THERE IS NO BETTER ALLEVIATION FOR THE SUFFERINGS OF MANKIND EXCEPT VERACITY OF THOUGHT AND OF ACTION.

HOW ODDLY SATISFYING IT IS TO SEE THIS LOCOMOTIVE, TRULY A PRODUCT OF SCIENCE AND TECHNOLOGY, SAVE MANKIND FROM WHAT COULD ONLY HAVE BEEN THE WORST OF ALL POSSIBLE FATES.

HAH! SPOKEN LIKE A TRUE SCIENTIST!

LET'S GET THESE ZARBI OUT OF HERE BEFORE THIS PORTAL CLOSES!

THEY'RE QUITE DOCILE WHEN NOT BEING MANIPULATED.

COME ALONG NOW.

THAT'S A GOOD ZARBI.

THANK YOU FOR YOUR HELP, DOCTOR. MY STUDENTS OWE YOU A GREAT DEBT.

NONSENSE, IT'S WE, AND THE WHOLE WORLD, THAT OWES YOU A DEBT, THOMAS.

WITHOUT YOU, WE NEVER WOULD HAVE BEEN ALERTED TO THE ANIMUS' PRESENCE.

IT'S A SHAME NO ONE EVER KNOW OF IT.

WHAT? BUT THE DISCOVERIES THAT WERE MADE!

YOU CAN'T SUGGEST I—

LOOK AROUND, MY FRIEND. ALL THE EVIDENCE IS GONE, OR SOON WILL BE.

IS MANKIND EVOLVED ENOUGH TO TAKE THESE SORT OF REVELATIONS SIMPLY ON YOUR WORD ALONE?

HOW DIFFICULT HAVE YOU FOUND IT CONVINCING THE POPULACE OF THE VERACITY OF NATURAL SELECTION?

NOW IMAGINE THEIR REACTION TO 'UNNATURAL' ALIEN LIFE. THEY'RE NOT READY. YOU, AND YOUR STUDENTS, MUST REMAIN SILENT. PROMISE ME.

VERY WELL, DOCTOR.

NEITHER I NOR MY STUDENTS SHALL BREATHE A WORD OF THE HORRORS WE'VE SEEN.

YOU SHOULD GET YOUR STUDENTS TO SAFETY, THOMAS, WHILE WE MAKE CERTAIN NO TRACES REMAIN OF OUR RECENT VISITORS.

VERY WELL, DOCTOR, ALTHOUGH I HATE TO LEAVE YOU ALONE DOWN HERE.

OH, DON'T WORRY. I'M HARDLY ALONE.

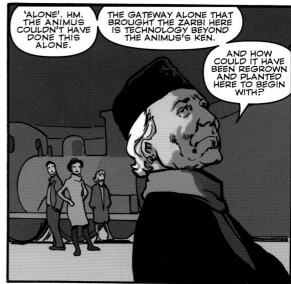

'ALONE'. HM. THE ANIMUS COULDN'T HAVE DONE THIS ALONE.

THE GATEWAY ALONE THAT BROUGHT THE ZARBI HERE IS TECHNOLOGY BEYOND THE ANIMUS'S KEN.

AND HOW COULD IT HAVE BEEN REGROWN AND PLANTED HERE TO BEGIN WITH?

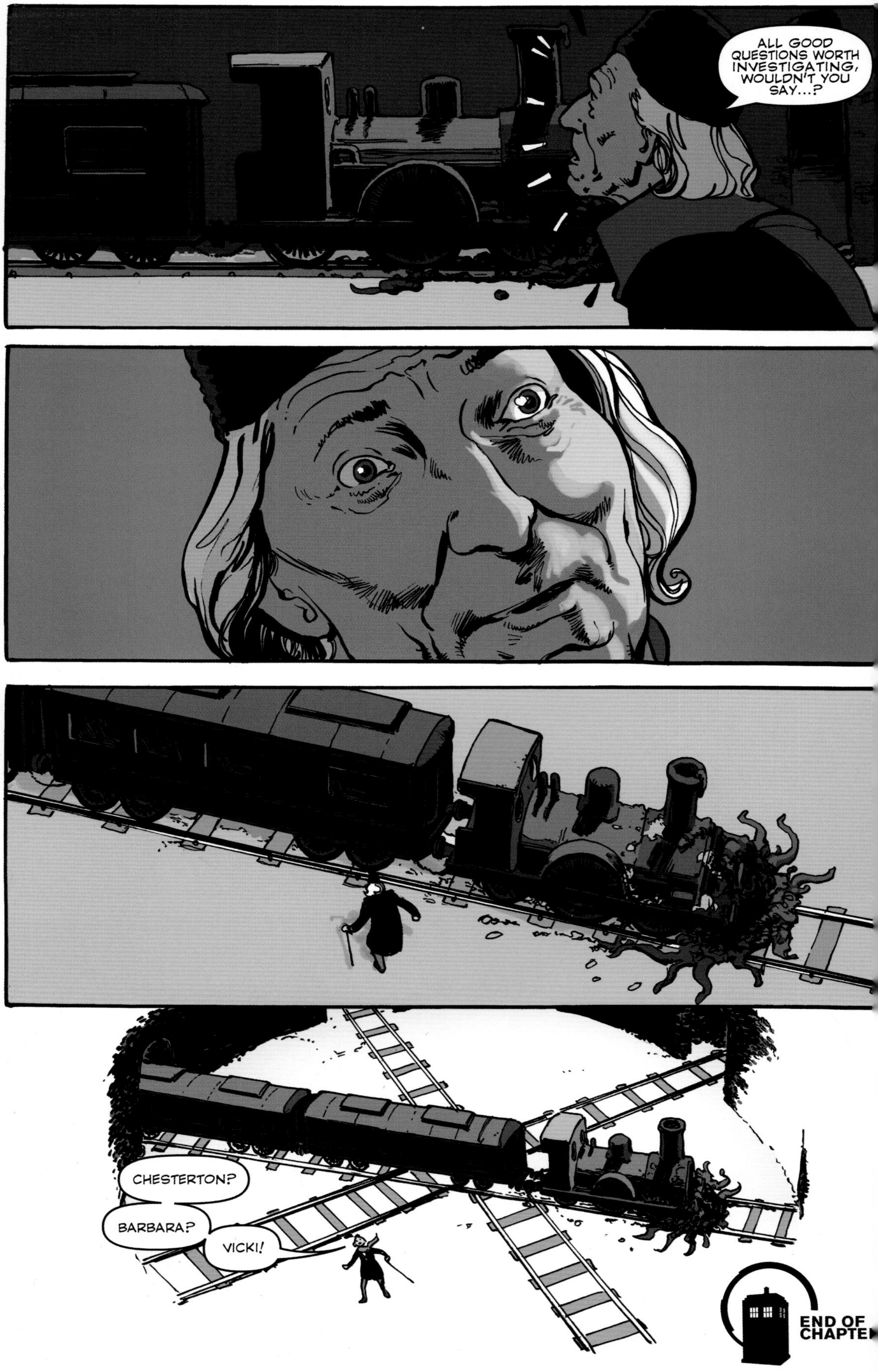
ALL GOOD QUESTIONS WORTH INVESTIGATING, WOULDN'T YOU SAY...?
CHESTERTON?
BARBARA?
VICKI!
END OF CHAPTE

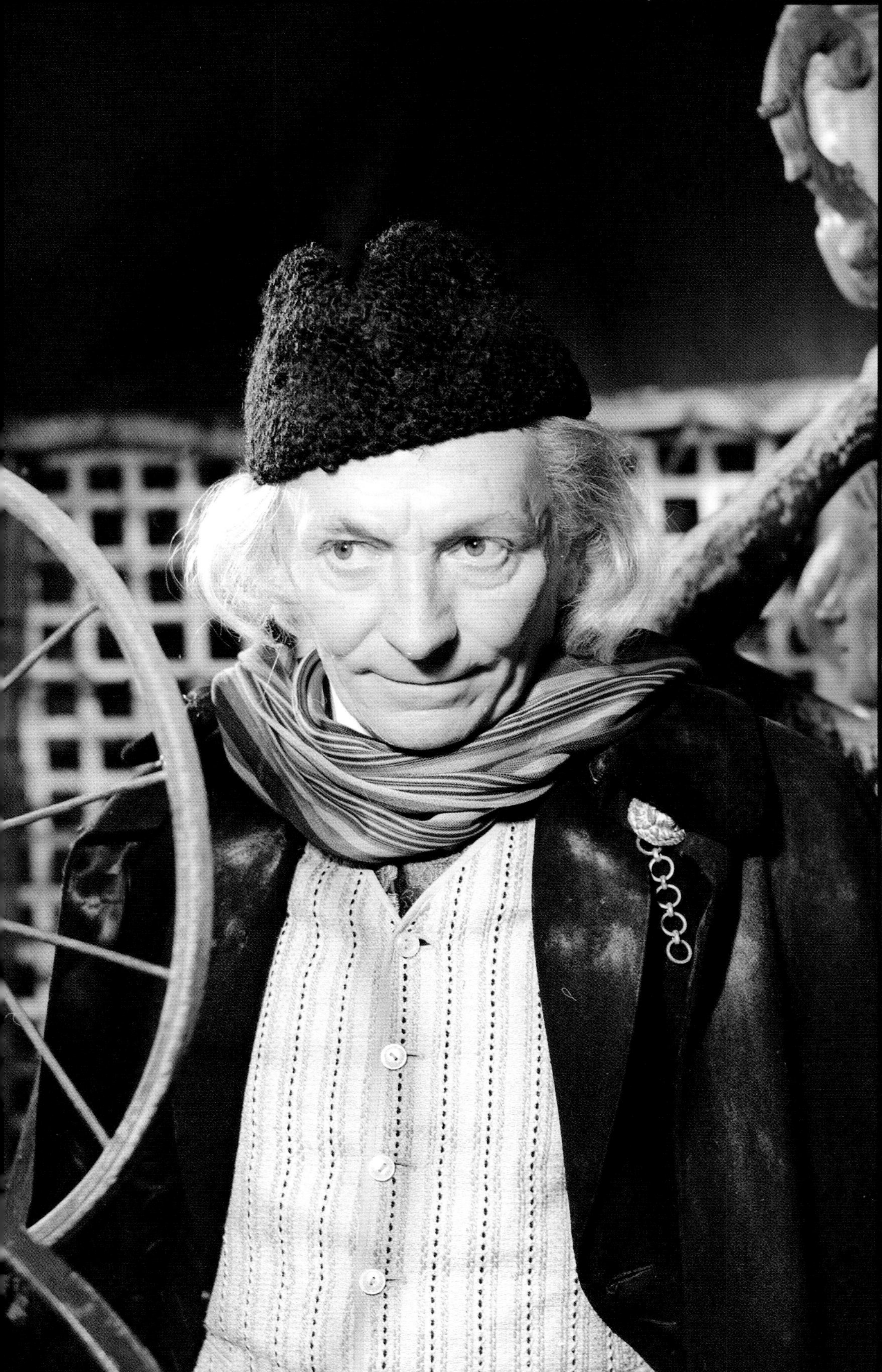

CHAPTER 2
"Bazaar Adventures"
Cover Art by Francesco Francavilla

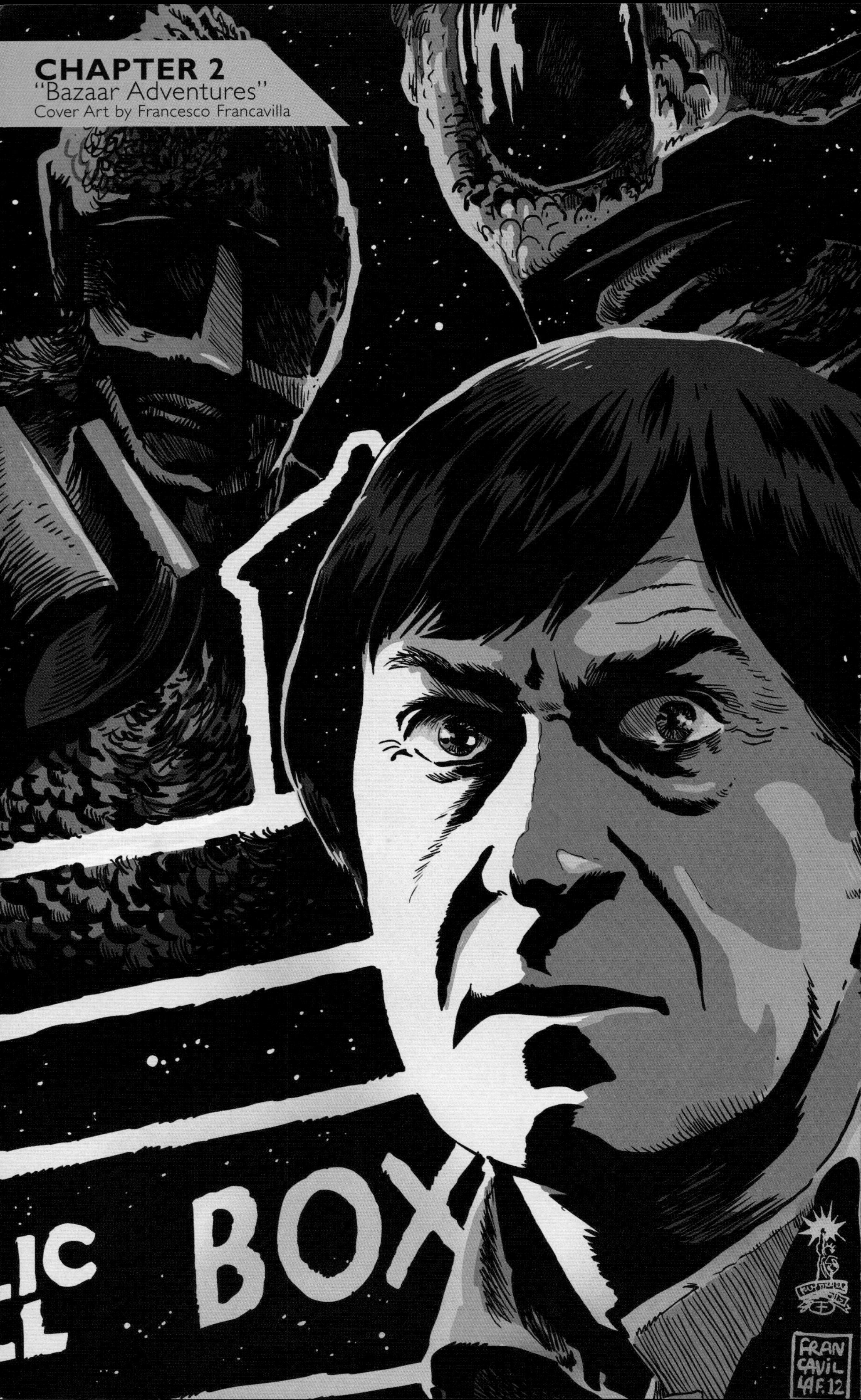
LIC
BOX
FRAN
CAVIL
LA F.12

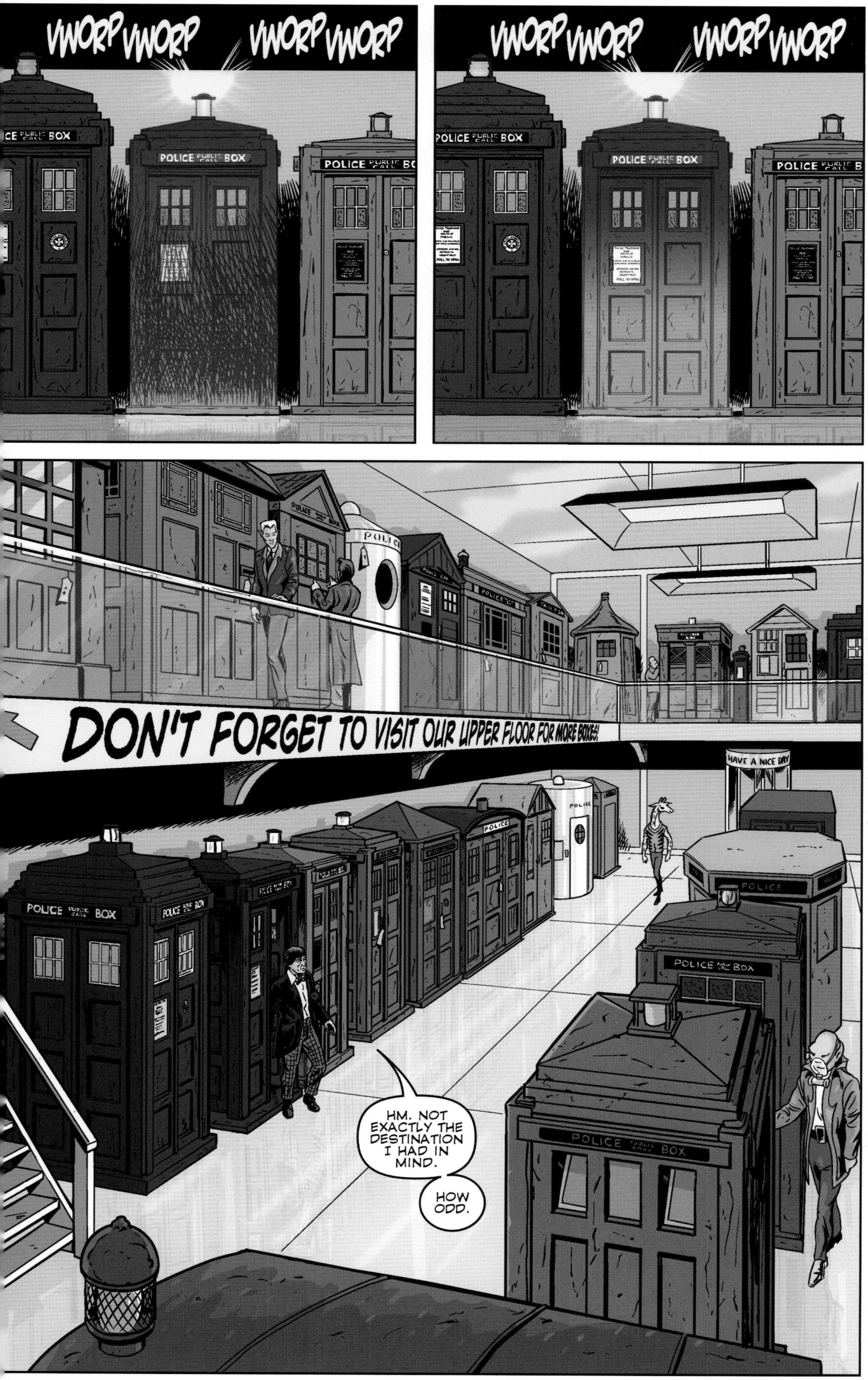
VWORP VWORP VWORP VWORP
VWORP VWORP VWORP VWORP
DON'T FORGET TO VISIT OUR UPPER FLOOR FOR MORE BOXES!
HAVE A NICE DAY
HM. NOT EXACTLY THE DESTINATION I HAD IN MIND.
HOW ODD.

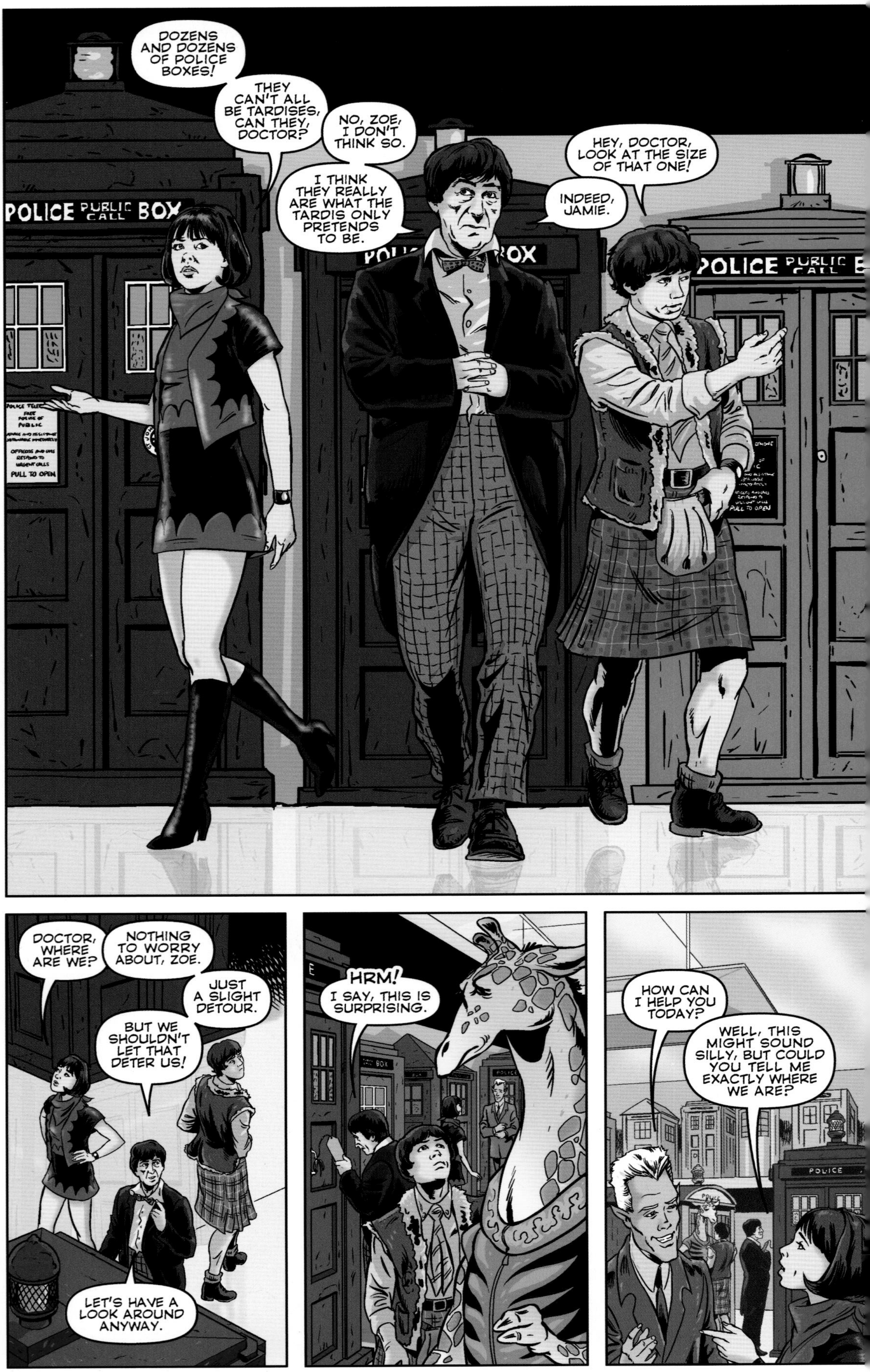
DOZENS AND DOZENS OF POLICE BOXES!
THEY CAN'T ALL BE TARDISES, CAN THEY, DOCTOR?
NO, ZOE, I DON'T THINK SO.
I THINK THEY REALLY ARE WHAT THE TARDIS ONLY PRETENDS TO BE.
HEY, DOCTOR, LOOK AT THE SIZE OF THAT ONE!
INDEED, JAMIE.
POLICE PUBLIC CALL BOX
PULL TO OPEN
DOCTOR, WHERE ARE WE?
NOTHING TO WORRY ABOUT, ZOE.
JUST A SLIGHT DETOUR.
BUT WE SHOULDN'T LET THAT DETER US!
LET'S HAVE A LOOK AROUND ANYWAY.
HRM!
I SAY, THIS IS SURPRISING.
HOW CAN I HELP YOU TODAY?
WELL, THIS MIGHT SOUND SILLY, BUT COULD YOU TELL ME EXACTLY WHERE WE ARE?
POLICE

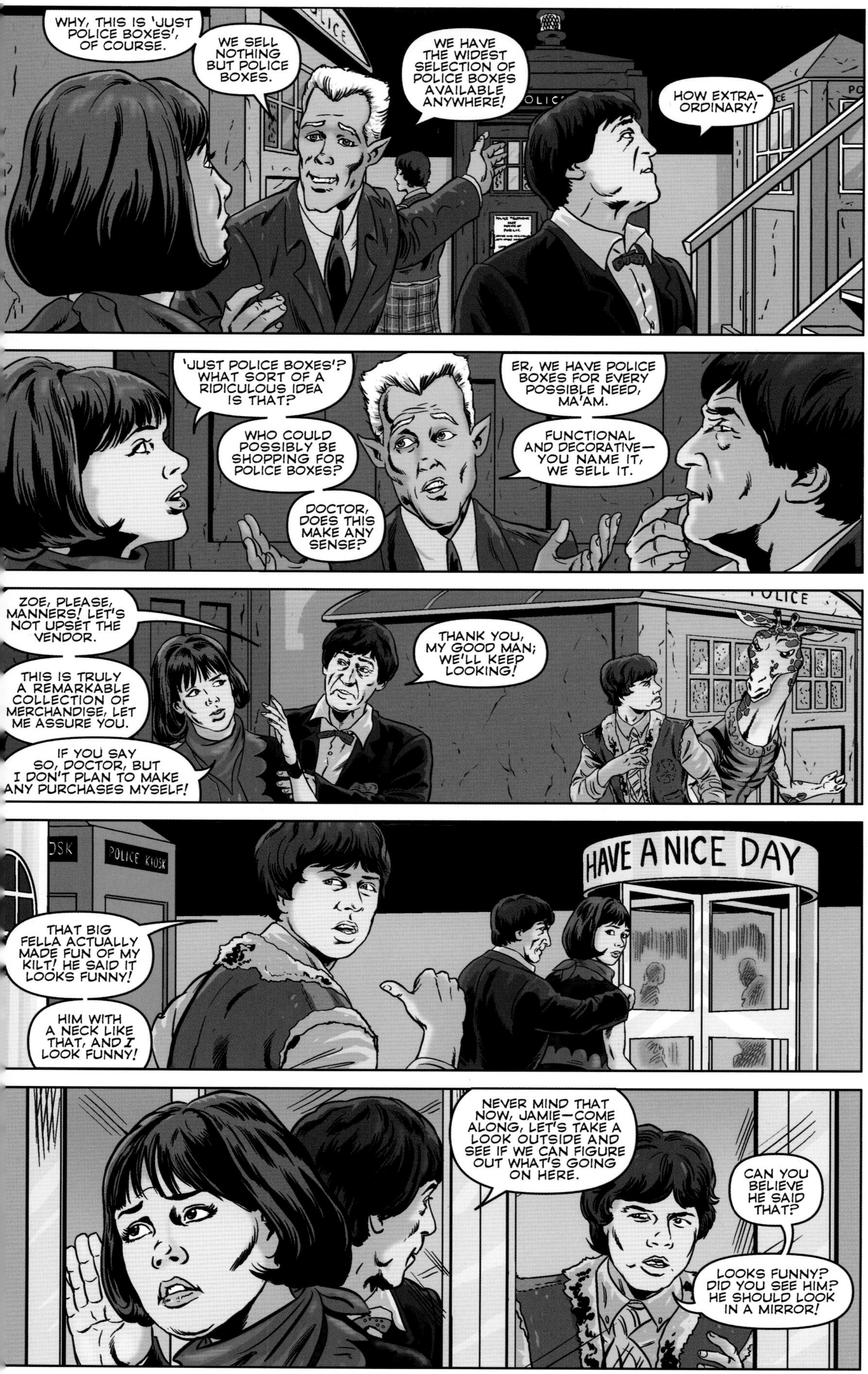
WHY, THIS IS 'JUST POLICE BOXES', OF COURSE.
WE SELL NOTHING BUT POLICE BOXES.
WE HAVE THE WIDEST SELECTION OF POLICE BOXES AVAILABLE ANYWHERE!
HOW EXTRA-ORDINARY!
'JUST POLICE BOXES'? WHAT SORT OF A RIDICULOUS IDEA IS THAT?
WHO COULD POSSIBLY BE SHOPPING FOR POLICE BOXES?
DOCTOR, DOES THIS MAKE ANY SENSE?
ER, WE HAVE POLICE BOXES FOR EVERY POSSIBLE NEED, MA'AM.
FUNCTIONAL AND DECORATIVE— YOU NAME IT, WE SELL IT.
ZOE, PLEASE, MANNERS! LET'S NOT UPSET THE VENDOR.
THIS IS TRULY A REMARKABLE COLLECTION OF MERCHANDISE, LET ME ASSURE YOU.
THANK YOU, MY GOOD MAN; WE'LL KEEP LOOKING!
IF YOU SAY SO, DOCTOR, BUT I DON'T PLAN TO MAKE ANY PURCHASES MYSELF!
POLICE KIOSK
HAVE A NICE DAY
THAT BIG FELLA ACTUALLY MADE FUN OF MY KILT! HE SAID IT LOOKS FUNNY!
HIM WITH A NECK LIKE THAT, AND *I* LOOK FUNNY!
NEVER MIND THAT NOW, JAMIE—COME ALONG, LET'S TAKE A LOOK OUTSIDE AND SEE IF WE CAN FIGURE OUT WHAT'S GOING ON HERE.
CAN YOU BELIEVE HE SAID THAT?
LOOKS FUNNY? DID YOU SEE HIM? HE SHOULD LOOK IN A MIRROR!

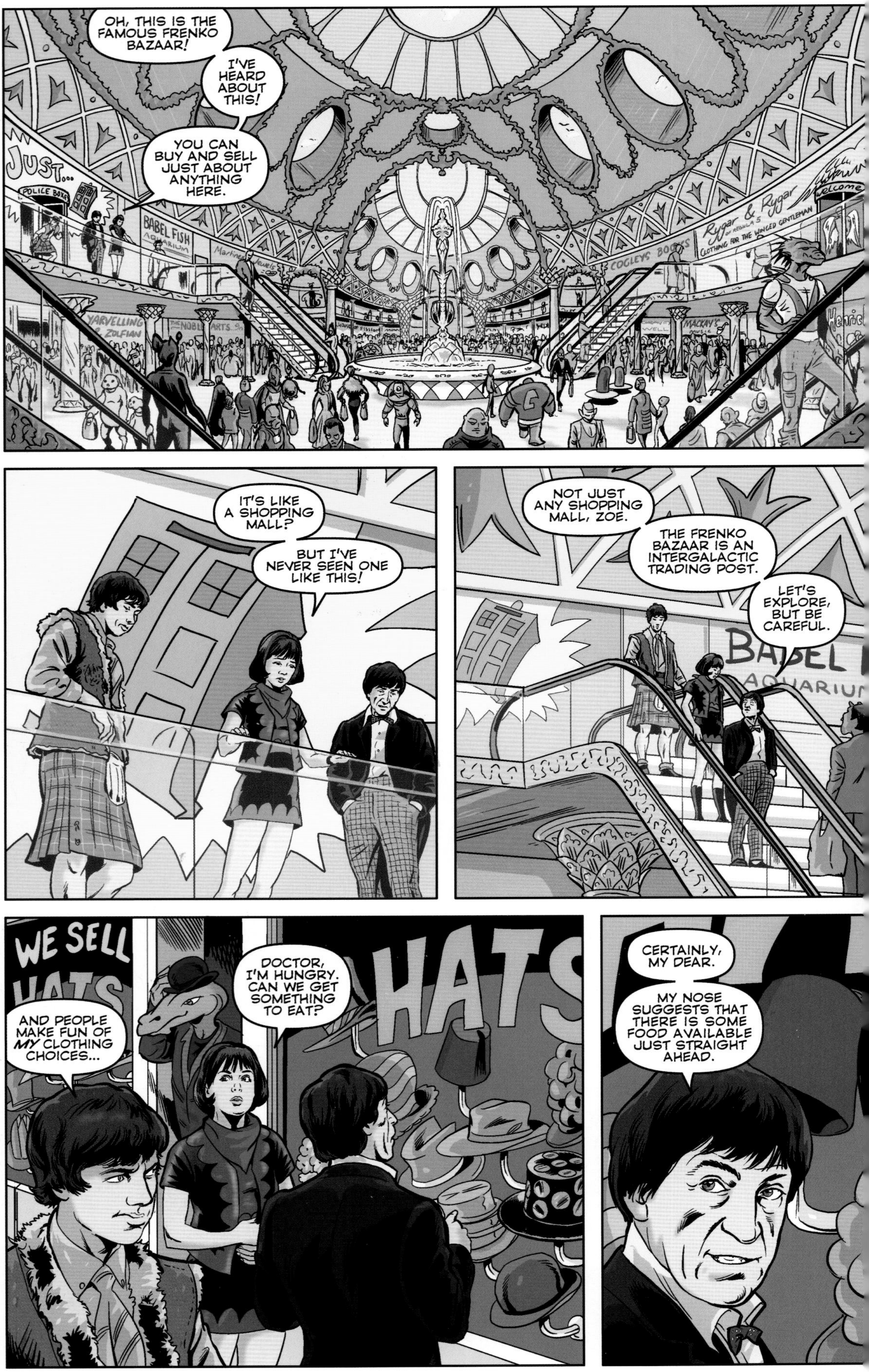
OH, THIS IS THE FAMOUS FRENKO BAZAAR!
I'VE HEARD ABOUT THIS!
YOU CAN BUY AND SELL JUST ABOUT ANYTHING HERE.
JUST...
POLICE BOXES
BABEL FISH AQUARIUM
Rygar & Rygar
CLOTHING FOR THE WINGED GENTLEMAN
Welcome
COGLEYS BOOTS
YARVELLING & ZOLFIAN
MACKAY'S
IT'S LIKE A SHOPPING MALL?
BUT I'VE NEVER SEEN ONE LIKE THIS!
NOT JUST ANY SHOPPING MALL, ZOE.
THE FRENKO BAZAAR IS AN INTERGALACTIC TRADING POST.
LET'S EXPLORE, BUT BE CAREFUL.
BABEL
AQUARIU
WE SELL HATS
HATS
AND PEOPLE MAKE FUN OF *MY* CLOTHING CHOICES...
DOCTOR, I'M HUNGRY. CAN WE GET SOMETHING TO EAT?
CERTAINLY, MY DEAR.
MY NOSE SUGGESTS THAT THERE IS SOME FOOD AVAILABLE JUST STRAIGHT AHEAD.

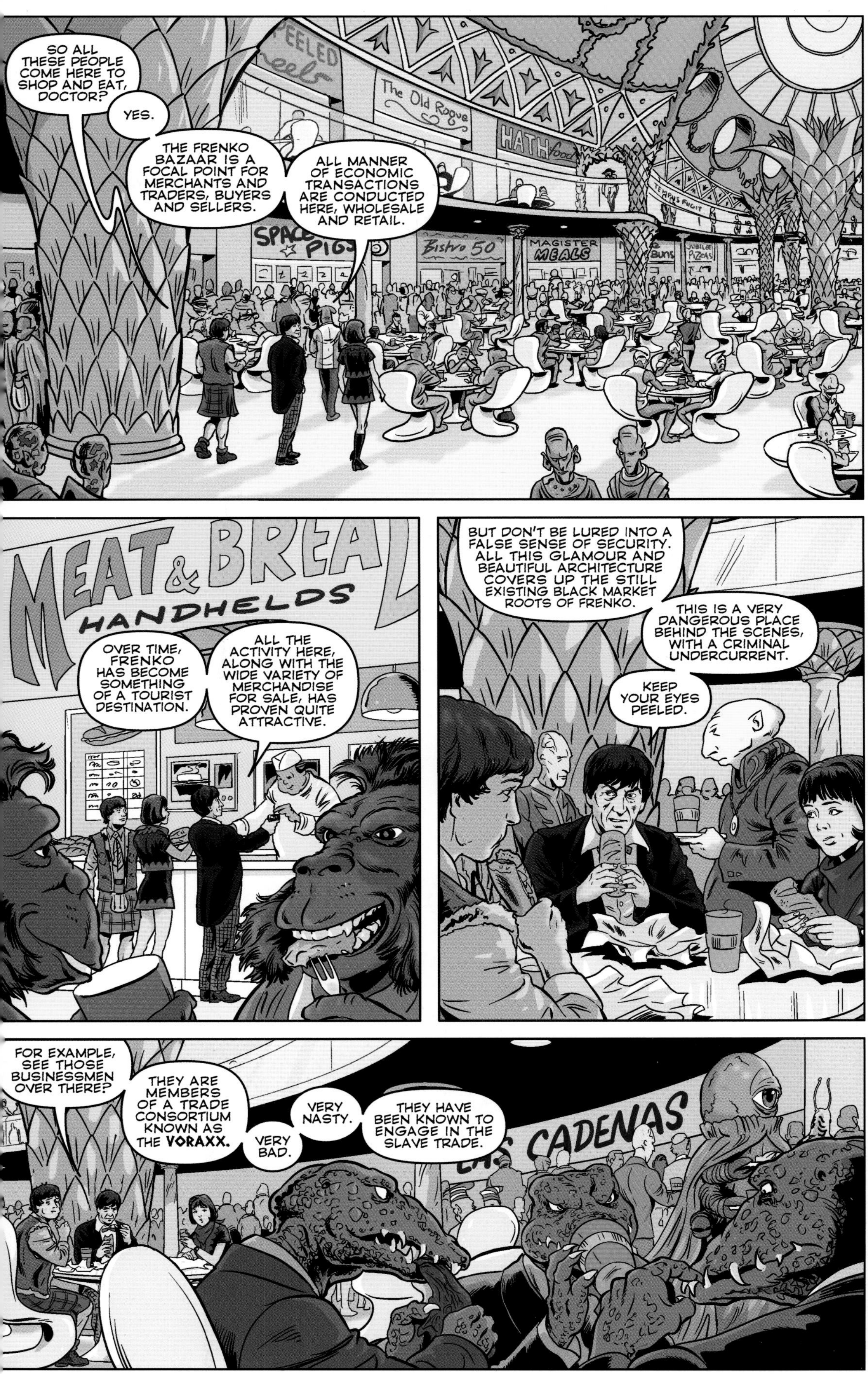
SO ALL THESE PEOPLE COME HERE TO SHOP AND EAT, DOCTOR?
YES.
THE FRENKO BAZAAR IS A FOCAL POINT FOR MERCHANTS AND TRADERS, BUYERS AND SELLERS.
ALL MANNER OF ECONOMIC TRANSACTIONS ARE CONDUCTED HERE, WHOLESALE AND RETAIL.
PEELED
The Old Rogue
HATH food
TEMPUS FUGIT
Bistro 50
MAGISTER MEALS
JUBILEE PIZZAS
MEAT & BREA
HANDHELDS
OVER TIME, FRENKO HAS BECOME SOMETHING OF A TOURIST DESTINATION.
ALL THE ACTIVITY HERE, ALONG WITH THE WIDE VARIETY OF MERCHANDISE FOR SALE, HAS PROVEN QUITE ATTRACTIVE.
BUT DON'T BE LURED INTO A FALSE SENSE OF SECURITY. ALL THIS GLAMOUR AND BEAUTIFUL ARCHITECTURE COVERS UP THE STILL EXISTING BLACK MARKET ROOTS OF FRENKO.
THIS IS A VERY DANGEROUS PLACE BEHIND THE SCENES, WITH A CRIMINAL UNDERCURRENT.
KEEP YOUR EYES PEELED.
FOR EXAMPLE, SEE THOSE BUSINESSMEN OVER THERE?
THEY ARE MEMBERS OF A TRADE CONSORTIUM KNOWN AS THE **VORAXX.**
VERY BAD.
VERY NASTY.
THEY HAVE BEEN KNOWN TO ENGAGE IN THE SLAVE TRADE.
CADENAS

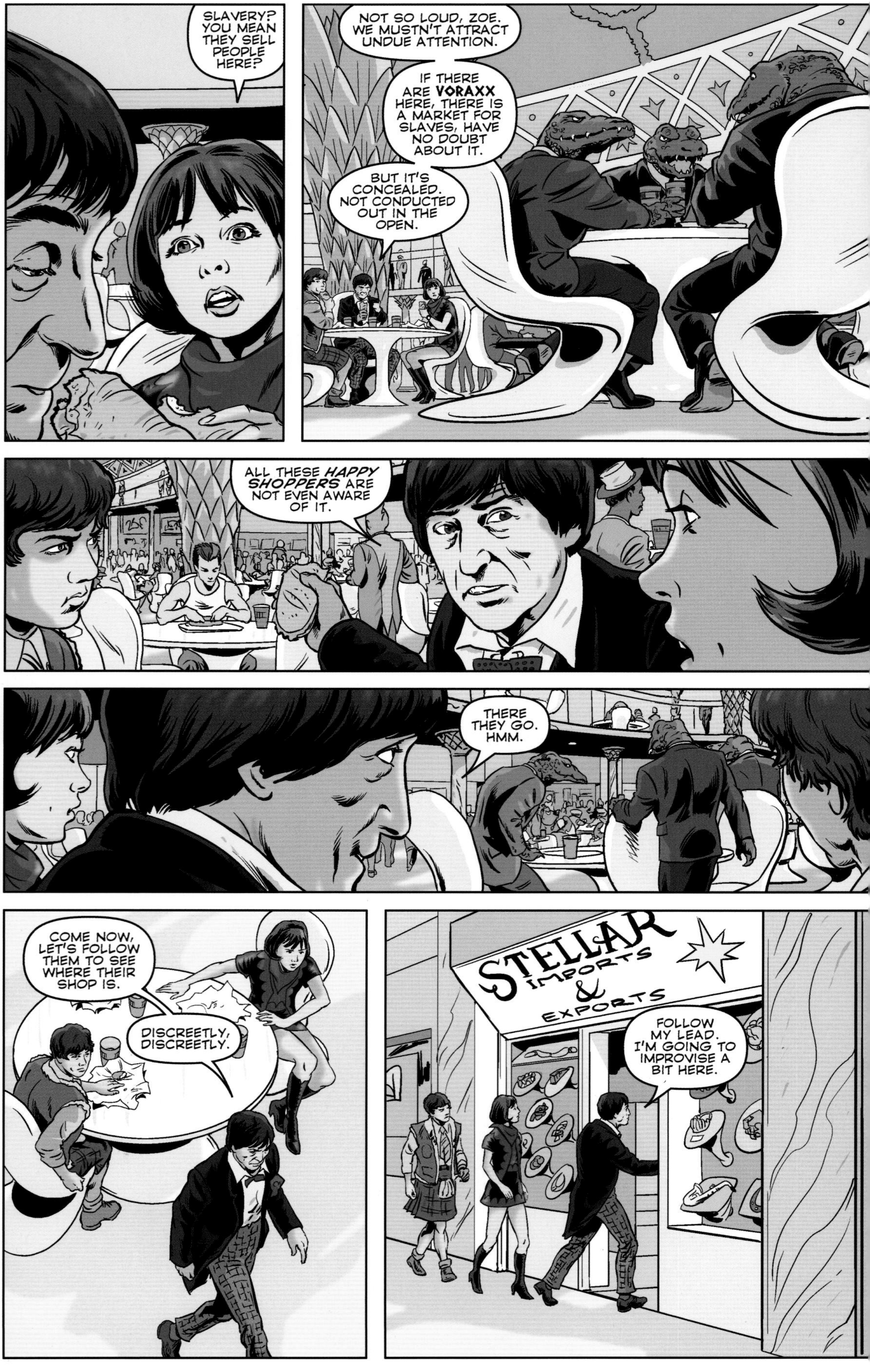
SLAVERY? YOU MEAN THEY SELL PEOPLE HERE?
NOT SO LOUD, ZOE. WE MUSTN'T ATTRACT UNDUE ATTENTION.
IF THERE ARE VORAXX HERE, THERE IS A MARKET FOR SLAVES, HAVE NO DOUBT ABOUT IT.
BUT IT'S CONCEALED. NOT CONDUCTED OUT IN THE OPEN.
ALL THESE HAPPY SHOPPERS ARE NOT EVEN AWARE OF IT.
THERE THEY GO. HMM.
COME NOW, LET'S FOLLOW THEM TO SEE WHERE THEIR SHOP IS.
DISCREETLY, DISCREETLY.
STELLAR IMPORTS & EXPORTS
FOLLOW MY LEAD. I'M GOING TO IMPROVISE A BIT HERE.

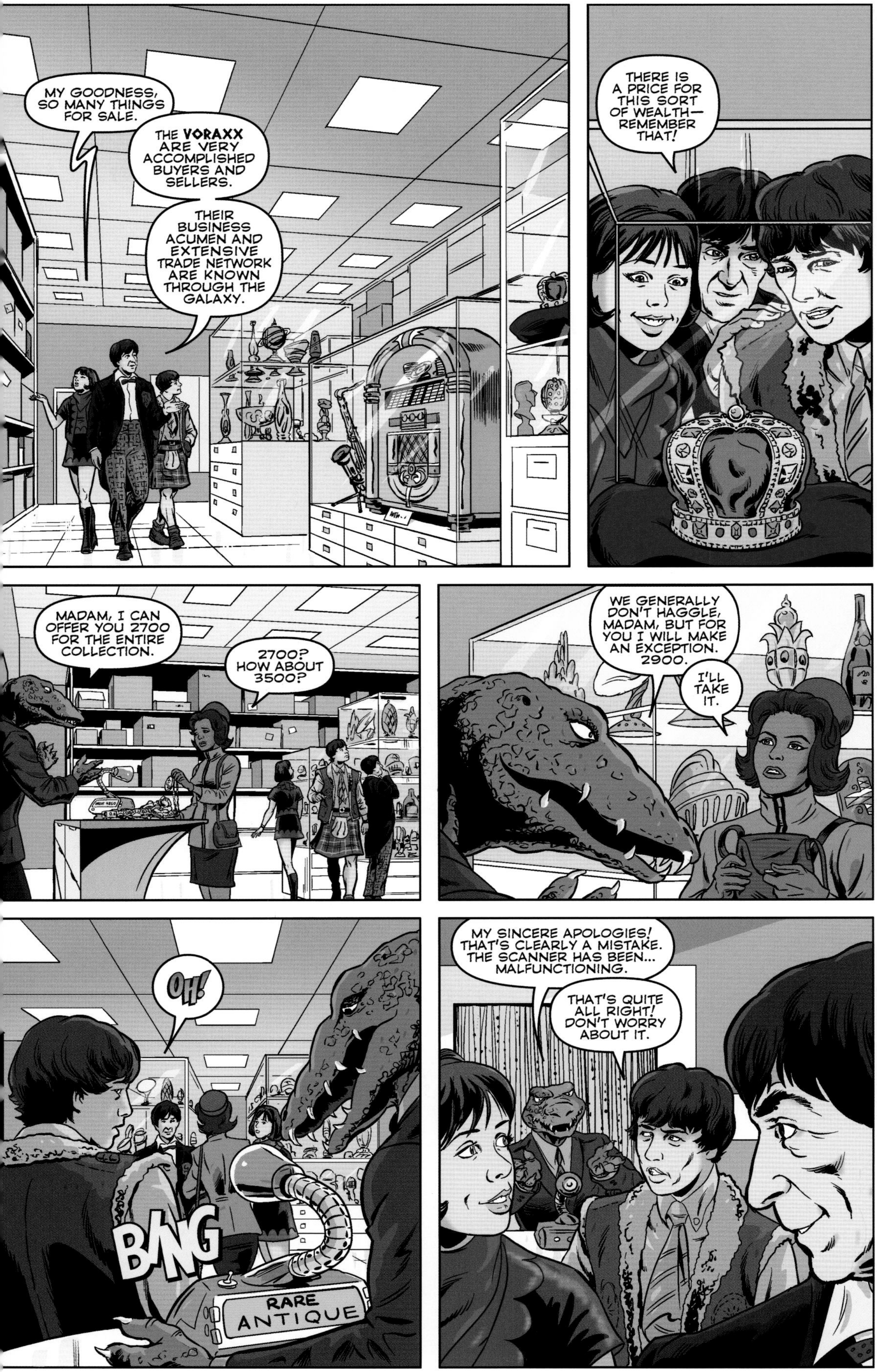

MY GOODNESS, SO MANY THINGS FOR SALE.
THE VORAXX ARE VERY ACCOMPLISHED BUYERS AND SELLERS.
THEIR BUSINESS ACUMEN AND EXTENSIVE TRADE NETWORK ARE KNOWN THROUGH THE GALAXY.
THERE IS A PRICE FOR THIS SORT OF WEALTH— REMEMBER THAT!
MADAM, I CAN OFFER YOU 2700 FOR THE ENTIRE COLLECTION.
2700? HOW ABOUT 3500?
WE GENERALLY DON'T HAGGLE, MADAM, BUT FOR YOU I WILL MAKE AN EXCEPTION. 2900.
I'LL TAKE IT.
OH!
BANG
RARE ANTIQUE
MY SINCERE APOLOGIES! THAT'S CLEARLY A MISTAKE. THE SCANNER HAS BEEN... MALFUNCTIONING.
THAT'S QUITE ALL RIGHT! DON'T WORRY ABOUT IT.

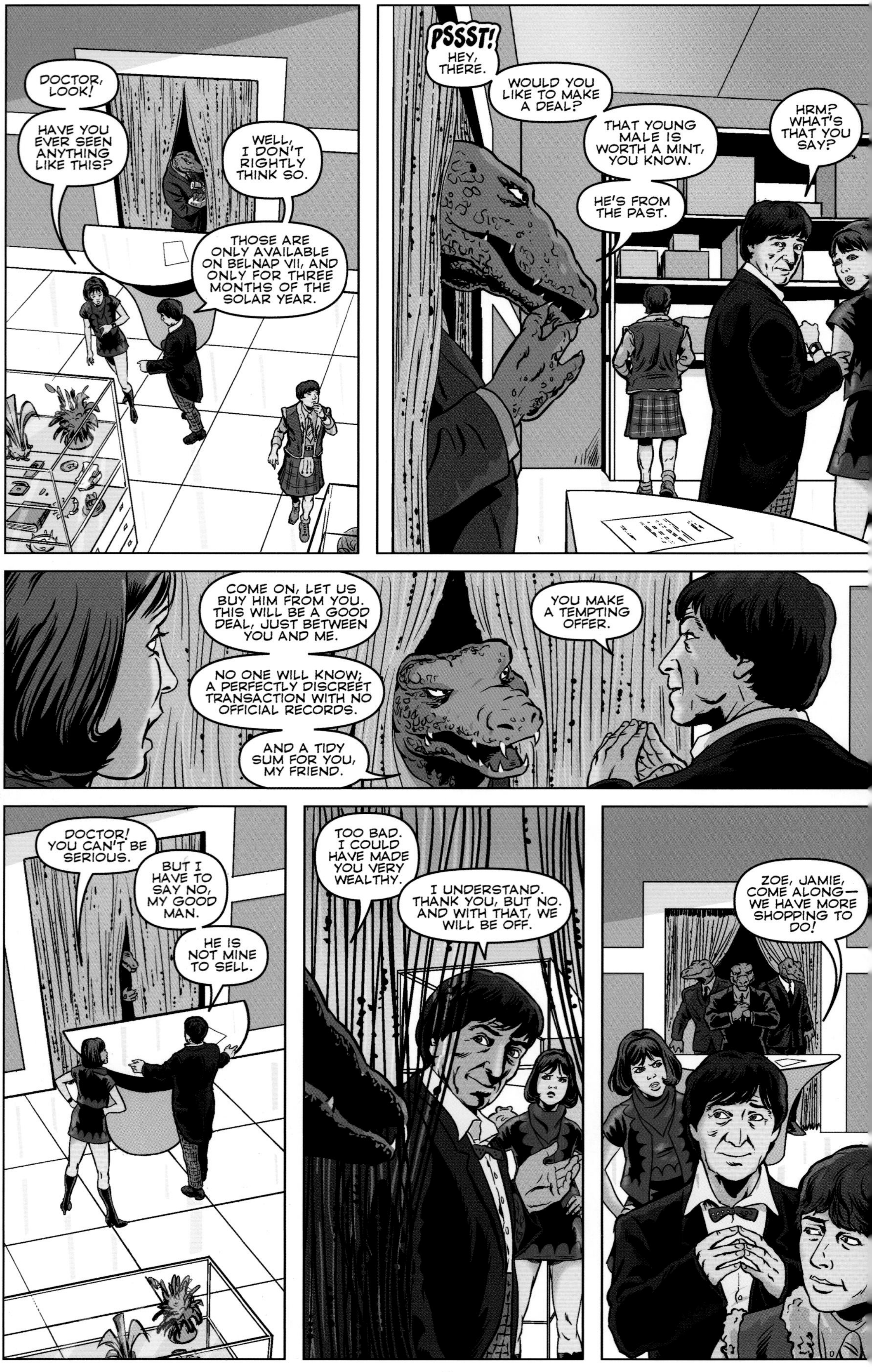
DOCTOR, LOOK!
HAVE YOU EVER SEEN ANYTHING LIKE THIS?
WELL, I DON'T RIGHTLY THINK SO.
THOSE ARE ONLY AVAILABLE ON BELNAP VII, AND ONLY FOR THREE MONTHS OF THE SOLAR YEAR.
PSSST!
HEY, THERE.
WOULD YOU LIKE TO MAKE A DEAL?
THAT YOUNG MALE IS WORTH A MINT, YOU KNOW.
HE'S FROM THE PAST.
HRM? WHAT'S THAT YOU SAY?
COME ON, LET US BUY HIM FROM YOU. THIS WILL BE A GOOD DEAL, JUST BETWEEN YOU AND ME.
NO ONE WILL KNOW; A PERFECTLY DISCREET TRANSACTION WITH NO OFFICIAL RECORDS.
AND A TIDY SUM FOR YOU, MY FRIEND.
YOU MAKE A TEMPTING OFFER.
DOCTOR! YOU CAN'T BE SERIOUS.
BUT I HAVE TO SAY NO, MY GOOD MAN.
HE IS NOT MINE TO SELL.
TOO BAD. I COULD HAVE MADE YOU VERY WEALTHY.
I UNDERSTAND. THANK YOU, BUT NO. AND WITH THAT, WE WILL BE OFF.
ZOE, JAMIE, COME ALONG— WE HAVE MORE SHOPPING TO DO!

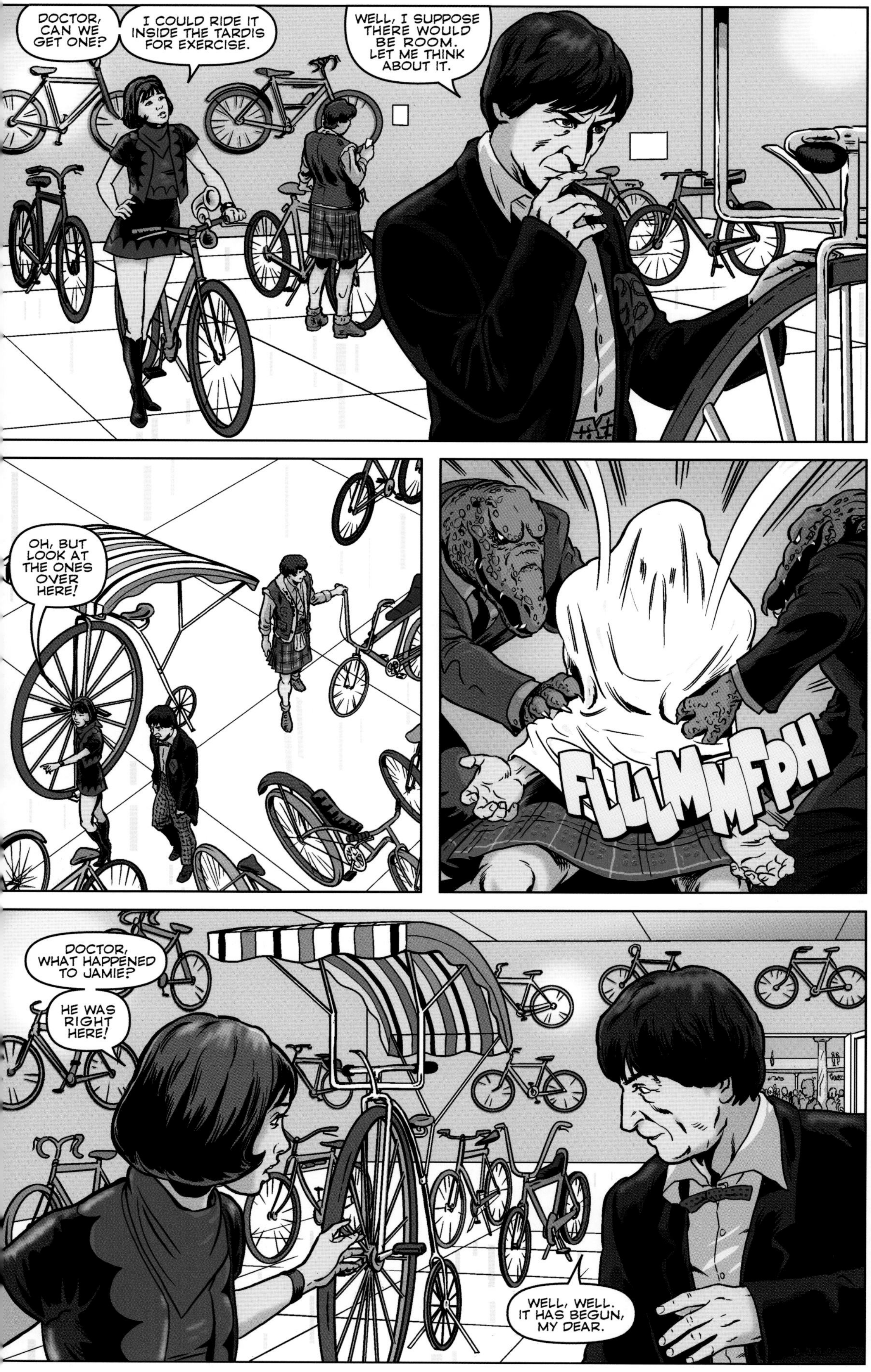
DOCTOR, CAN WE GET ONE?
I COULD RIDE IT INSIDE THE TARDIS FOR EXERCISE.
WELL, I SUPPOSE THERE WOULD BE ROOM. LET ME THINK ABOUT IT.
OH, BUT LOOK AT THE ONES OVER HERE!
FLLLMMFPH
DOCTOR, WHAT HAPPENED TO JAMIE?
HE WAS RIGHT HERE!
WELL, WELL. IT HAS BEGUN, MY DEAR.

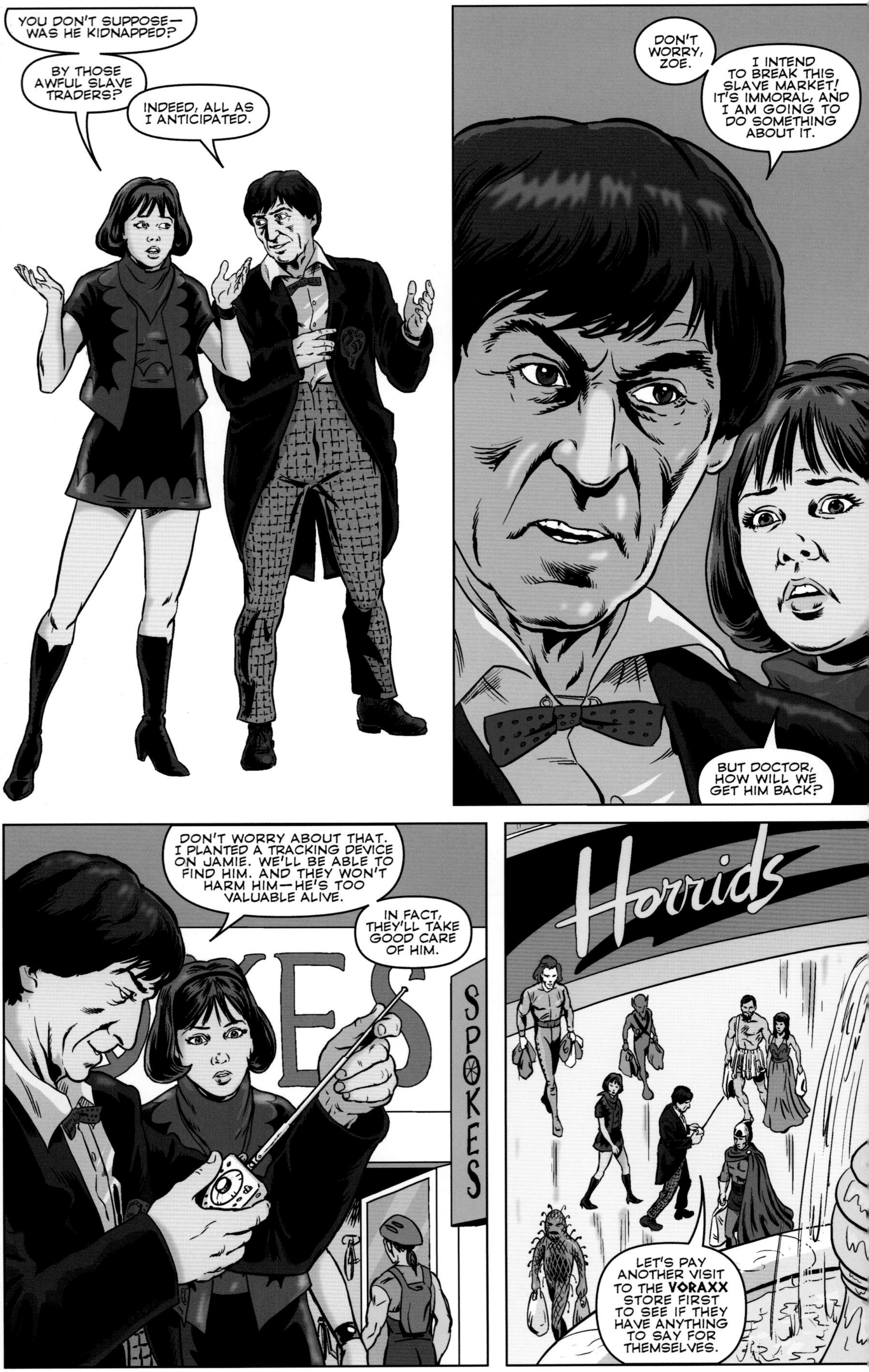
YOU DON'T SUPPOSE— WAS HE KIDNAPPED?
BY THOSE AWFUL SLAVE TRADERS?
INDEED, ALL AS I ANTICIPATED.
DON'T WORRY, ZOE.
I INTEND TO BREAK THIS SLAVE MARKET! IT'S IMMORAL, AND I AM GOING TO DO SOMETHING ABOUT IT.
BUT DOCTOR, HOW WILL WE GET HIM BACK?
DON'T WORRY ABOUT THAT. I PLANTED A TRACKING DEVICE ON JAMIE. WE'LL BE ABLE TO FIND HIM. AND THEY WON'T HARM HIM—HE'S TOO VALUABLE ALIVE.
IN FACT, THEY'LL TAKE GOOD CARE OF HIM.
SPOKES
Horrids
LET'S PAY ANOTHER VISIT TO THE **VORAXX** STORE FIRST TO SEE IF THEY HAVE ANYTHING TO SAY FOR THEMSELVES.

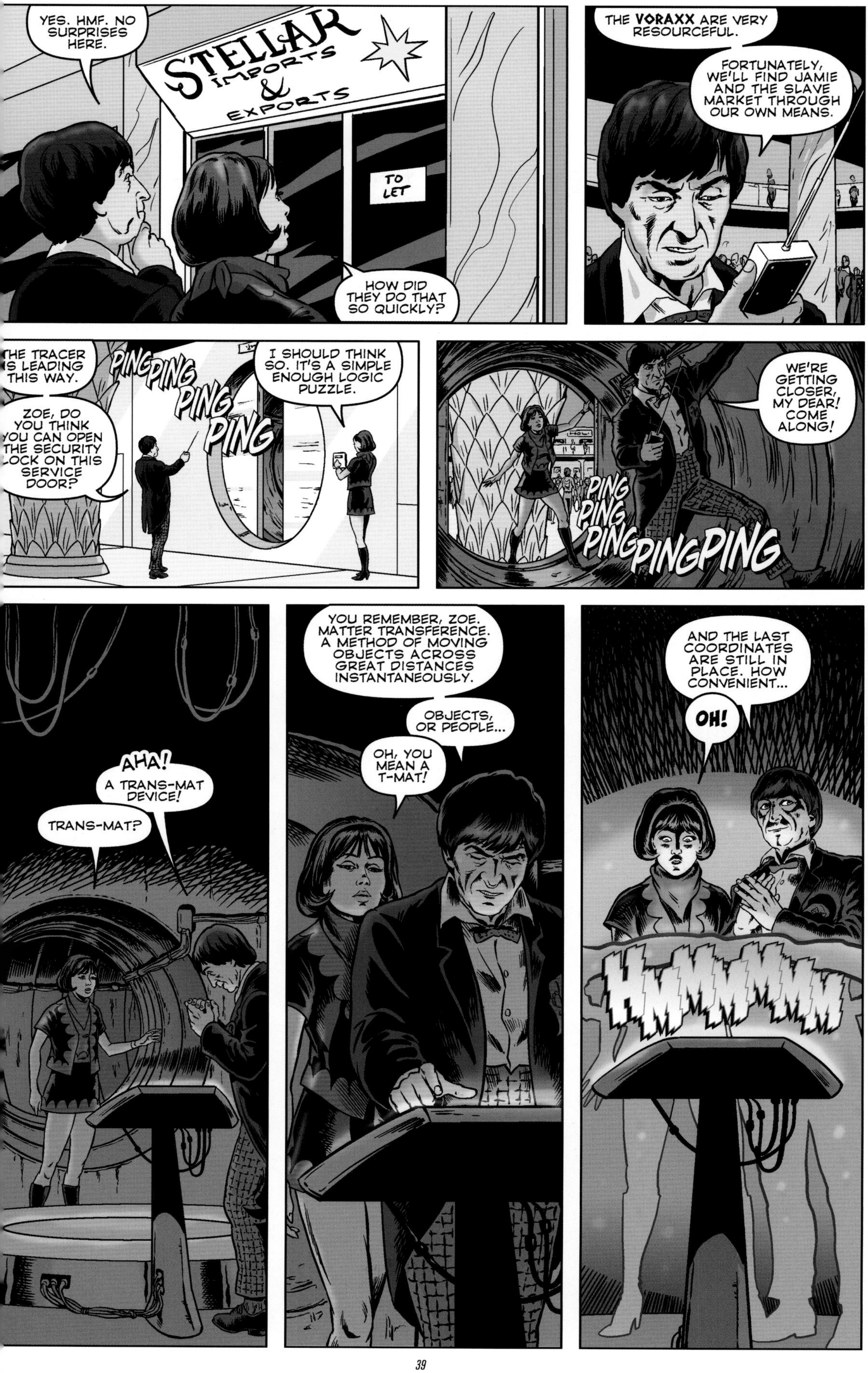
YES. HMF. NO SURPRISES HERE.
STELLAR IMPORTS & EXPORTS
TO LET
HOW DID THEY DO THAT SO QUICKLY?
THE VORAXX ARE VERY RESOURCEFUL.
FORTUNATELY, WE'LL FIND JAMIE AND THE SLAVE MARKET THROUGH OUR OWN MEANS.
THE TRACER IS LEADING THIS WAY.
PING PING PING PING
ZOE, DO YOU THINK YOU CAN OPEN THE SECURITY LOCK ON THIS SERVICE DOOR?
I SHOULD THINK SO. IT'S A SIMPLE ENOUGH LOGIC PUZZLE.
WE'RE GETTING CLOSER, MY DEAR! COME ALONG!
PING PING PINGPINGPING
AHA! A TRANS-MAT DEVICE!
TRANS-MAT?
YOU REMEMBER, ZOE. MATTER TRANSFERENCE. A METHOD OF MOVING OBJECTS ACROSS GREAT DISTANCES INSTANTANEOUSLY.
OBJECTS, OR PEOPLE...
OH, YOU MEAN A T-MAT!
AND THE LAST COORDINATES ARE STILL IN PLACE. HOW CONVENIENT...
OH!
HMMMMMM

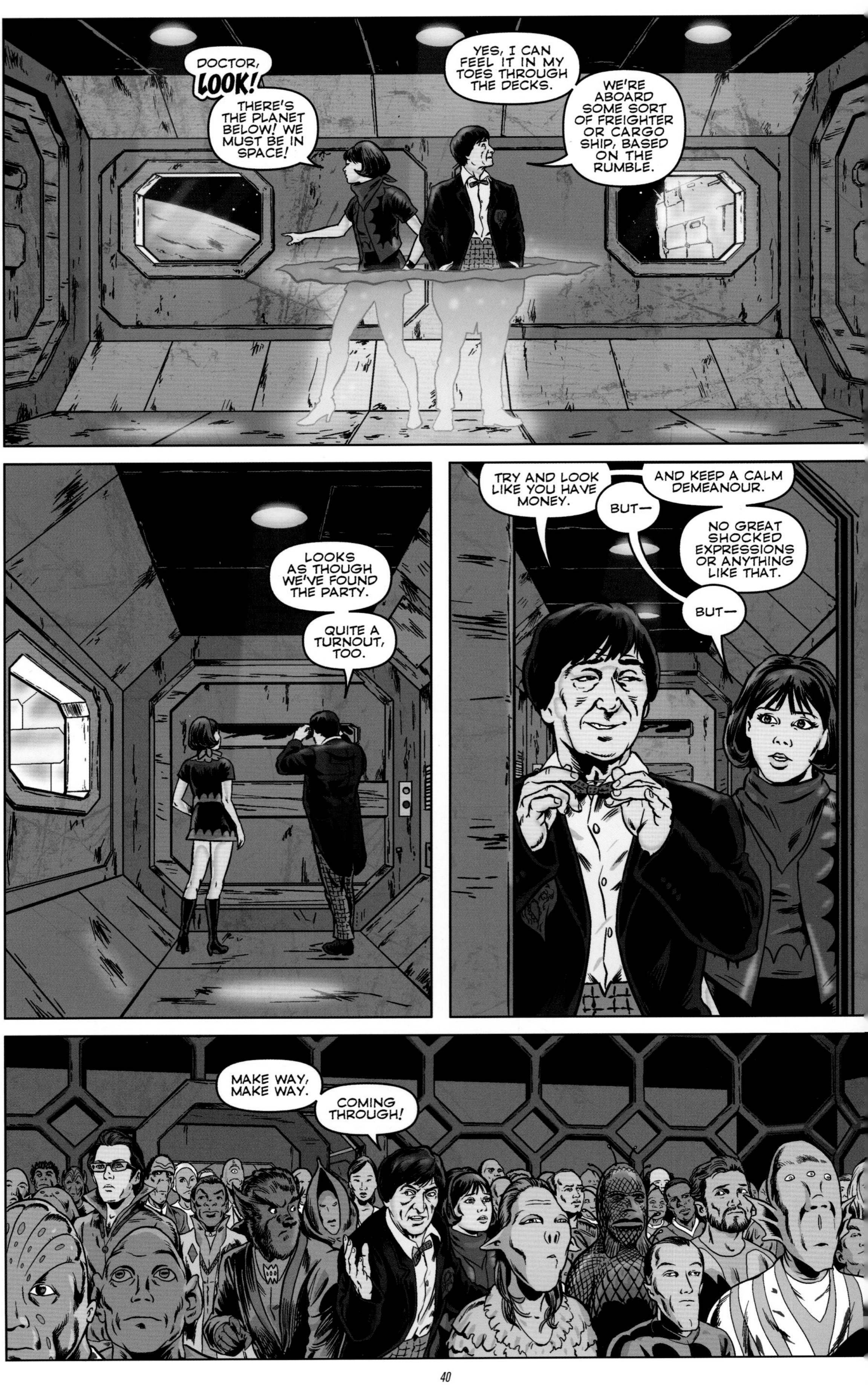
DOCTOR, LOOK!
THERE'S THE PLANET BELOW! WE MUST BE IN SPACE!
YES, I CAN FEEL IT IN MY TOES THROUGH THE DECKS.
WE'RE ABOARD SOME SORT OF FREIGHTER OR CARGO SHIP, BASED ON THE RUMBLE.
LOOKS AS THOUGH WE'VE FOUND THE PARTY.
QUITE A TURNOUT, TOO.
TRY AND LOOK LIKE YOU HAVE MONEY.
AND KEEP A CALM DEMEANOUR.
BUT—
NO GREAT SHOCKED EXPRESSIONS OR ANYTHING LIKE THAT.
BUT—
MAKE WAY, MAKE WAY.
COMING THROUGH!

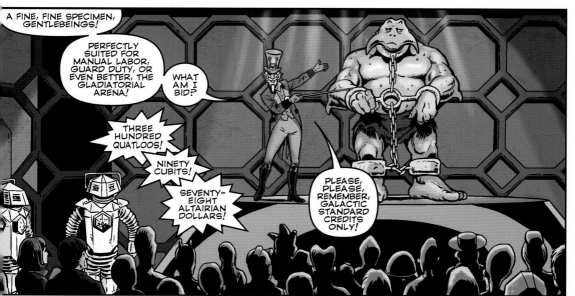

A FINE, FINE SPECIMEN, GENTLEBEINGS!

PERFECTLY SUITED FOR MANUAL LABOR, GUARD DUTY, OR EVEN BETTER, THE GLADIATORIAL ARENA!

WHAT AM I BID?

THREE HUNDRED QUATLOOS!

NINETY CUBITS!

SEVENTY-EIGHT ALTAIRIAN DOLLARS!

PLEASE, PLEASE, REMEMBER, GALACTIC STANDARD CREDITS ONLY!

UTTERLY BARBARIC! THIS SIMPLY WON'T DO!

OH, WHY, THANK YOU!

DOCTOR, LOOK AT THIS.

THAT ROBOT HANDED ME THIS—IT'S AN AUCTION SCHEDULE AND MANIFEST.

IT SAYS HERE THAT JAMIE IS SCHEDULED FOR AUCTION IN THE SECOND SESSION, LATER TODAY!

SPLENDID! CAN YOU FIND A MAP ON THERE AS WELL?

FOUND IT! 'MERCHANDISE VIEWING'!

THEN LEAD THE WAY, ZOE!

IT SHOULD BE BEHIND THIS DOOR...

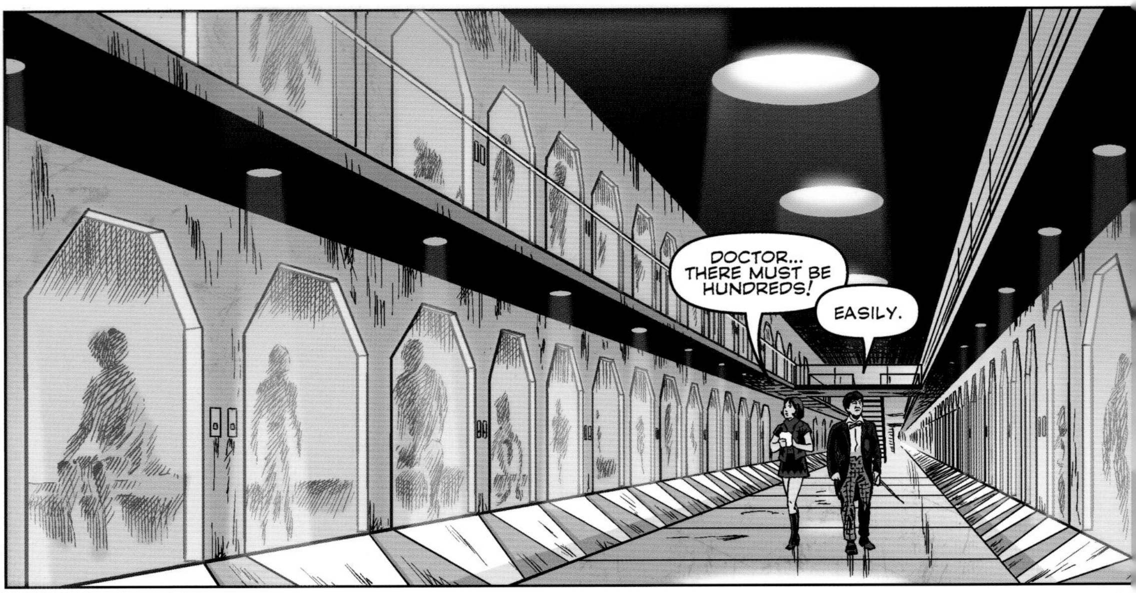
DOCTOR... THERE MUST BE HUNDREDS!
EASILY.

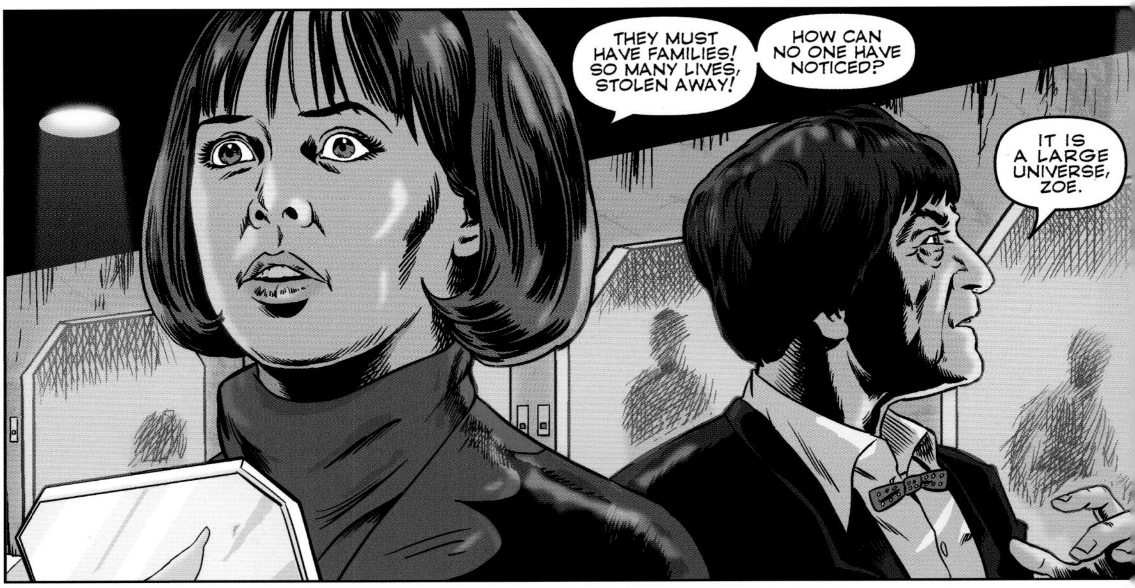
THEY MUST HAVE FAMILIES! SO MANY LIVES, STOLEN AWAY!
HOW CAN NO ONE HAVE NOTICED?
IT IS A LARGE UNIVERSE, ZOE.

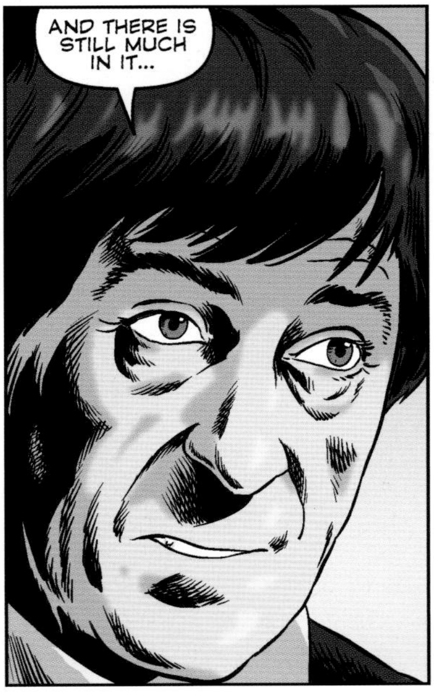
AND THERE IS STILL MUCH IN IT...

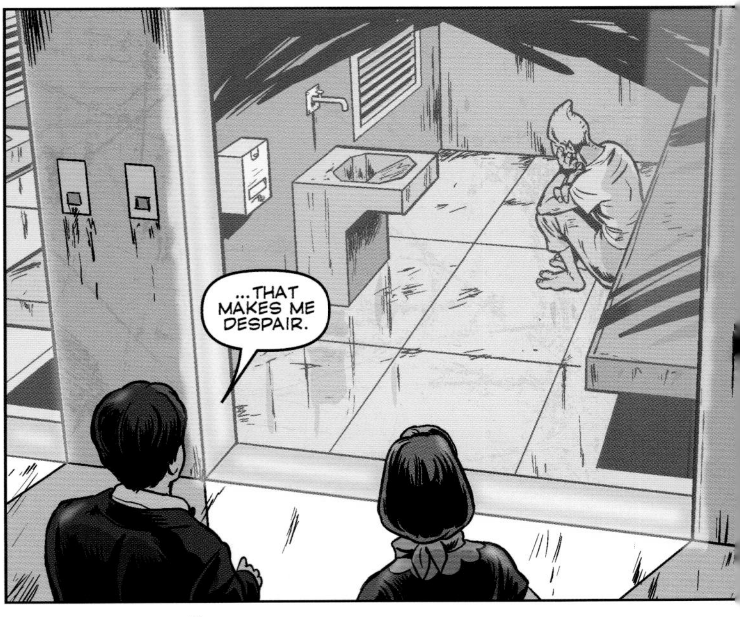
...THAT MAKES ME DESPAIR.

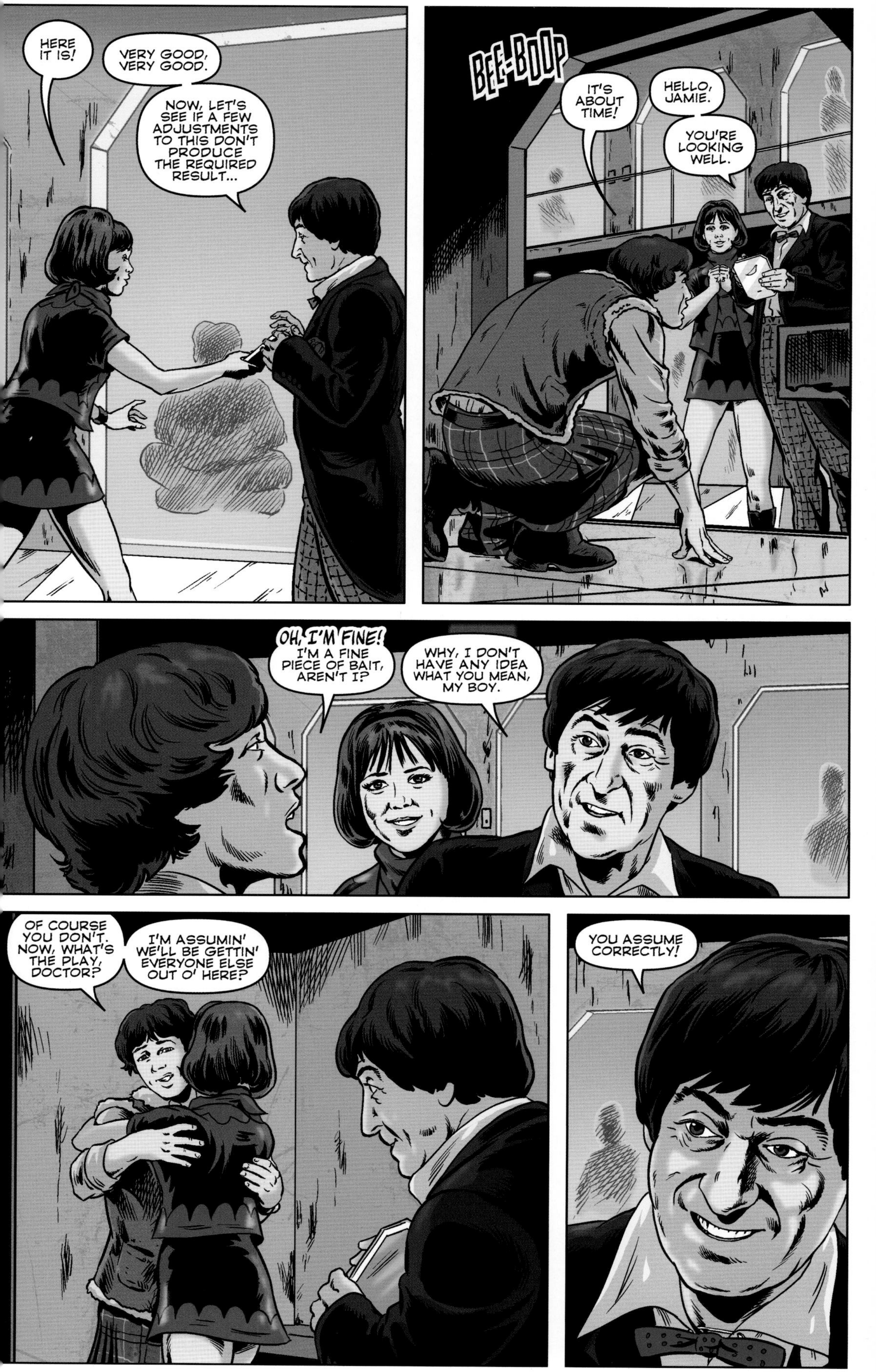
HERE IT IS!
VERY GOOD, VERY GOOD.
NOW, LET'S SEE IF A FEW ADJUSTMENTS TO THIS DON'T PRODUCE THE REQUIRED RESULT...
BEE-BOOP
IT'S ABOUT TIME!
HELLO, JAMIE.
YOU'RE LOOKING WELL.
OH, I'M FINE! I'M A FINE PIECE OF BAIT, AREN'T I?
WHY, I DON'T HAVE ANY IDEA WHAT YOU MEAN, MY BOY.
OF COURSE YOU DON'T. NOW, WHAT'S THE PLAY, DOCTOR?
I'M ASSUMIN' WE'LL BE GETTIN' EVERYONE ELSE OUT O' HERE?
YOU ASSUME CORRECTLY!

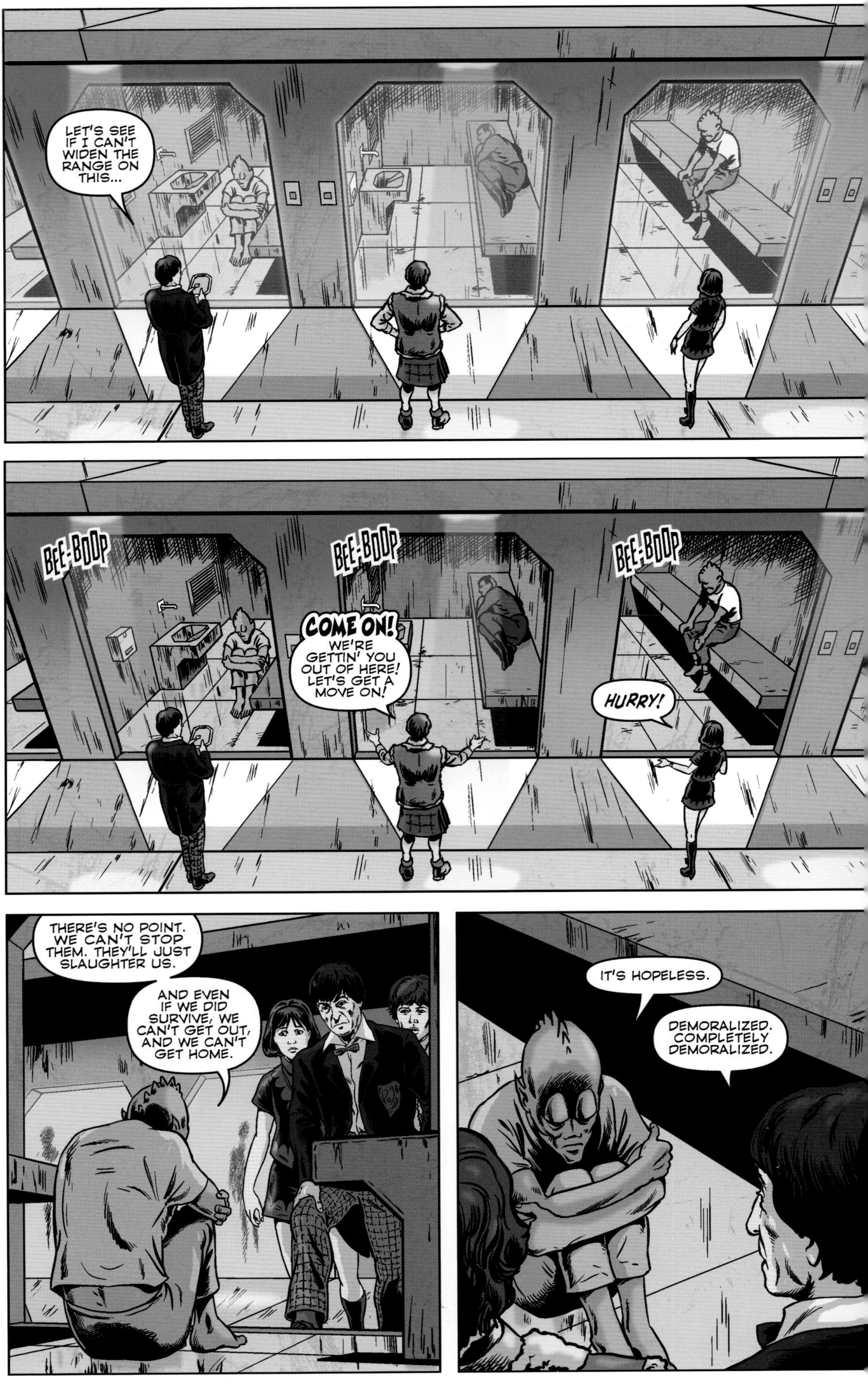

LET'S SEE IF I CAN'T WIDEN THE RANGE ON THIS...
BEE-BOOP
BEE-BOOP
COME ON! WE'RE GETTIN' YOU OUT OF HERE! LET'S GET A MOVE ON!
BEE-BOOP
HURRY!
THERE'S NO POINT. WE CAN'T STOP THEM. THEY'LL JUST SLAUGHTER US.
AND EVEN IF WE DID SURVIVE, WE CAN'T GET OUT, AND WE CAN'T GET HOME.
IT'S HOPELESS.
DEMORALIZED. COMPLETELY DEMORALIZED.

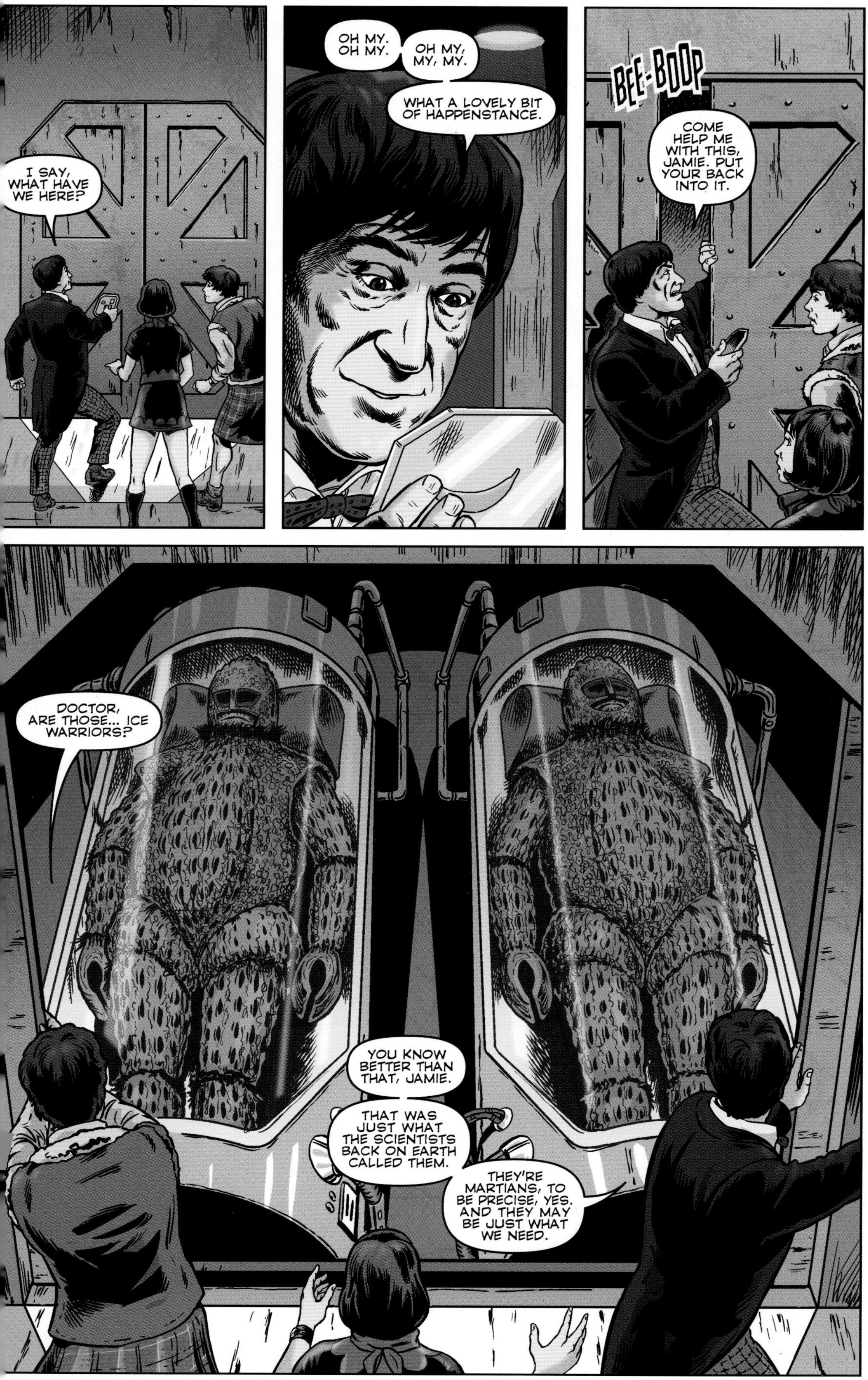
I SAY, WHAT HAVE WE HERE?
OH MY. OH MY.
OH MY, MY, MY.
WHAT A LOVELY BIT OF HAPPENSTANCE.
BEE-BOOP
COME HELP ME WITH THIS, JAMIE. PUT YOUR BACK INTO IT.
DOCTOR, ARE THOSE... ICE WARRIORS?
YOU KNOW BETTER THAN THAT, JAMIE.
THAT WAS JUST WHAT THE SCIENTISTS BACK ON EARTH CALLED THEM.
THEY'RE MARTIANS, TO BE PRECISE, YES. AND THEY MAY BE JUST WHAT WE NEED.

...WHERE... ARE WE?

YOU ARE CAPTIVES ABOARD A SLAVER SHIP.

ARE YOU... OUR ENSSSS-SLAVER?

NOT AT ALL. I CAN FREE YOU.

THERE ARE MANY HERE HELD ENSLAVED, BUT THEY LACK THE WILL TO RISE UP. THEY NEED INSPIRATION.

I AM CALLED... ARAXUS... HELP ME UP... AND I WILL TURN YOUR RABBLE INTO AN ARMY.

BUZZZ BUZZZ BUZZZ BUZZZ

ALERT! ALERT! MERCHANDISE HAS ESCAPED THEIR CELLS!

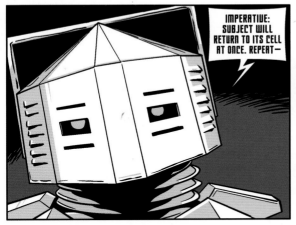

IMPERATIVE: SUBJECT WILL RETURN TO ITS CELL AT ONCE. REPEAT—

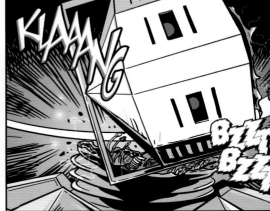

KLAAANG

BZZT BZZT

LET USSSSSSS FIGHT!

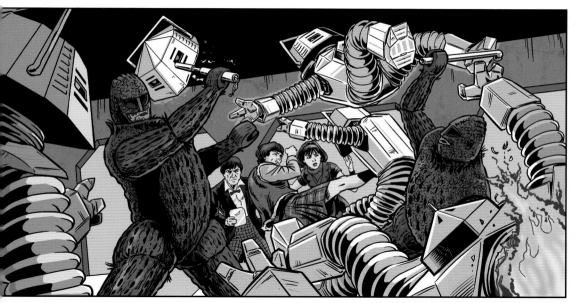

RRRAAGGGH!

FREEDOM!

YAAAAHH!

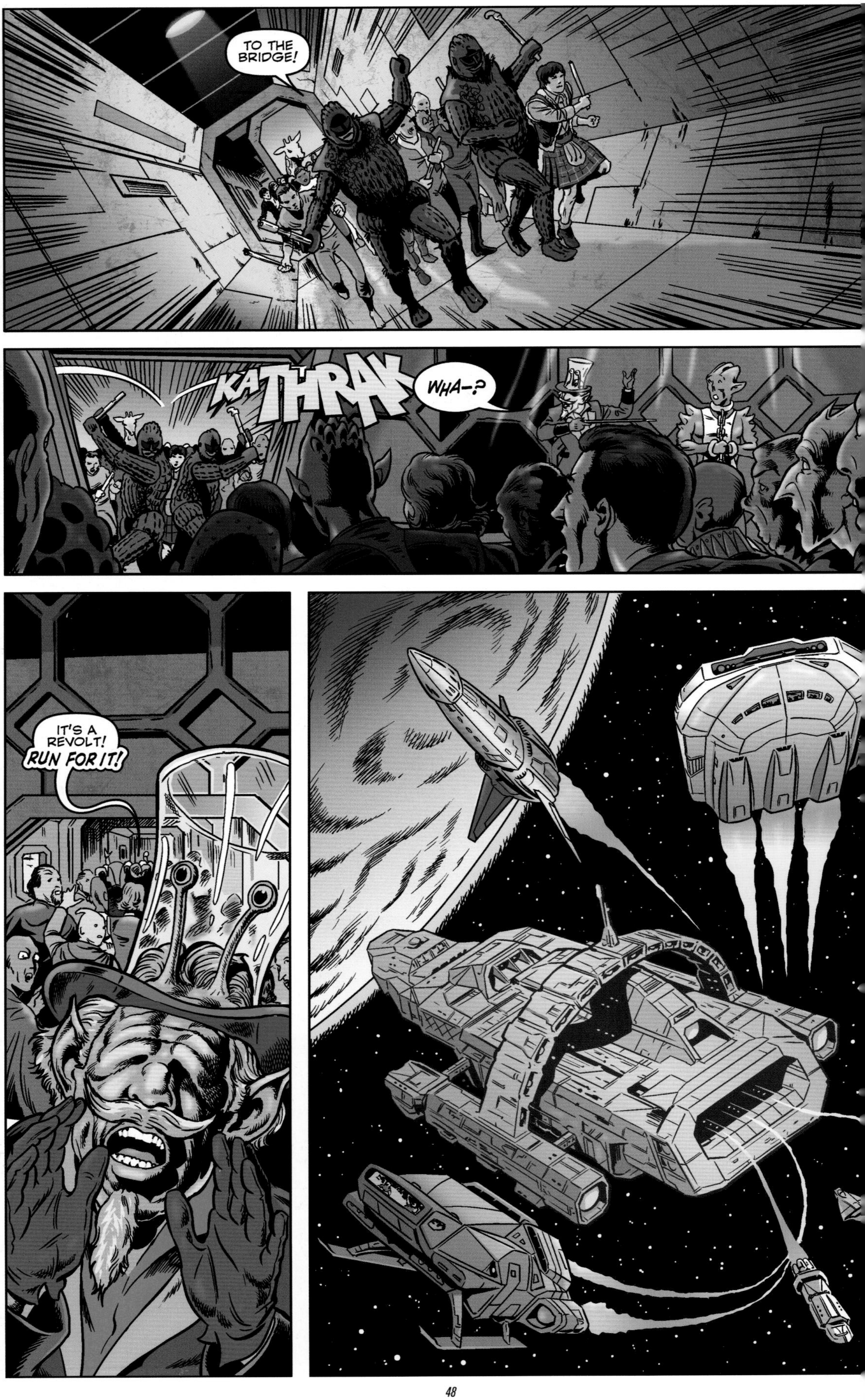
TO THE BRIDGE!
KATHRAK
WHA--?
IT'S A REVOLT! RUN FOR IT!

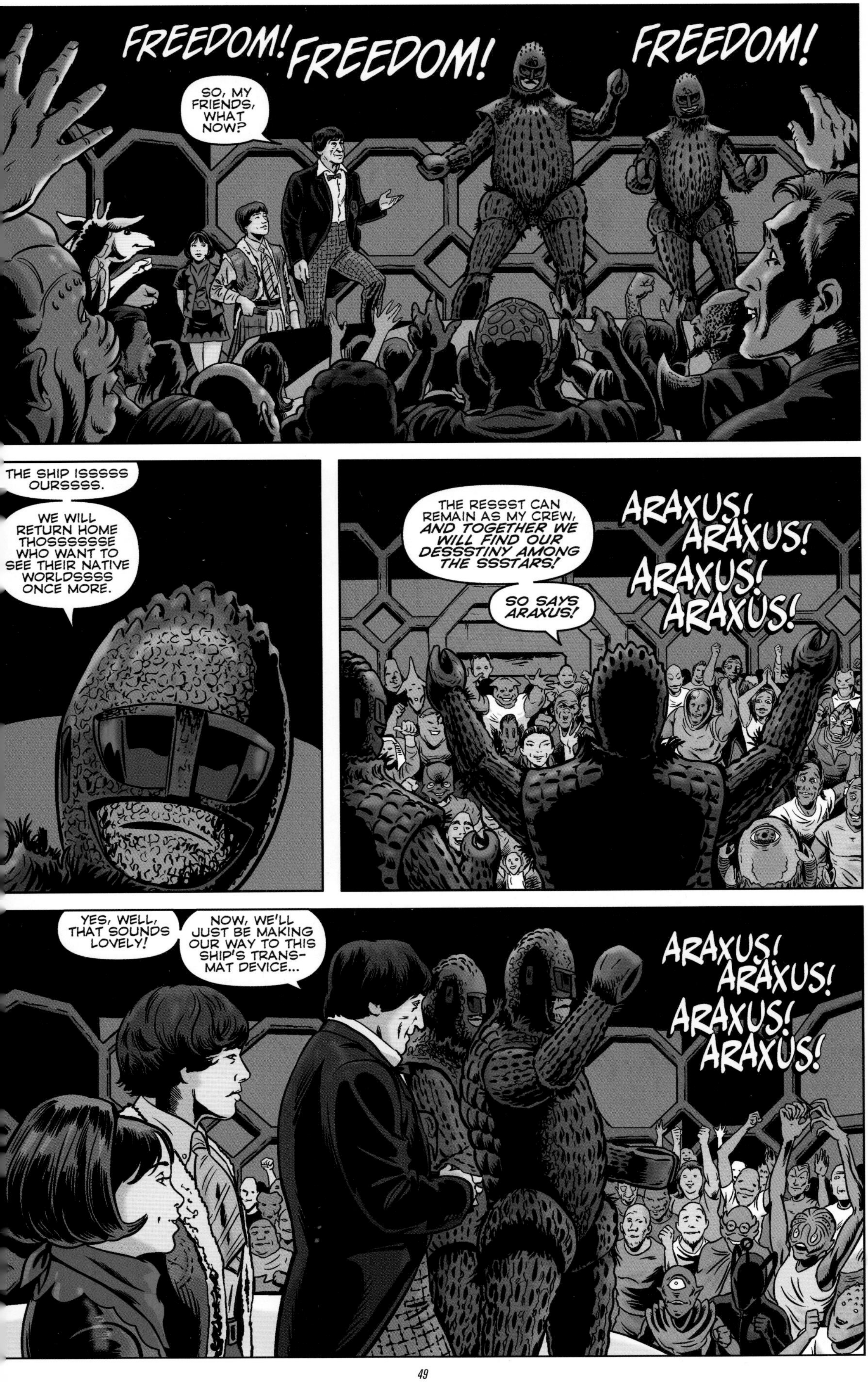
FREEDOM! FREEDOM! FREEDOM!
SO, MY FRIENDS, WHAT NOW?
THE SHIP ISSSSS OURSSSS.
WE WILL RETURN HOME THOSSSSSSE WHO WANT TO SEE THEIR NATIVE WORLDSSSS ONCE MORE.
THE RESSST CAN REMAIN AS MY CREW, AND TOGETHER WE WILL FIND OUR DESSSTINY AMONG THE SSSTARS!
SO SAYS ARAXUS!
ARAXUS! ARAXUS! ARAXUS! ARAXUS!
YES, WELL, THAT SOUNDS LOVELY!
NOW, WE'LL JUST BE MAKING OUR WAY TO THIS SHIP'S TRANS-MAT DEVICE...
ARAXUS! ARAXUS! ARAXUS! ARAXUS!

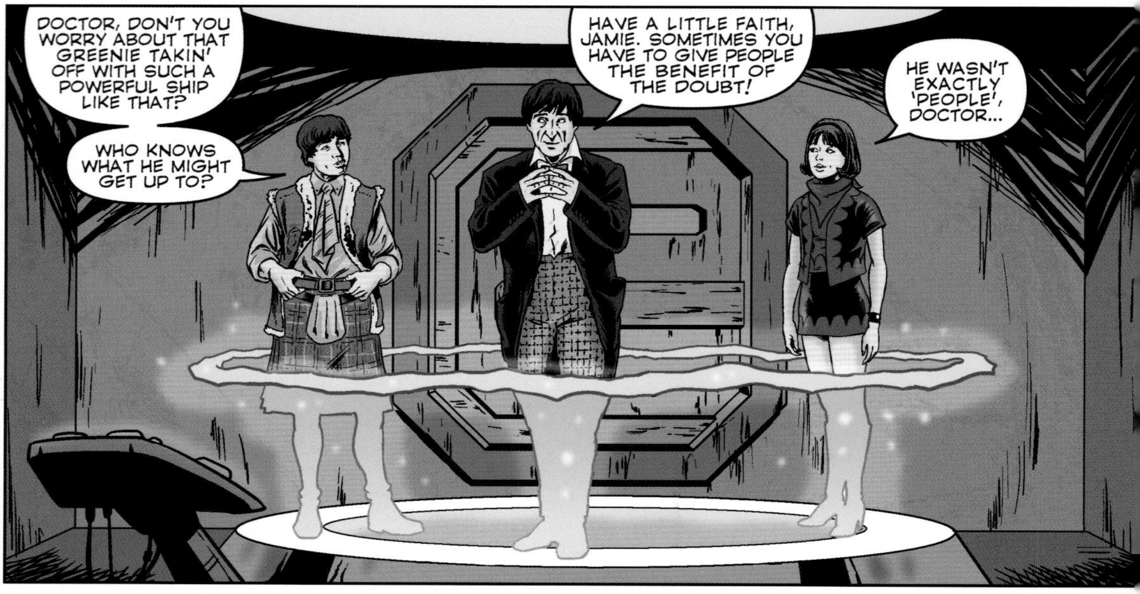
DOCTOR, DON'T YOU WORRY ABOUT THAT GREENIE TAKIN' OFF WITH SUCH A POWERFUL SHIP LIKE THAT?
WHO KNOWS WHAT HE MIGHT GET UP TO?
HAVE A LITTLE FAITH, JAMIE. SOMETIMES YOU HAVE TO GIVE PEOPLE THE BENEFIT OF THE DOUBT!
HE WASN'T EXACTLY 'PEOPLE', DOCTOR...

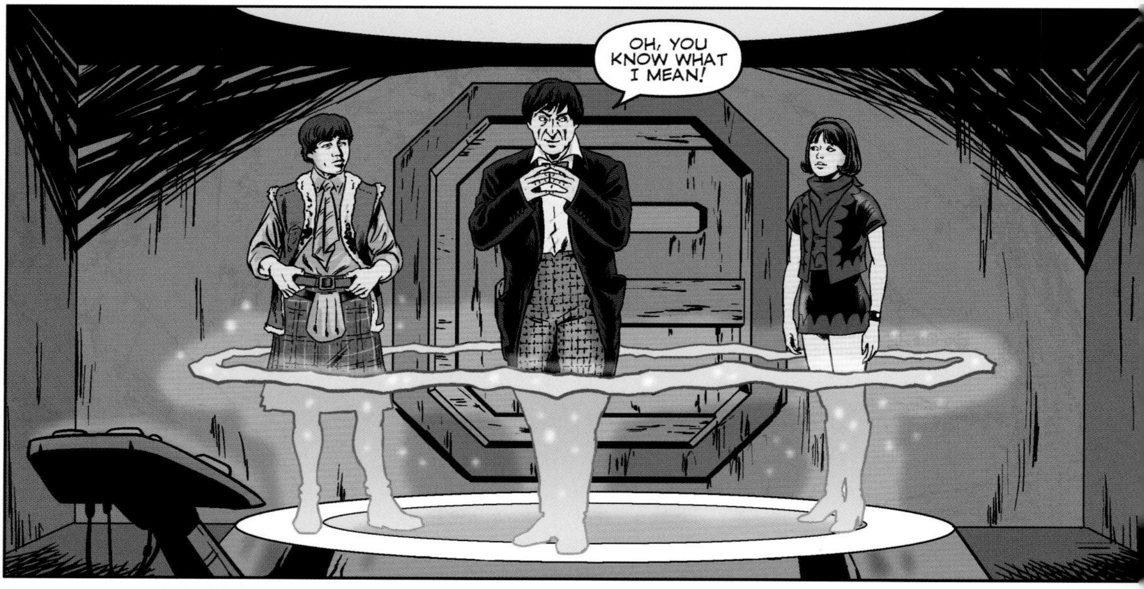
OH, YOU KNOW WHAT I MEAN!

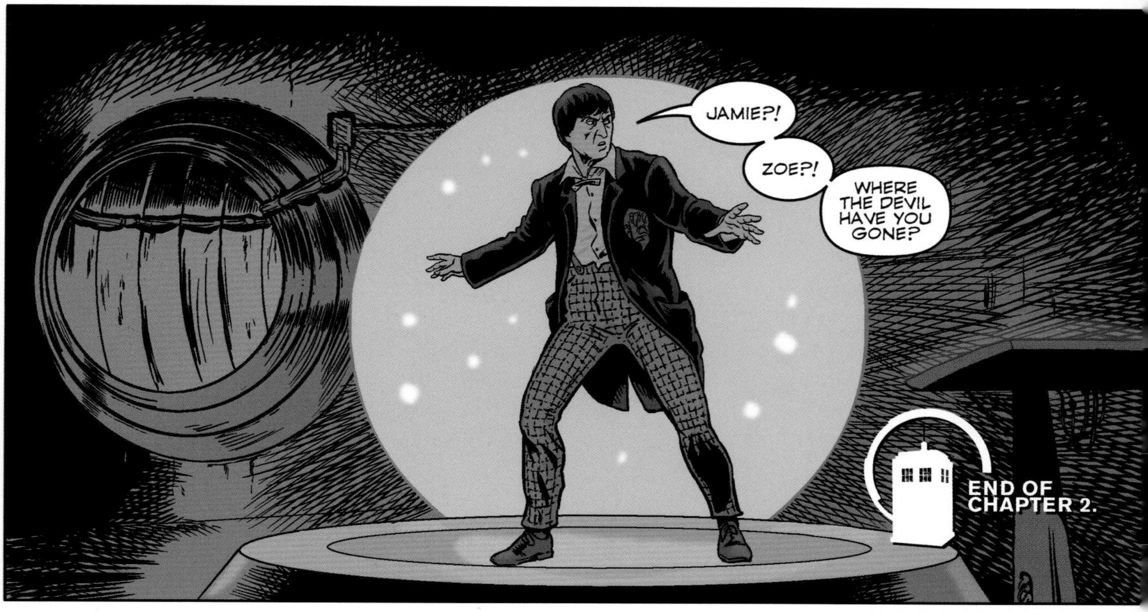
JAMIE?!
ZOE?!
WHERE THE DEVIL HAVE YOU GONE?
END OF CHAPTER 2.

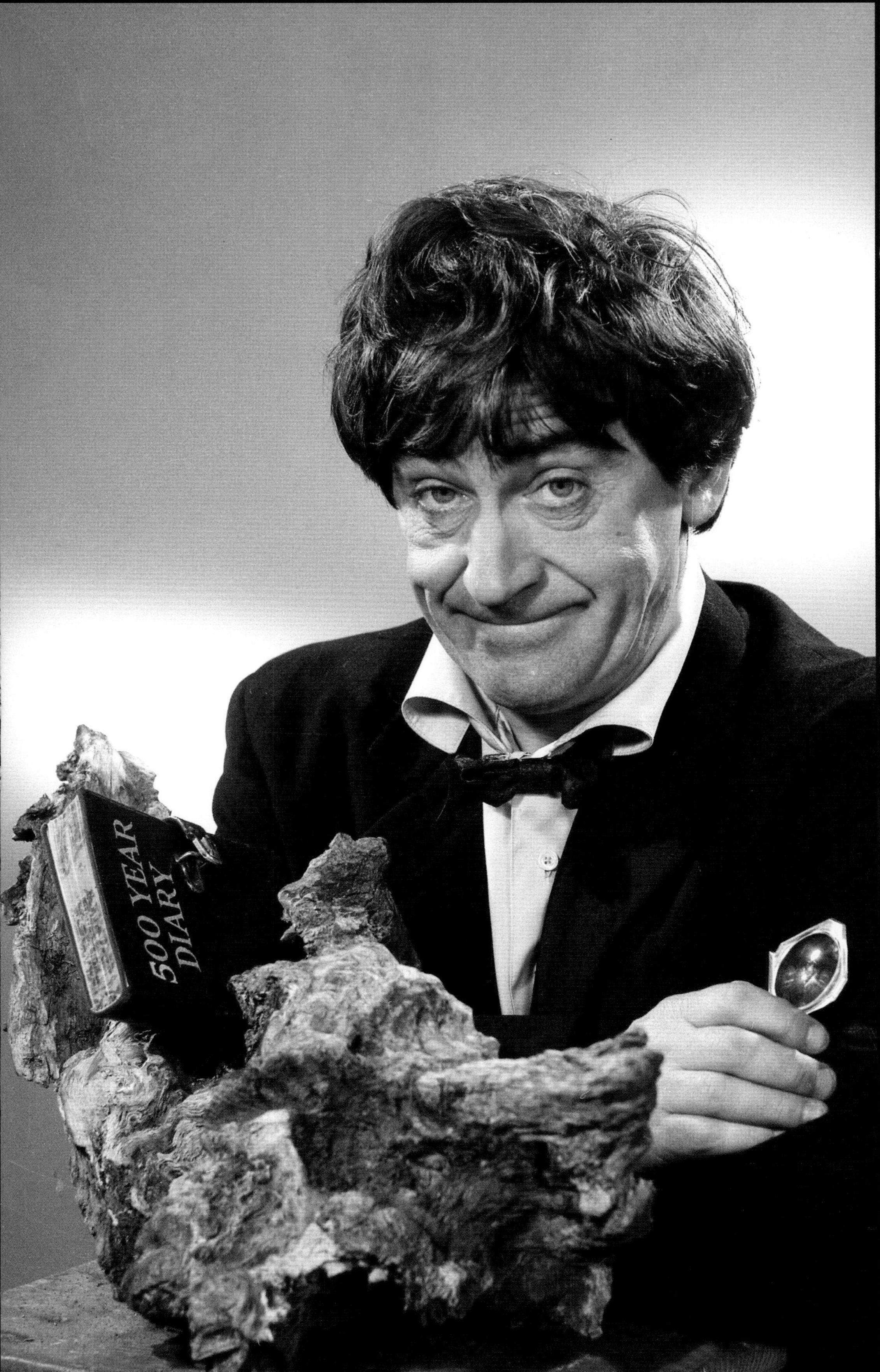
500 YEAR
DIARY

CHAPTER 3
"In With the Tide"
Cover Art by Francesco Francavilla

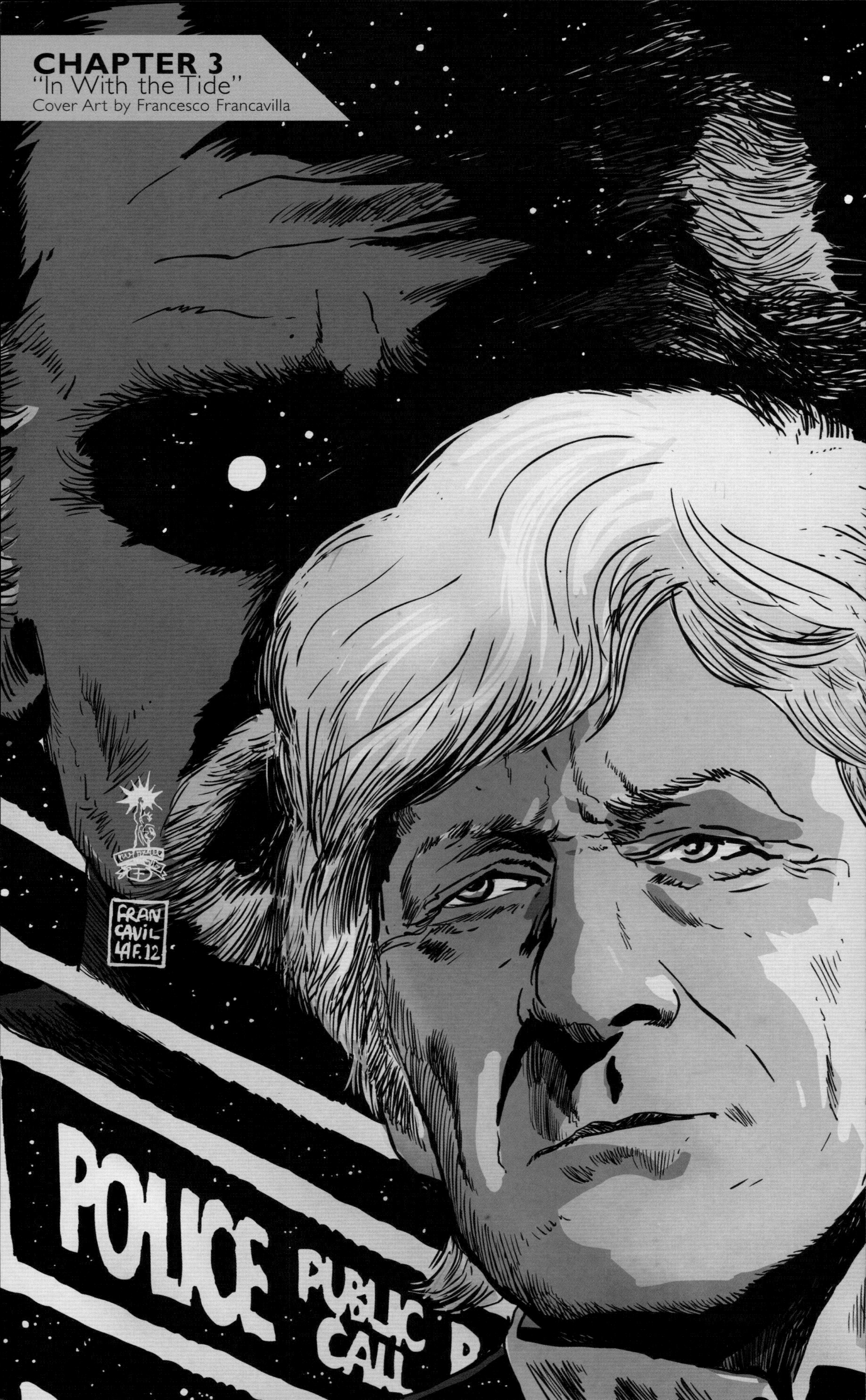
FRAN CAVIL LA F. 12
POLICE
PUBLIC CALL

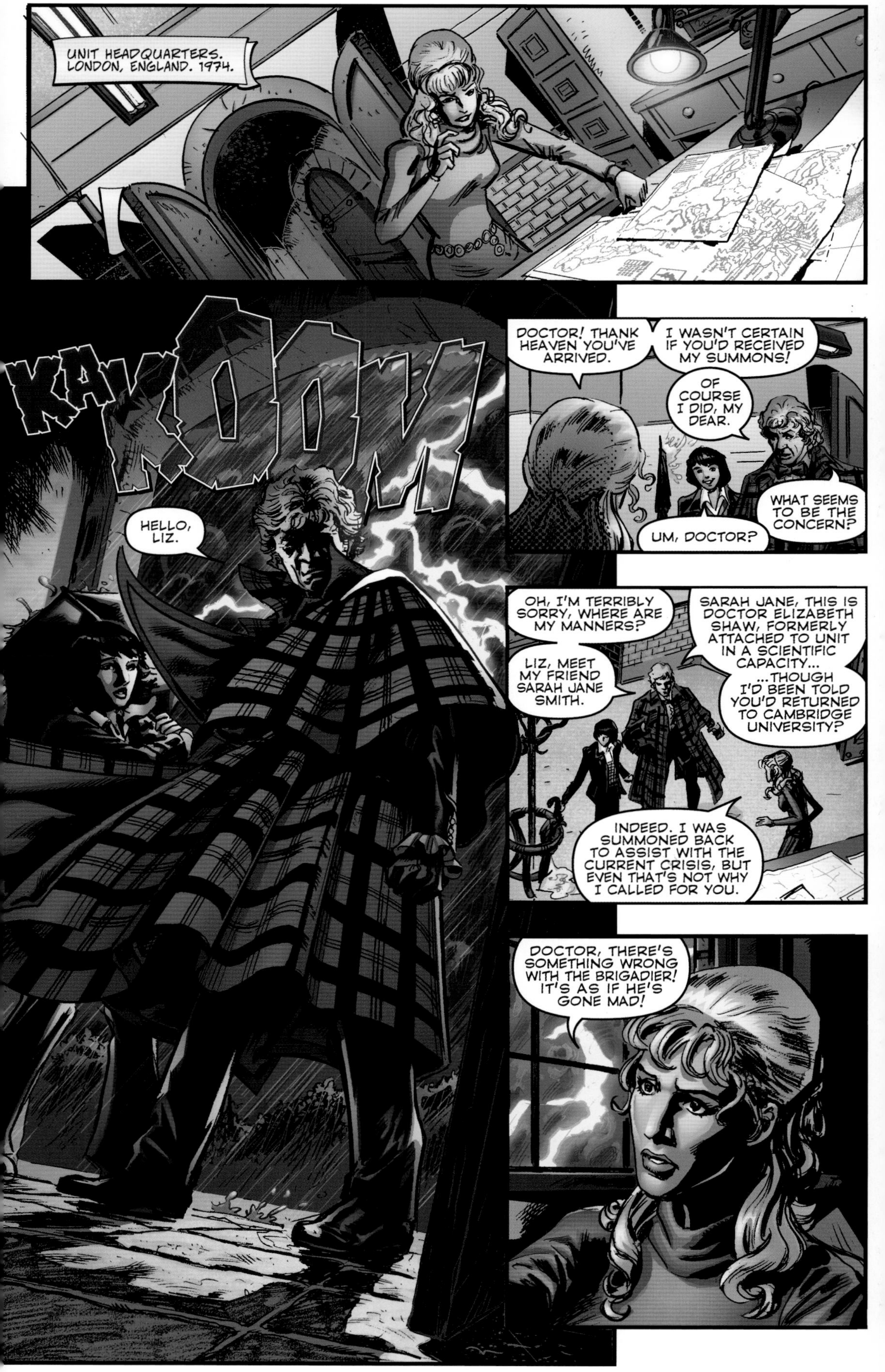
UNIT HEADQUARTERS. LONDON, ENGLAND. 1974.
KA-KOOM
HELLO, LIZ.
DOCTOR! THANK HEAVEN YOU'VE ARRIVED.
I WASN'T CERTAIN IF YOU'D RECEIVED MY SUMMONS!
OF COURSE I DID, MY DEAR.
WHAT SEEMS TO BE THE CONCERN?
UM, DOCTOR?
OH, I'M TERRIBLY SORRY, WHERE ARE MY MANNERS?
LIZ, MEET MY FRIEND SARAH JANE SMITH.
SARAH JANE, THIS IS DOCTOR ELIZABETH SHAW, FORMERLY ATTACHED TO UNIT IN A SCIENTIFIC CAPACITY...
...THOUGH I'D BEEN TOLD YOU'D RETURNED TO CAMBRIDGE UNIVERSITY?
INDEED. I WAS SUMMONED BACK TO ASSIST WITH THE CURRENT CRISIS, BUT EVEN THAT'S NOT WHY I CALLED FOR YOU.
DOCTOR, THERE'S SOMETHING WRONG WITH THE BRIGADIER! IT'S AS IF HE'S GONE MAD!

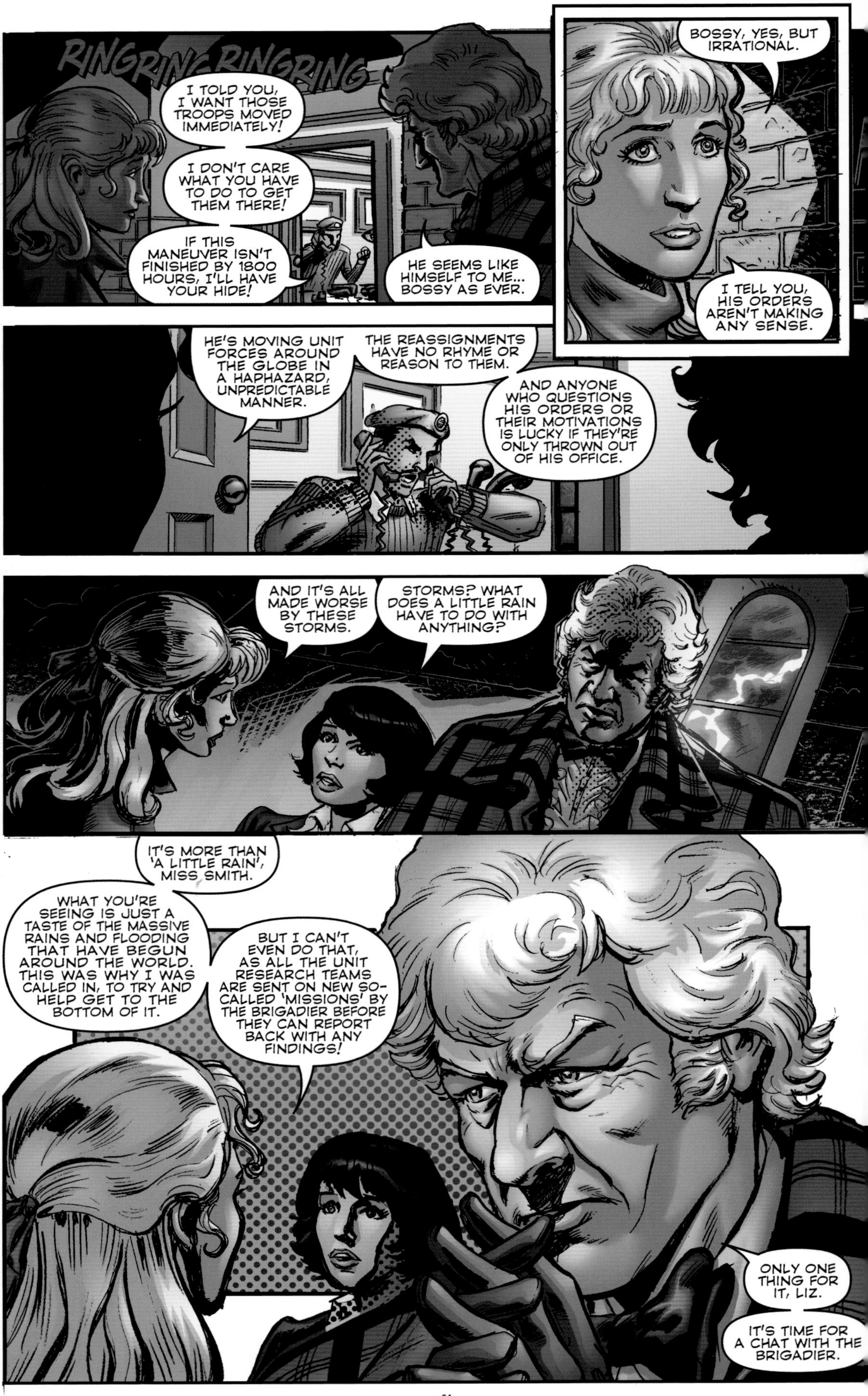
RINGRING RINGRING
I TOLD YOU, I WANT THOSE TROOPS MOVED IMMEDIATELY!
I DON'T CARE WHAT YOU HAVE TO DO TO GET THEM THERE!
IF THIS MANEUVER ISN'T FINISHED BY 1800 HOURS, I'LL HAVE YOUR HIDE!
HE SEEMS LIKE HIMSELF TO ME... BOSSY AS EVER.
BOSSY, YES, BUT IRRATIONAL.
I TELL YOU, HIS ORDERS AREN'T MAKING ANY SENSE.
HE'S MOVING UNIT FORCES AROUND THE GLOBE IN A HAPHAZARD, UNPREDICTABLE MANNER.
THE REASSIGNMENTS HAVE NO RHYME OR REASON TO THEM.
AND ANYONE WHO QUESTIONS HIS ORDERS OR THEIR MOTIVATIONS IS LUCKY IF THEY'RE ONLY THROWN OUT OF HIS OFFICE.
AND IT'S ALL MADE WORSE BY THESE STORMS.
STORMS? WHAT DOES A LITTLE RAIN HAVE TO DO WITH ANYTHING?
IT'S MORE THAN 'A LITTLE RAIN', MISS SMITH.
WHAT YOU'RE SEEING IS JUST A TASTE OF THE MASSIVE RAINS AND FLOODING THAT HAVE BEGUN AROUND THE WORLD. THIS WAS WHY I WAS CALLED IN, TO TRY AND HELP GET TO THE BOTTOM OF IT.
BUT I CAN'T EVEN DO THAT, AS ALL THE UNIT RESEARCH TEAMS ARE SENT ON NEW SO-CALLED 'MISSIONS' BY THE BRIGADIER BEFORE THEY CAN REPORT BACK WITH ANY FINDINGS!
ONLY ONE THING FOR IT, LIZ.
IT'S TIME FOR A CHAT WITH THE BRIGADIER.

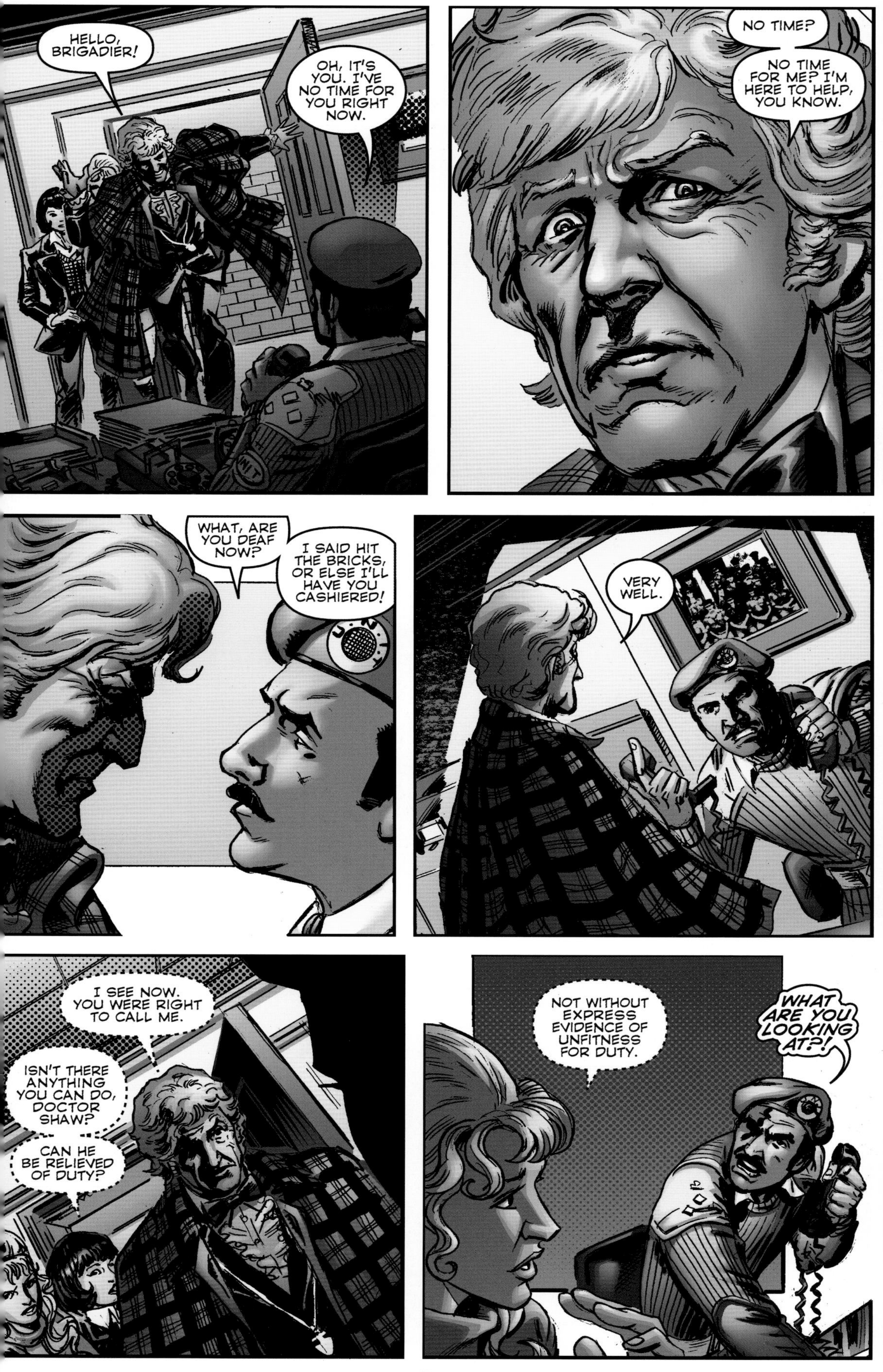
HELLO, BRIGADIER!
OH, IT'S YOU. I'VE NO TIME FOR YOU RIGHT NOW.
NO TIME?
NO TIME FOR ME? I'M HERE TO HELP, YOU KNOW.
WHAT, ARE YOU DEAF NOW?
I SAID HIT THE BRICKS, OR ELSE I'LL HAVE YOU CASHIERED!
VERY WELL.
I SEE NOW. YOU WERE RIGHT TO CALL ME.
ISN'T THERE ANYTHING YOU CAN DO, DOCTOR SHAW?
CAN HE BE RELIEVED OF DUTY?
NOT WITHOUT EXPRESS EVIDENCE OF UNFITNESS FOR DUTY.
WHAT ARE YOU LOOKING AT?!

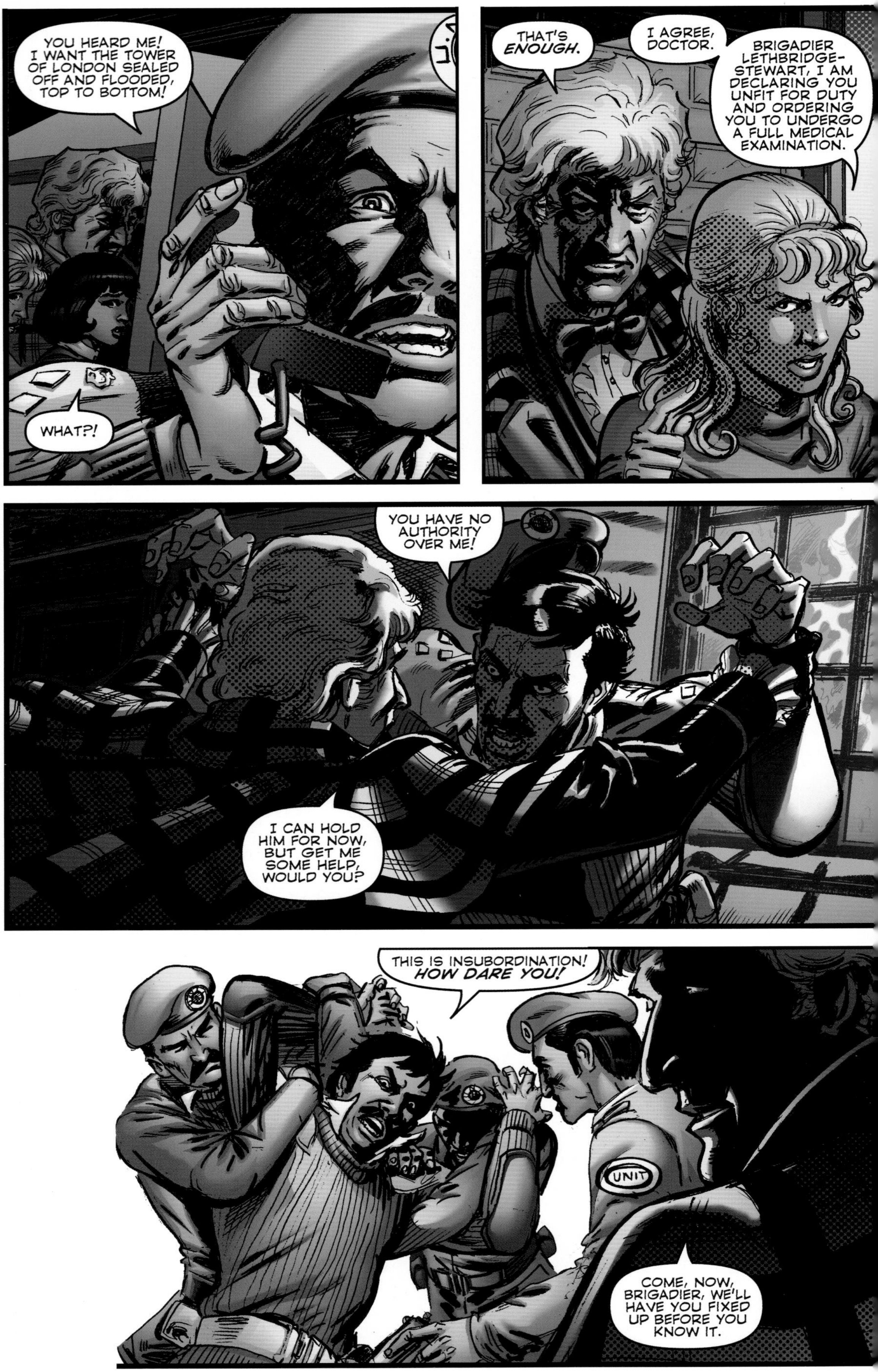
YOU HEARD ME! I WANT THE TOWER OF LONDON SEALED OFF AND FLOODED, TOP TO BOTTOM!
WHAT?!
THAT'S *ENOUGH*.
I AGREE, DOCTOR.
BRIGADIER LETHBRIDGE-STEWART, I AM DECLARING YOU UNFIT FOR DUTY AND ORDERING YOU TO UNDERGO A FULL MEDICAL EXAMINATION.
YOU HAVE NO AUTHORITY OVER ME!
I CAN HOLD HIM FOR NOW, BUT GET ME SOME HELP, WOULD YOU?
THIS IS INSUBORDINATION! *HOW DARE YOU!*
UNIT
COME, NOW, BRIGADIER, WE'LL HAVE YOU FIXED UP BEFORE YOU KNOW IT.

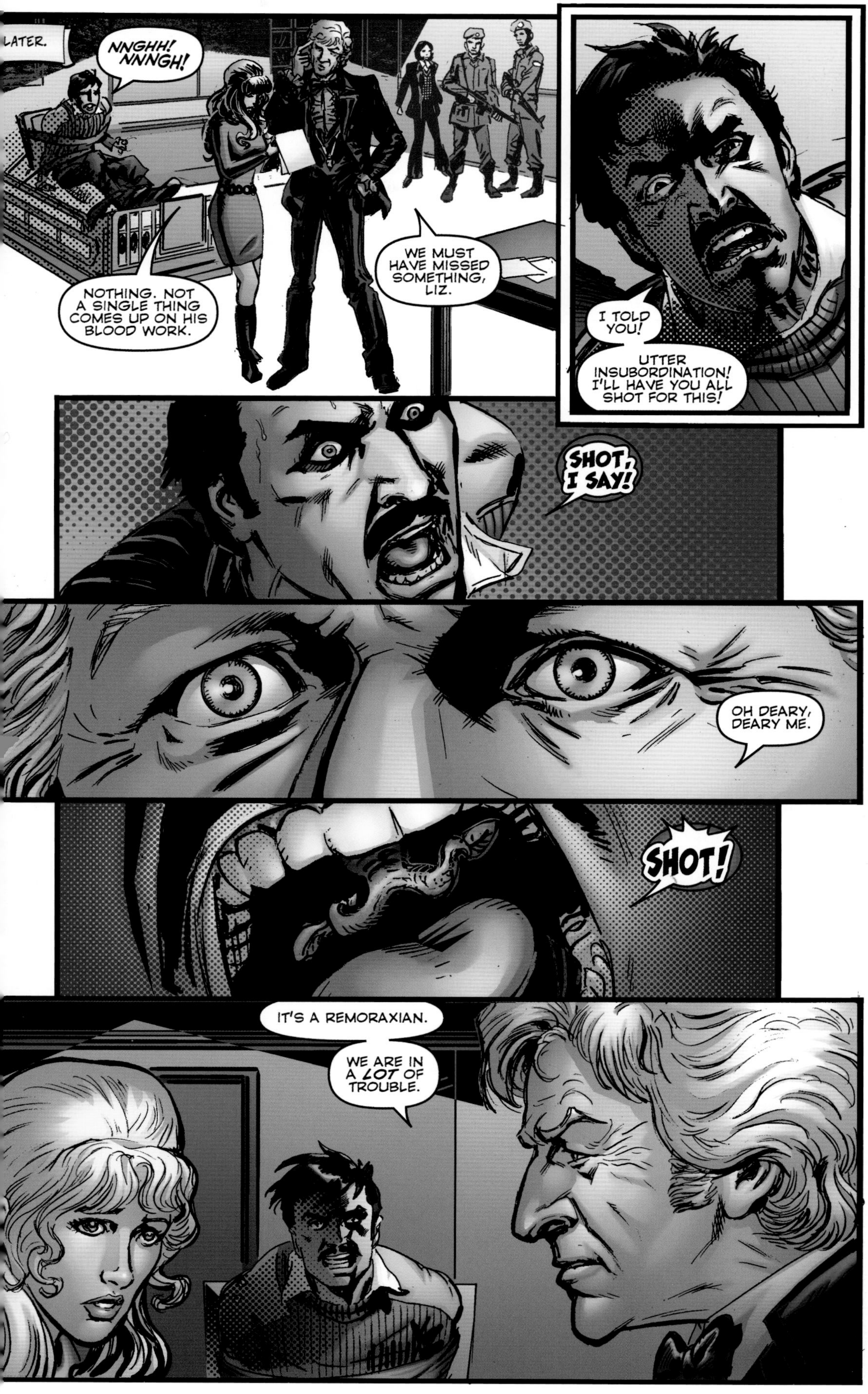
LATER.
NNGHH! NNNGH!
NOTHING. NOT A SINGLE THING COMES UP ON HIS BLOOD WORK.
WE MUST HAVE MISSED SOMETHING, LIZ.
I TOLD YOU!
UTTER INSUBORDINATION! I'LL HAVE YOU ALL SHOT FOR THIS!
SHOT, I SAY!
OH DEARY, DEARY ME.
SHOT!
IT'S A REMORAXIAN.
WE ARE IN A *LOT* OF TROUBLE.

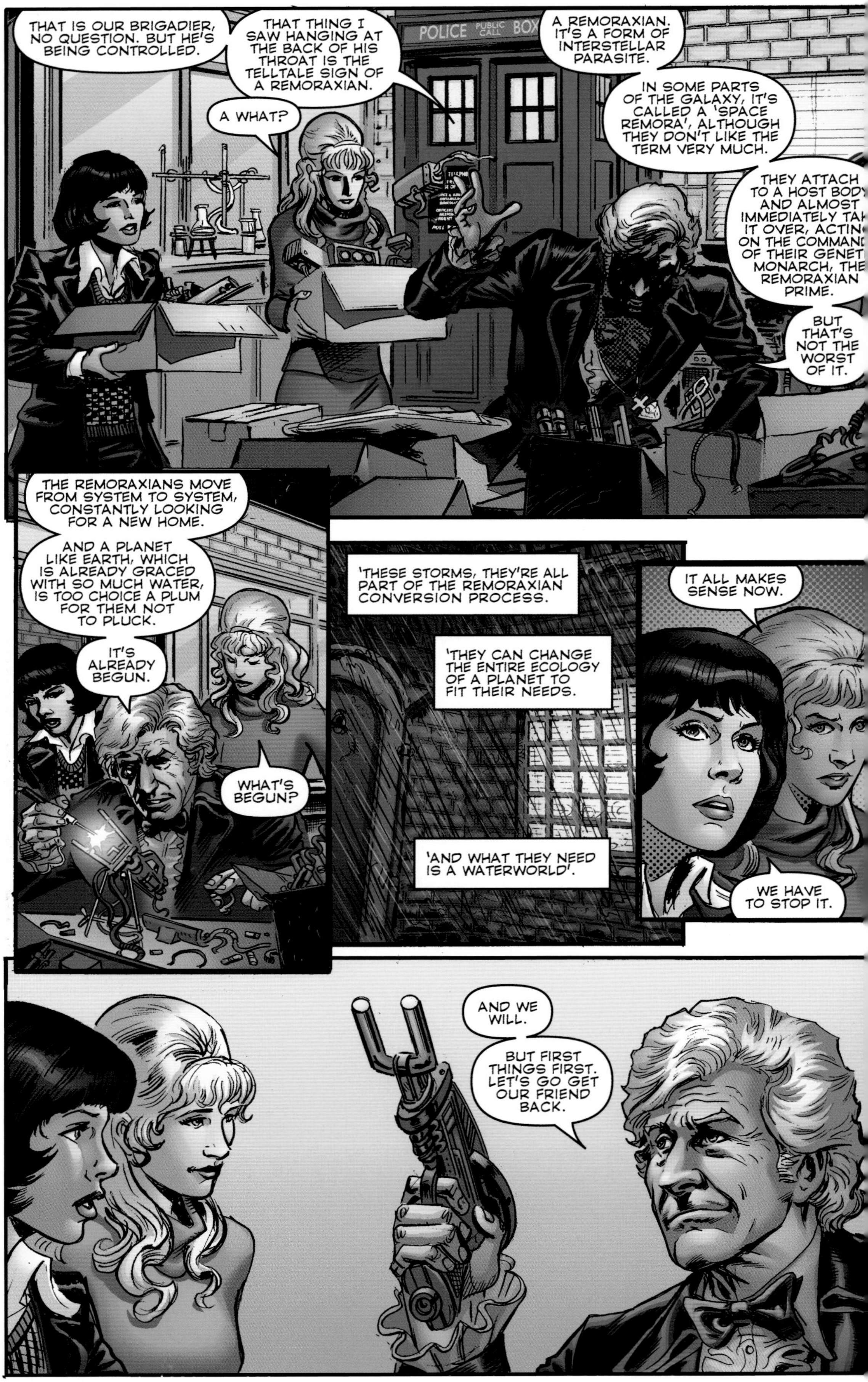
THAT IS OUR BRIGADIER, NO QUESTION. BUT HE'S BEING CONTROLLED.
THAT THING I SAW HANGING AT THE BACK OF HIS THROAT IS THE TELLTALE SIGN OF A REMORAXIAN.
A WHAT?
POLICE PUBLIC CALL BOX
A REMORAXIAN. IT'S A FORM OF INTERSTELLAR PARASITE.
IN SOME PARTS OF THE GALAXY, IT'S CALLED A 'SPACE REMORA', ALTHOUGH THEY DON'T LIKE THE TERM VERY MUCH.
THEY ATTACH TO A HOST BODY AND ALMOST IMMEDIATELY TAK IT OVER, ACTIN ON THE COMMAND OF THEIR GENET MONARCH, THE REMORAXIAN PRIME.
BUT THAT'S NOT THE WORST OF IT.
THE REMORAXIANS MOVE FROM SYSTEM TO SYSTEM, CONSTANTLY LOOKING FOR A NEW HOME.
AND A PLANET LIKE EARTH, WHICH IS ALREADY GRACED WITH SO MUCH WATER, IS TOO CHOICE A PLUM FOR THEM NOT TO PLUCK.
IT'S ALREADY BEGUN.
WHAT'S BEGUN?
'THESE STORMS, THEY'RE ALL PART OF THE REMORAXIAN CONVERSION PROCESS.
'THEY CAN CHANGE THE ENTIRE ECOLOGY OF A PLANET TO FIT THEIR NEEDS.
'AND WHAT THEY NEED IS A WATERWORLD'.
IT ALL MAKES SENSE NOW.
WE HAVE TO STOP IT.
AND WE WILL.
BUT FIRST THINGS FIRST. LET'S GO GET OUR FRIEND BACK.

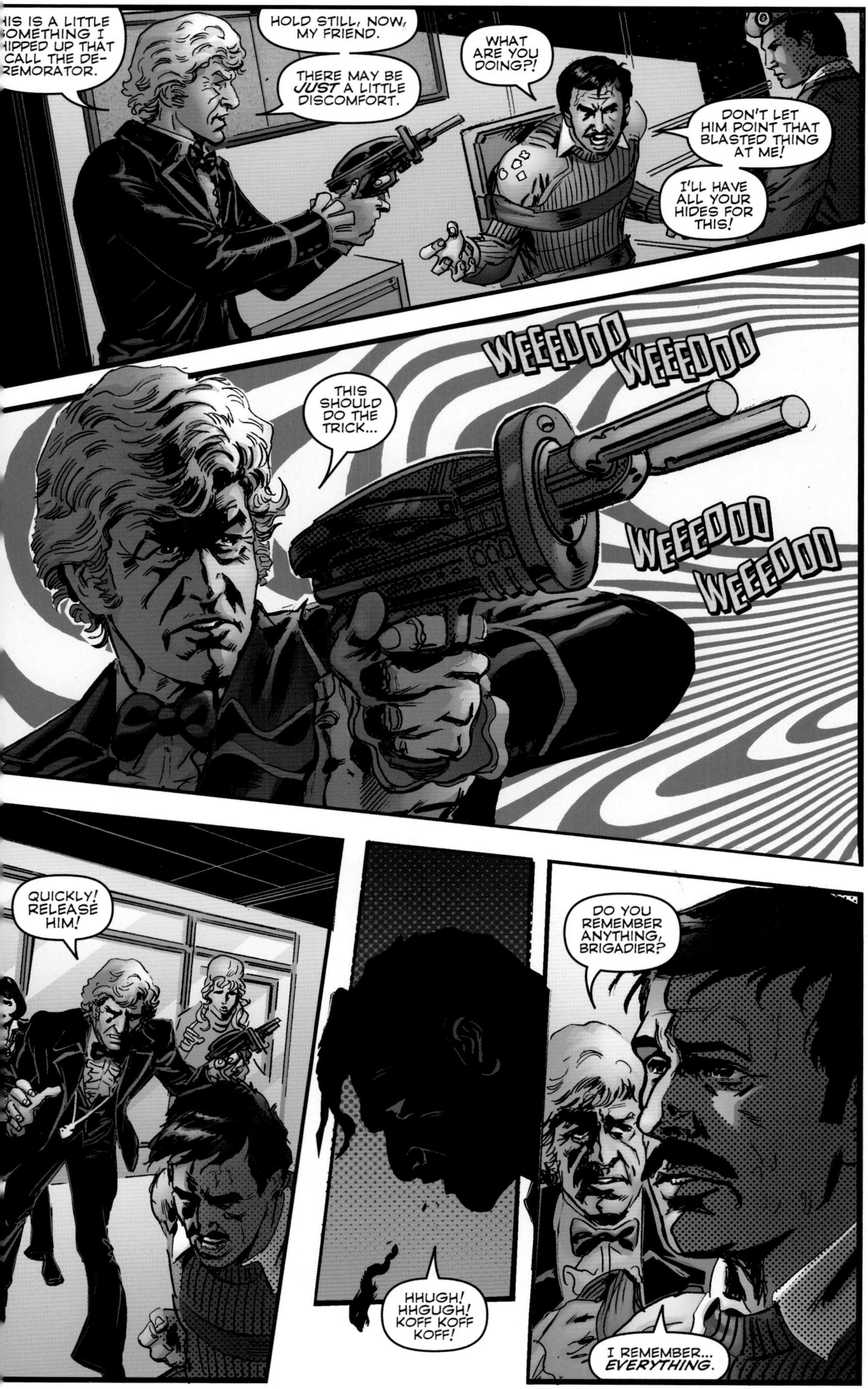
HIS IS A LITTLE SOMETHING I HIPPED UP THAT CALL THE DE-REMORATOR.
HOLD STILL, NOW, MY FRIEND.
THERE MAY BE *JUST* A LITTLE DISCOMFORT.
WHAT ARE YOU DOING?!
DON'T LET HIM POINT THAT BLASTED THING AT ME!
I'LL HAVE ALL YOUR HIDES FOR THIS!
WEEEDOO WEEEDOO
THIS SHOULD DO THE TRICK...
WEEEDOO WEEEDOO
QUICKLY! RELEASE HIM!
HHUGH! HHGUGH! KOFF KOFF KOFF!
DO YOU REMEMBER ANYTHING, BRIGADIER?
I REMEMBER... *EVERYTHING*.

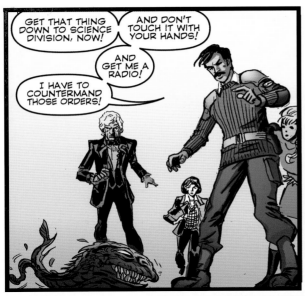

GET THAT THING DOWN TO SCIENCE DIVISION, NOW!

AND DON'T TOUCH IT WITH YOUR HANDS!

AND GET ME A RADIO!

I HAVE TO COUNTERMAND THOSE ORDERS!

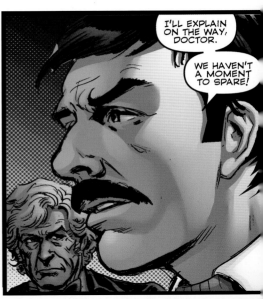

I'LL EXPLAIN ON THE WAY, DOCTOR.

WE HAVEN'T A MOMENT TO SPARE!

UNIT HAS A NAUTICAL RESEARCH FACILITY JUST OFF THE COAST.

BEEN TRAINING DOLPHINS THERE, AMONG OTHER THINGS.

BUT THOSE... *THINGS* HAVE TAKEN IT OVER.

THERE'S SOME SORT OF... MOTHER CREATURE THERE. I CAN SEE IT IN MY MIND'S EYE.

YES, I RATHER EXPECTED THERE TO BE A REMORAXIAN PRIME IN THE VICINITY.

THEY'VE BEEN ORCHESTRATING ALL OF THIS FROM THE SEALAB.

THEY'VE BEEN DISTRIBUTING THOSE PARASITES TO UNIT OFFICERS ALL OVER THE GLOBE.

THAT'S WHY THEY HAD ME REASSIGNING PERSONNEL SO MUCH.

I'D BEEN PUTTING THOSE DEVILS IN PLACE MYSELF, **DAMMIT!**

TAKE IT EASY, BRIGADIER. IT WASN'T YOUR FAULT.

THAT'S SMALL COMFORT TO ME NOW.

AND THAT'S NOT THE WORST OF IT—HOWEVER THEY'RE CHANGING THE WEATHER, IT'S ALL BEING CONTROLLED FROM THERE, TOO.

THEY WON'T STOP UNTIL THE OCEANS RISE ABOVE THE VERY TREES!

I KNOW. I'VE SEEN IT HAPPEN. BUT WE'RE ON TO THEM NOW.

WHO I

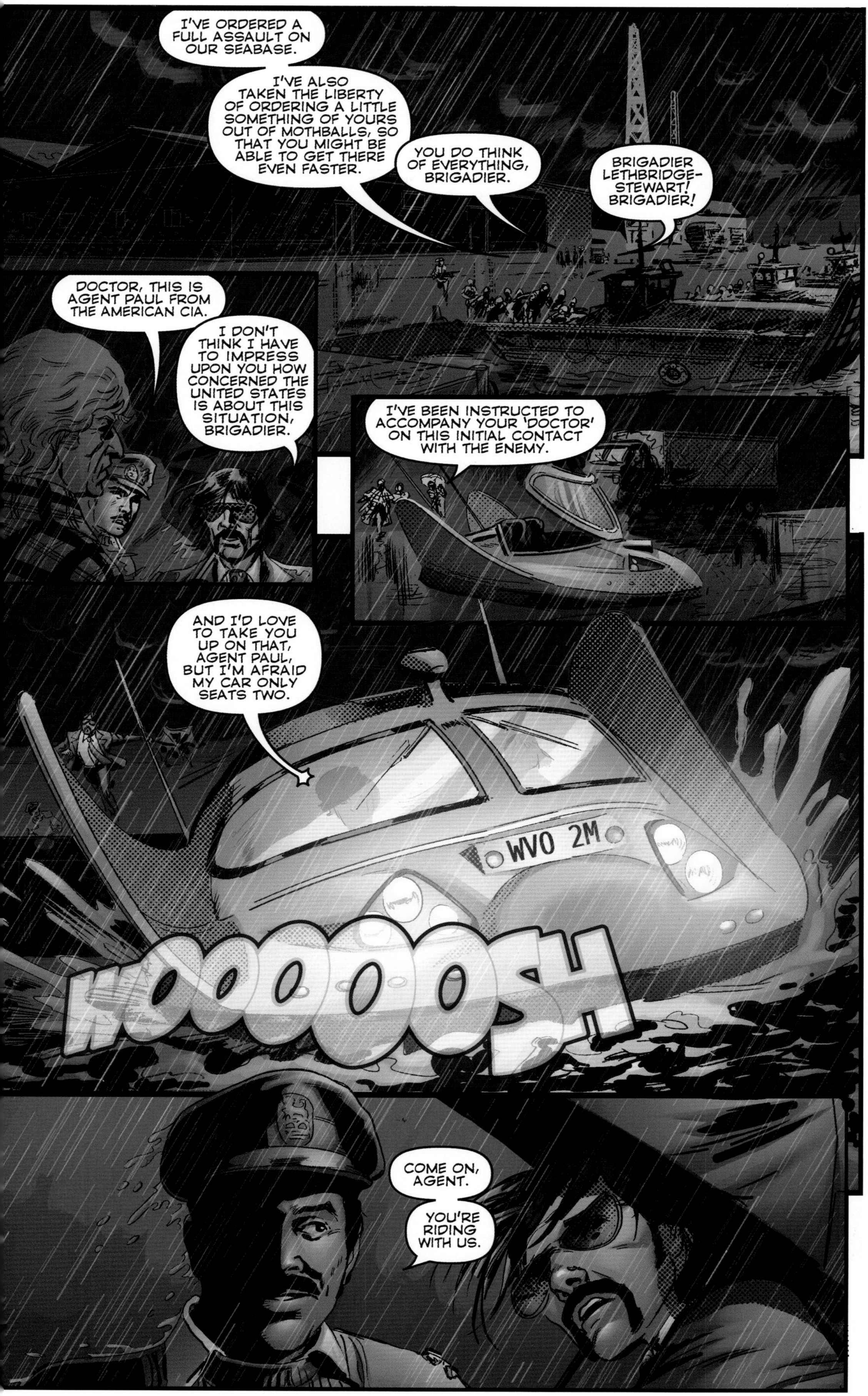

I'VE ORDERED A FULL ASSAULT ON OUR SEABASE.
I'VE ALSO TAKEN THE LIBERTY OF ORDERING A LITTLE SOMETHING OF YOURS OUT OF MOTHBALLS, SO THAT YOU MIGHT BE ABLE TO GET THERE EVEN FASTER.
YOU DO THINK OF EVERYTHING, BRIGADIER.
BRIGADIER LETHBRIDGE-STEWART! BRIGADIER!
DOCTOR, THIS IS AGENT PAUL FROM THE AMERICAN CIA.
I DON'T THINK I HAVE TO IMPRESS UPON YOU HOW CONCERNED THE UNITED STATES IS ABOUT THIS SITUATION, BRIGADIER.
I'VE BEEN INSTRUCTED TO ACCOMPANY YOUR 'DOCTOR' ON THIS INITIAL CONTACT WITH THE ENEMY.
AND I'D LOVE TO TAKE YOU UP ON THAT, AGENT PAUL, BUT I'M AFRAID MY CAR ONLY SEATS TWO.
WVO 2M
WOOOOOOSH
COME ON, AGENT.
YOU'RE RIDING WITH US.

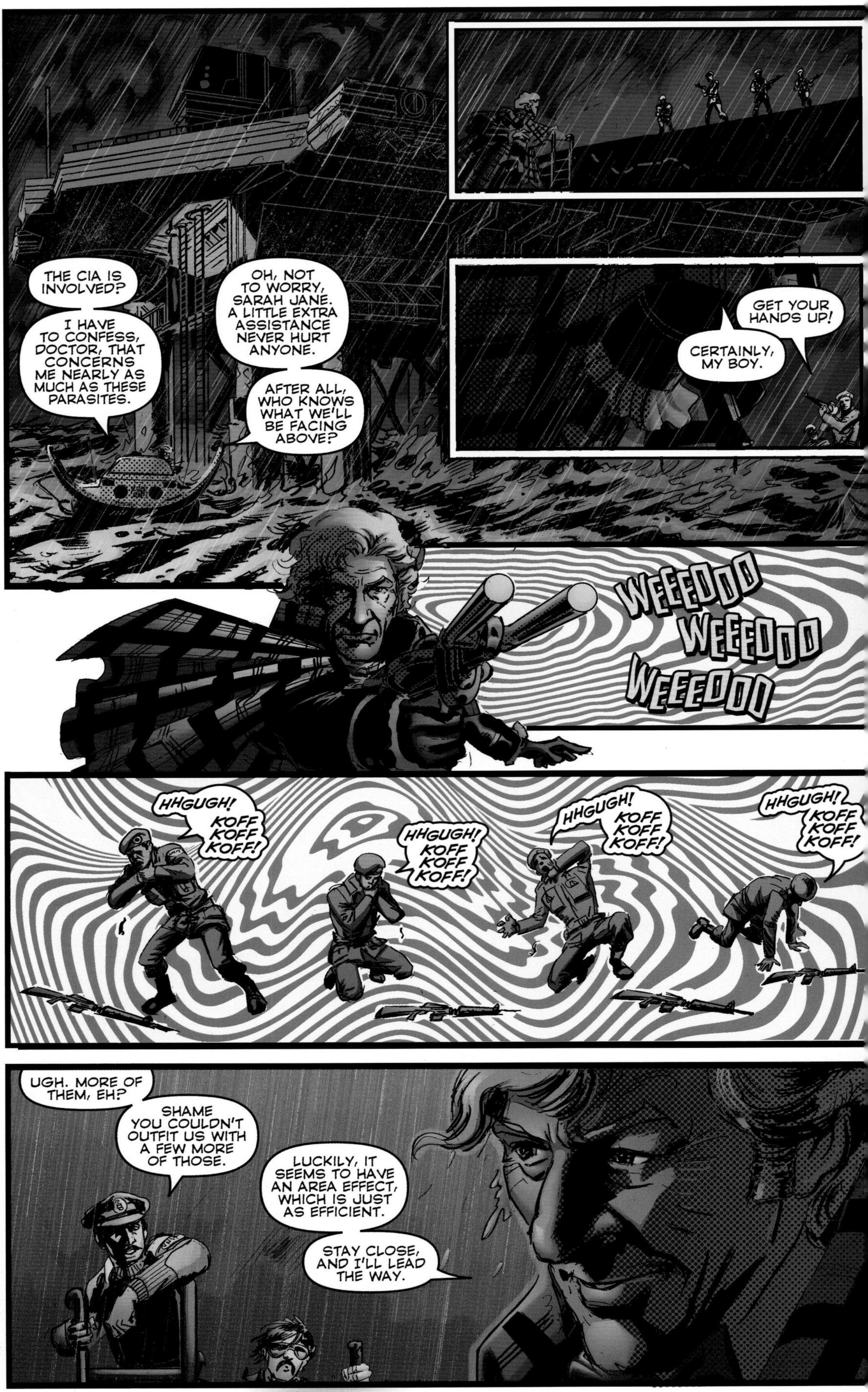
THE CIA IS INVOLVED?
I HAVE TO CONFESS, DOCTOR, THAT CONCERNS ME NEARLY AS MUCH AS THESE PARASITES.
OH, NOT TO WORRY, SARAH JANE. A LITTLE EXTRA ASSISTANCE NEVER HURT ANYONE.
AFTER ALL, WHO KNOWS WHAT WE'LL BE FACING ABOVE?
GET YOUR HANDS UP!
CERTAINLY, MY BOY.
WEEEDOO WEEEDOO WEEEDOO
HHGUGH! KOFF KOFF KOFF!
HHGUGH! KOFF KOFF KOFF!
HHGUGH! KOFF KOFF KOFF!
HHGUGH! KOFF KOFF KOFF!
UGH. MORE OF THEM, EH?
SHAME YOU COULDN'T OUTFIT US WITH A FEW MORE OF THOSE.
LUCKILY, IT SEEMS TO HAVE AN AREA EFFECT, WHICH IS JUST AS EFFICIENT.
STAY CLOSE, AND I'LL LEAD THE WAY.

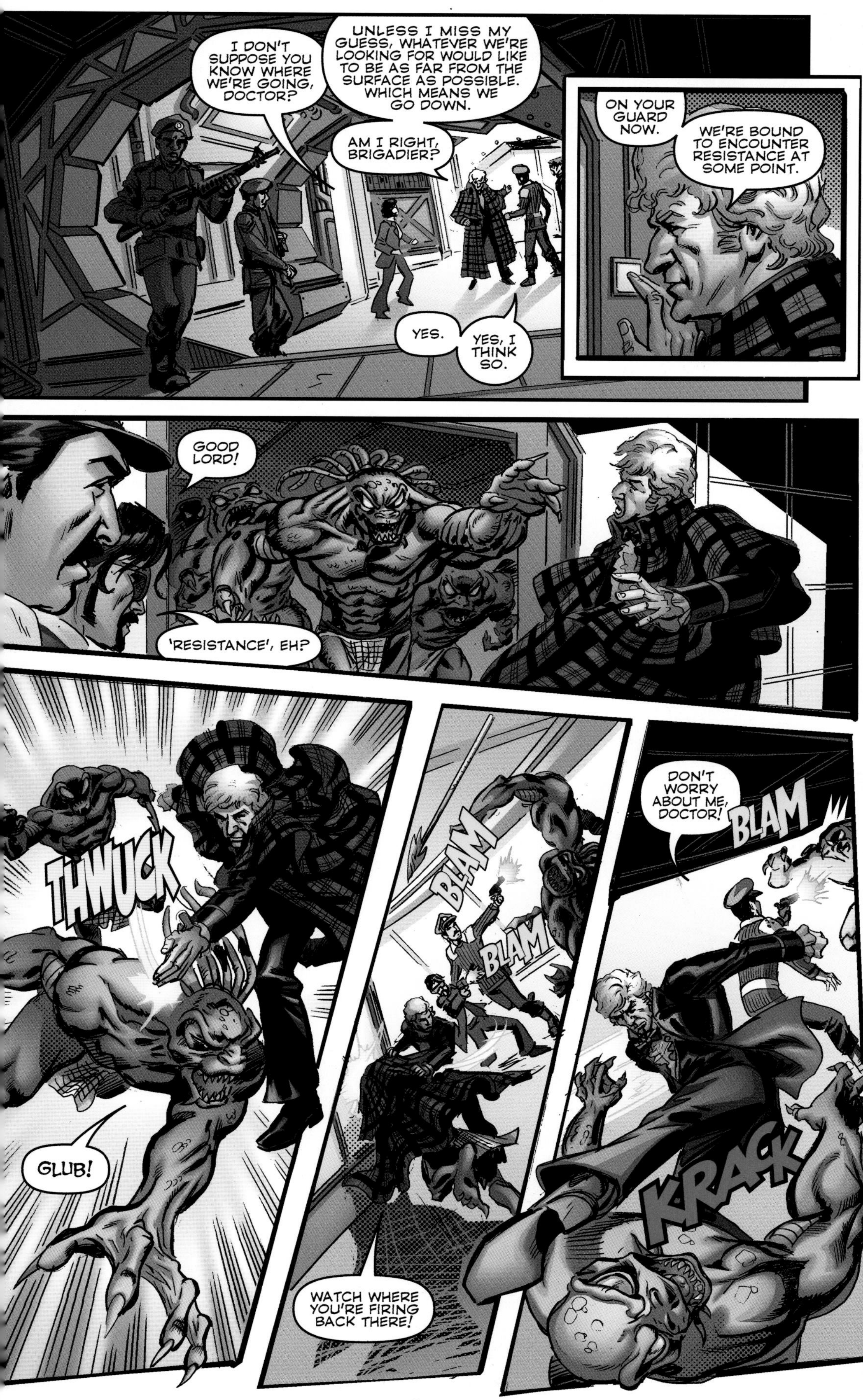
I DON'T SUPPOSE YOU KNOW WHERE WE'RE GOING, DOCTOR?
UNLESS I MISS MY GUESS, WHATEVER WE'RE LOOKING FOR WOULD LIKE TO BE AS FAR FROM THE SURFACE AS POSSIBLE. WHICH MEANS WE GO DOWN.
AM I RIGHT, BRIGADIER?
YES.
YES, I THINK SO.
ON YOUR GUARD NOW.
WE'RE BOUND TO ENCOUNTER RESISTANCE AT SOME POINT.
GOOD LORD!
'RESISTANCE', EH?
THWUCK
GLUB!
BLAM
BLAM
WATCH WHERE YOU'RE FIRING BACK THERE!
DON'T WORRY ABOUT ME, DOCTOR!
BLAM
KRACK

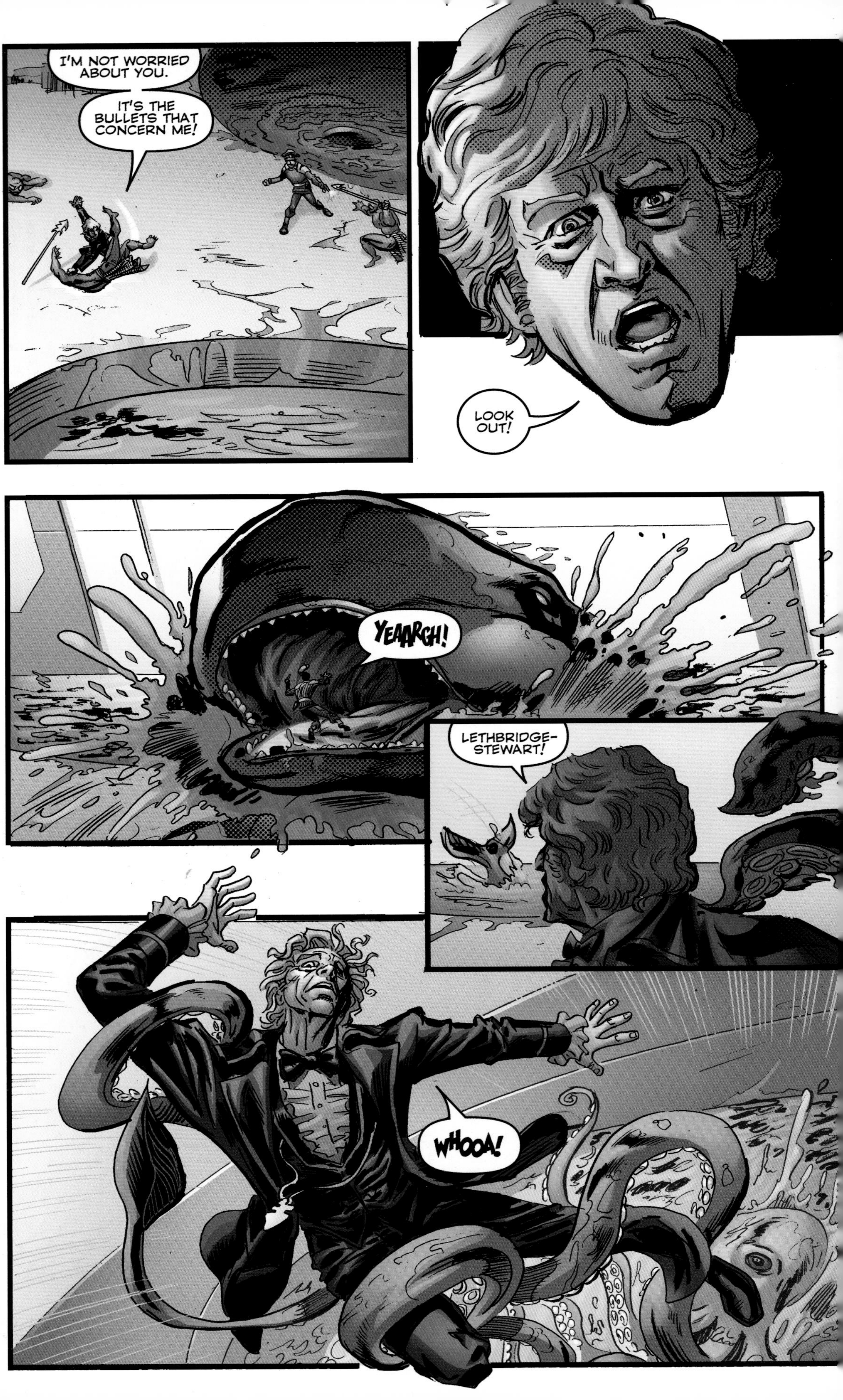
I'M NOT WORRIED ABOUT YOU.
IT'S THE BULLETS THAT CONCERN ME!
LOOK OUT!
YEAARGH!
LETHBRIDGE-STEWART!
WHOOA!

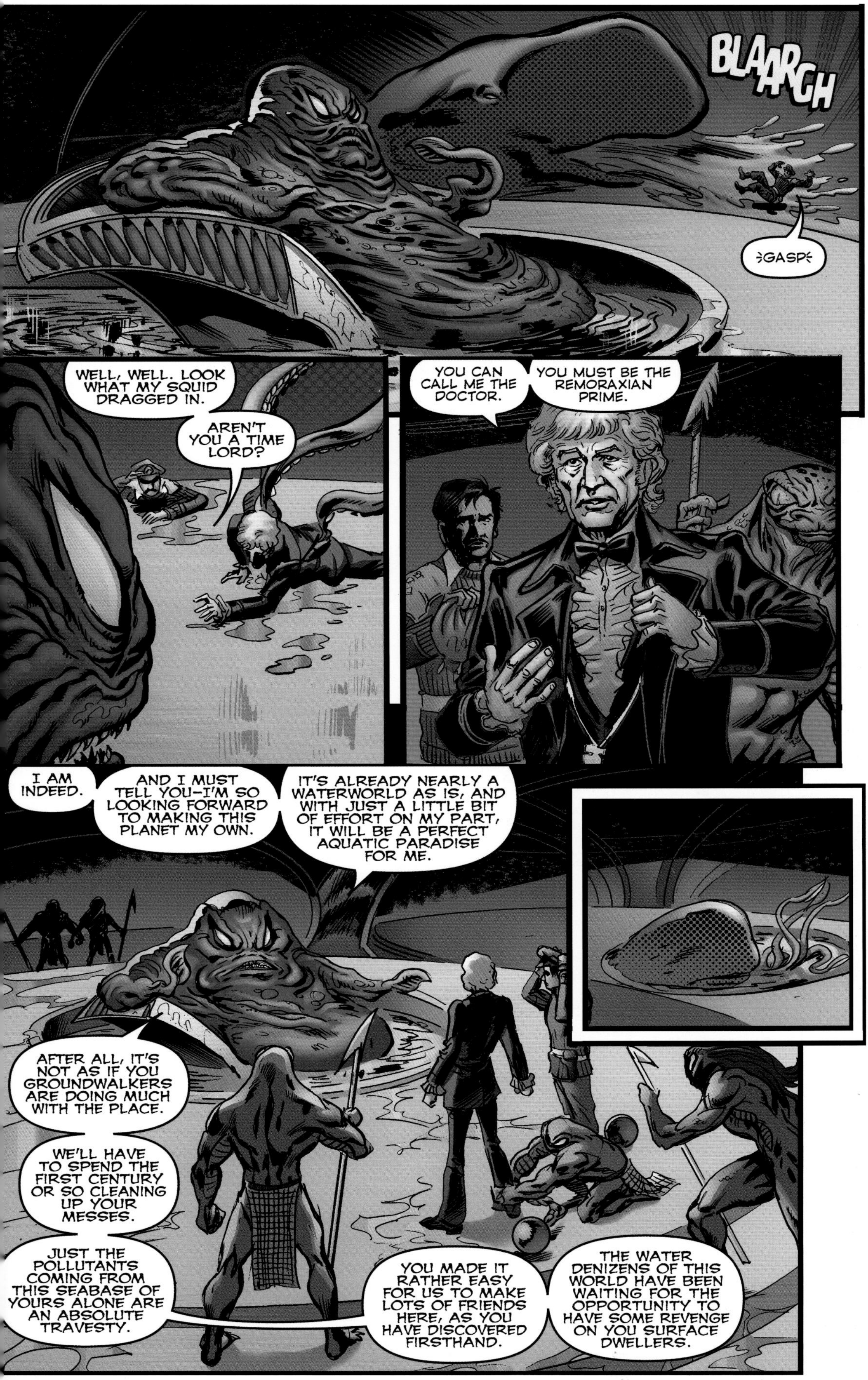
BLAARGH
GASP
WELL, WELL. LOOK WHAT MY SQUID DRAGGED IN.
AREN'T YOU A TIME LORD?
YOU CAN CALL ME THE DOCTOR.
YOU MUST BE THE REMORAXIAN PRIME.
I AM INDEED.
AND I MUST TELL YOU--I'M SO LOOKING FORWARD TO MAKING THIS PLANET MY OWN.
IT'S ALREADY NEARLY A WATERWORLD AS IS, AND WITH JUST A LITTLE BIT OF EFFORT ON MY PART, IT WILL BE A PERFECT AQUATIC PARADISE FOR ME.
AFTER ALL, IT'S NOT AS IF YOU GROUNDWALKERS ARE DOING MUCH WITH THE PLACE.
WE'LL HAVE TO SPEND THE FIRST CENTURY OR SO CLEANING UP YOUR MESSES.
JUST THE POLLUTANTS COMING FROM THIS SEABASE OF YOURS ALONE ARE AN ABSOLUTE TRAVESTY.
YOU MADE IT RATHER EASY FOR US TO MAKE LOTS OF FRIENDS HERE, AS YOU HAVE DISCOVERED FIRSTHAND.
THE WATER DENIZENS OF THIS WORLD HAVE BEEN WAITING FOR THE OPPORTUNITY TO HAVE SOME REVENGE ON YOU SURFACE DWELLERS.

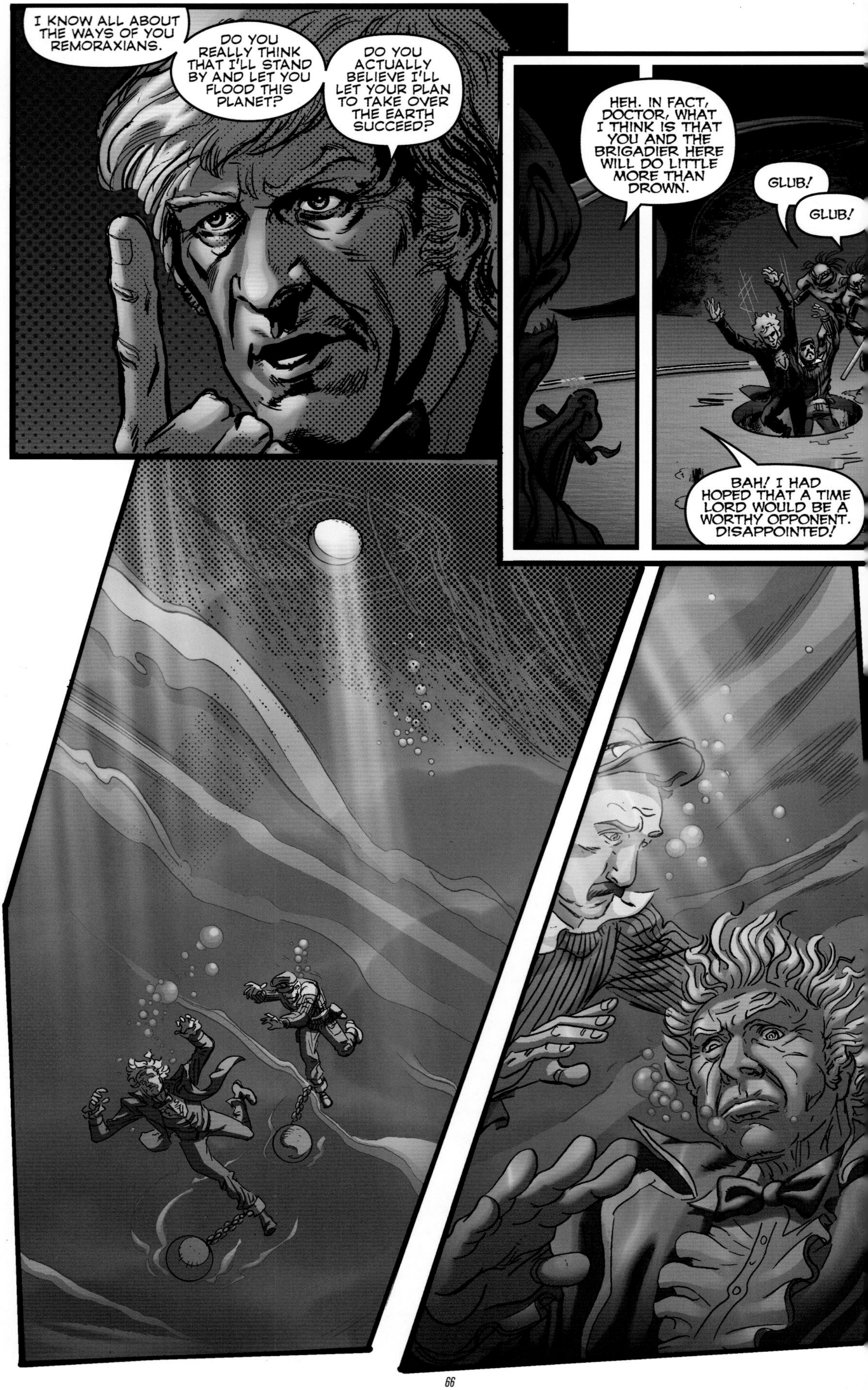
I KNOW ALL ABOUT THE WAYS OF YOU REMORAXIANS.
DO YOU REALLY THINK THAT I'LL STAND BY AND LET YOU FLOOD THIS PLANET?
DO YOU ACTUALLY BELIEVE I'LL LET YOUR PLAN TO TAKE OVER THE EARTH SUCCEED?
HEH. IN FACT, DOCTOR, WHAT I THINK IS THAT YOU AND THE BRIGADIER HERE WILL DO LITTLE MORE THAN DROWN.
GLUB!
GLUB!
BAH! I HAD HOPED THAT A TIME LORD WOULD BE A WORTHY OPPONENT. DISAPPOINTED!

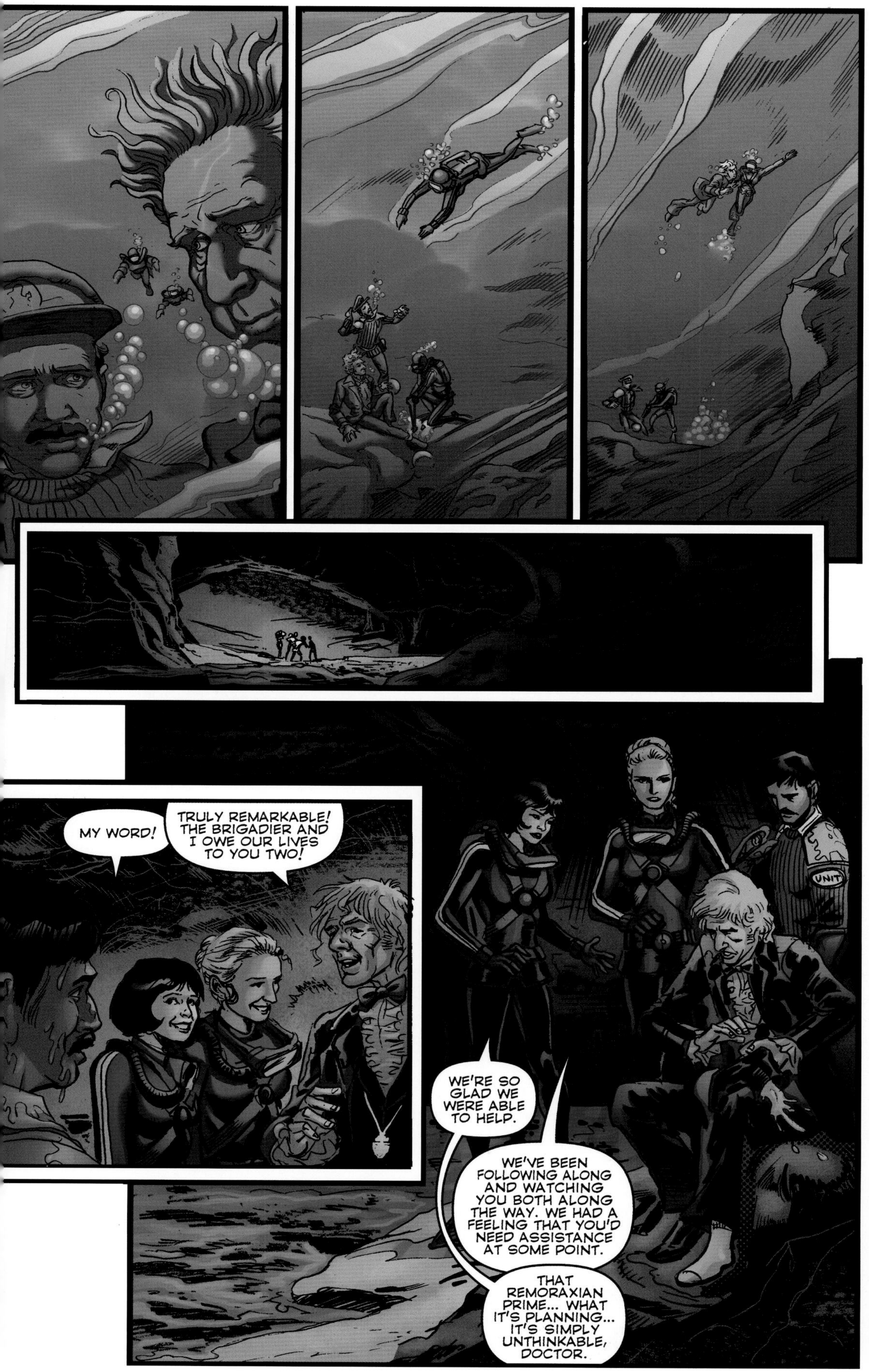
MY WORD!
TRULY REMARKABLE! THE BRIGADIER AND I OWE OUR LIVES TO YOU TWO!
UNIT
WE'RE SO GLAD WE WERE ABLE TO HELP.
WE'VE BEEN FOLLOWING ALONG AND WATCHING YOU BOTH ALONG THE WAY. WE HAD A FEELING THAT YOU'D NEED ASSISTANCE AT SOME POINT.
THAT REMORAXIAN PRIME... WHAT IT'S PLANNING... IT'S SIMPLY UNTHINKABLE, DOCTOR.

THAT IT IS, SARAH JANE. WE MUST STOP HIM AS QUICKLY AS POSSIBLE.

WHERE IS THE REST OF OUR TASK FORCE?

MANY HAVE BEEN CAPTURED OR KILLED.

HERE UP AHEAD, AGENT PAUL FROM THE CIA HAS ESTABLISHED A TEMPORARY COMMAND CENTER FOR OUR REMAINING FORCES.

GENTLEMEN! I SEE DR. SHAW AND MISS SMITH WERE ABLE TO RESCUE YOU FROM YOUR PREDICAMENT.

THEY WERE MOST INSISTENT ON FOLLOWING YOU.

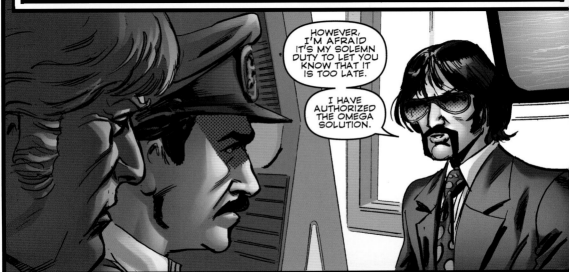

HOWEVER, I'M AFRAID IT'S MY SOLEMN DUTY TO LET YOU KNOW THAT IT IS TOO LATE.

I HAVE AUTHORIZED THE OMEGA SOLUTION.

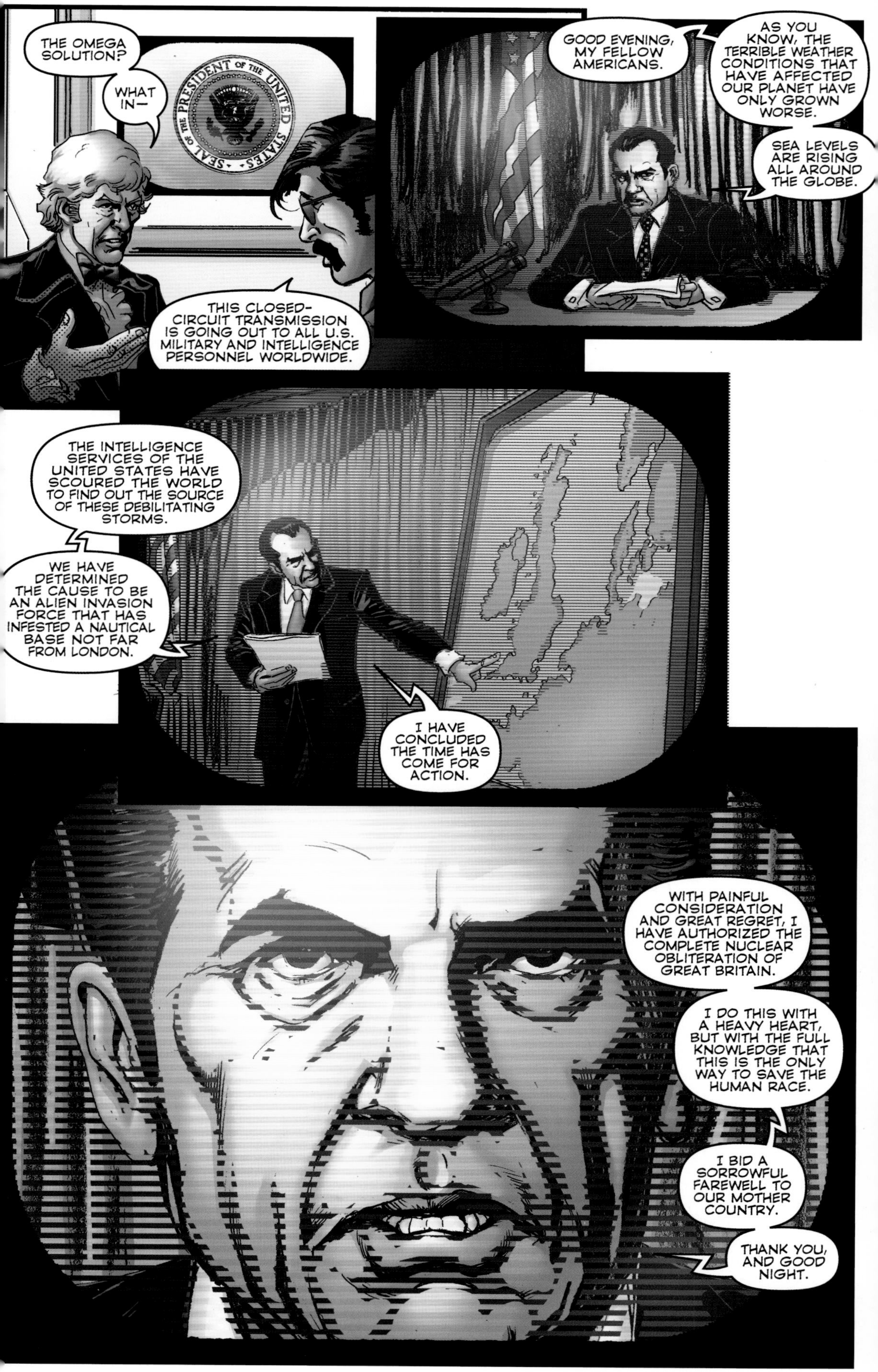

THE OMEGA SOLUTION?
WHAT IN—
SEAL OF THE PRESIDENT OF THE UNITED STATES
THIS CLOSED-CIRCUIT TRANSMISSION IS GOING OUT TO ALL U.S. MILITARY AND INTELLIGENCE PERSONNEL WORLDWIDE.
GOOD EVENING, MY FELLOW AMERICANS.
AS YOU KNOW, THE TERRIBLE WEATHER CONDITIONS THAT HAVE AFFECTED OUR PLANET HAVE ONLY GROWN WORSE.
SEA LEVELS ARE RISING ALL AROUND THE GLOBE.
THE INTELLIGENCE SERVICES OF THE UNITED STATES HAVE SCOURED THE WORLD TO FIND OUT THE SOURCE OF THESE DEBILITATING STORMS.
WE HAVE DETERMINED THE CAUSE TO BE AN ALIEN INVASION FORCE THAT HAS INFESTED A NAUTICAL BASE NOT FAR FROM LONDON.
I HAVE CONCLUDED THE TIME HAS COME FOR ACTION.
WITH PAINFUL CONSIDERATION AND GREAT REGRET, I HAVE AUTHORIZED THE COMPLETE NUCLEAR OBLITERATION OF GREAT BRITAIN.
I DO THIS WITH A HEAVY HEART, BUT WITH THE FULL KNOWLEDGE THAT THIS IS THE ONLY WAY TO SAVE THE HUMAN RACE.
I BID A SORROWFUL FAREWELL TO OUR MOTHER COUNTRY.
THANK YOU, AND GOOD NIGHT.

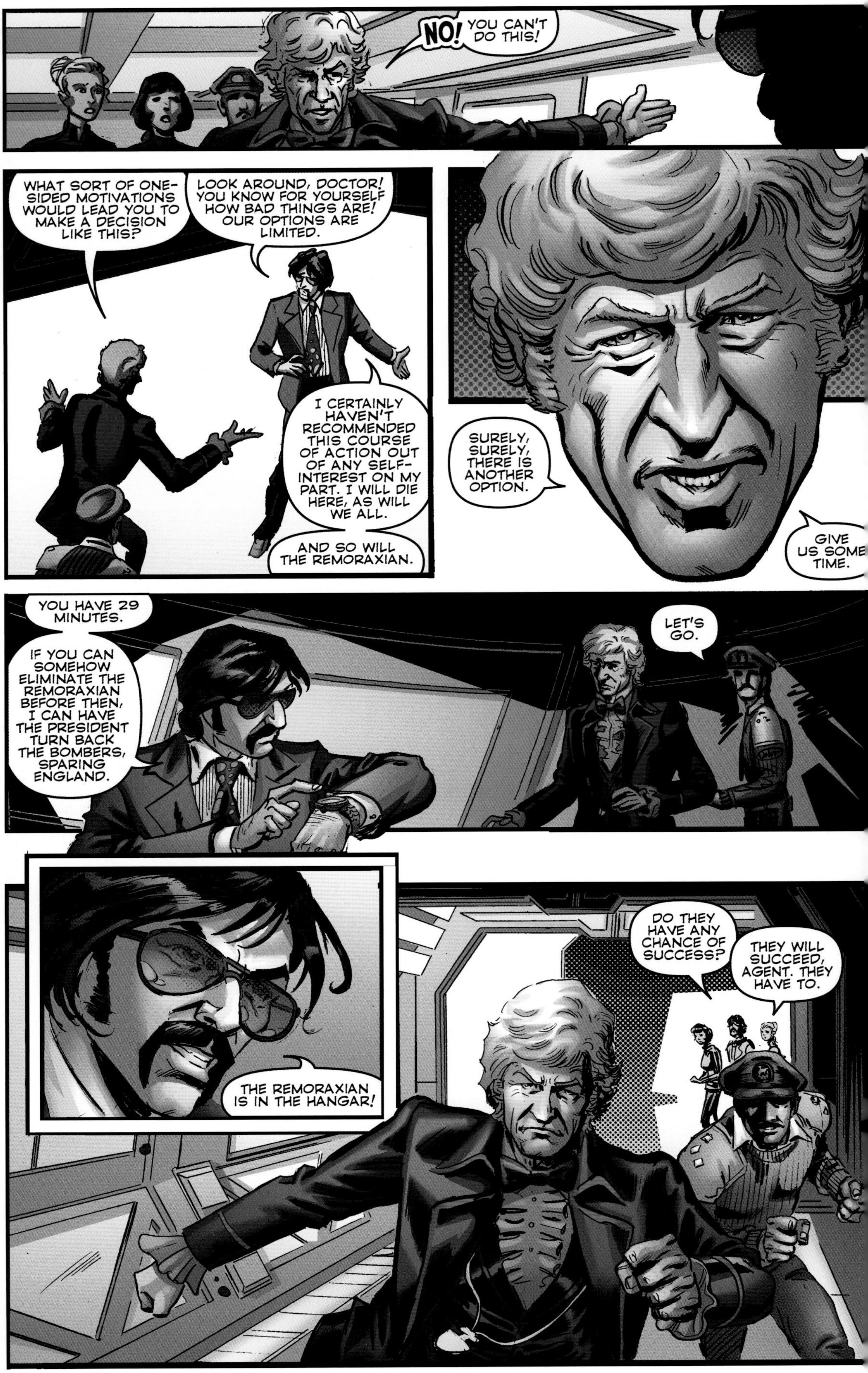
NO! YOU CAN'T DO THIS!
WHAT SORT OF ONE-SIDED MOTIVATIONS WOULD LEAD YOU TO MAKE A DECISION LIKE THIS?
LOOK AROUND, DOCTOR! YOU KNOW FOR YOURSELF HOW BAD THINGS ARE! OUR OPTIONS ARE LIMITED.
I CERTAINLY HAVEN'T RECOMMENDED THIS COURSE OF ACTION OUT OF ANY SELF-INTEREST ON MY PART. I WILL DIE HERE, AS WILL WE ALL.
AND SO WILL THE REMORAXIAN.
SURELY, SURELY, THERE IS ANOTHER OPTION.
GIVE US SOME TIME.
YOU HAVE 29 MINUTES.
IF YOU CAN SOMEHOW ELIMINATE THE REMORAXIAN BEFORE THEN, I CAN HAVE THE PRESIDENT TURN BACK THE BOMBERS, SPARING ENGLAND.
LET'S GO.
THE REMORAXIAN IS IN THE HANGAR!
DO THEY HAVE ANY CHANCE OF SUCCESS?
THEY WILL SUCCEED, AGENT. THEY HAVE TO.

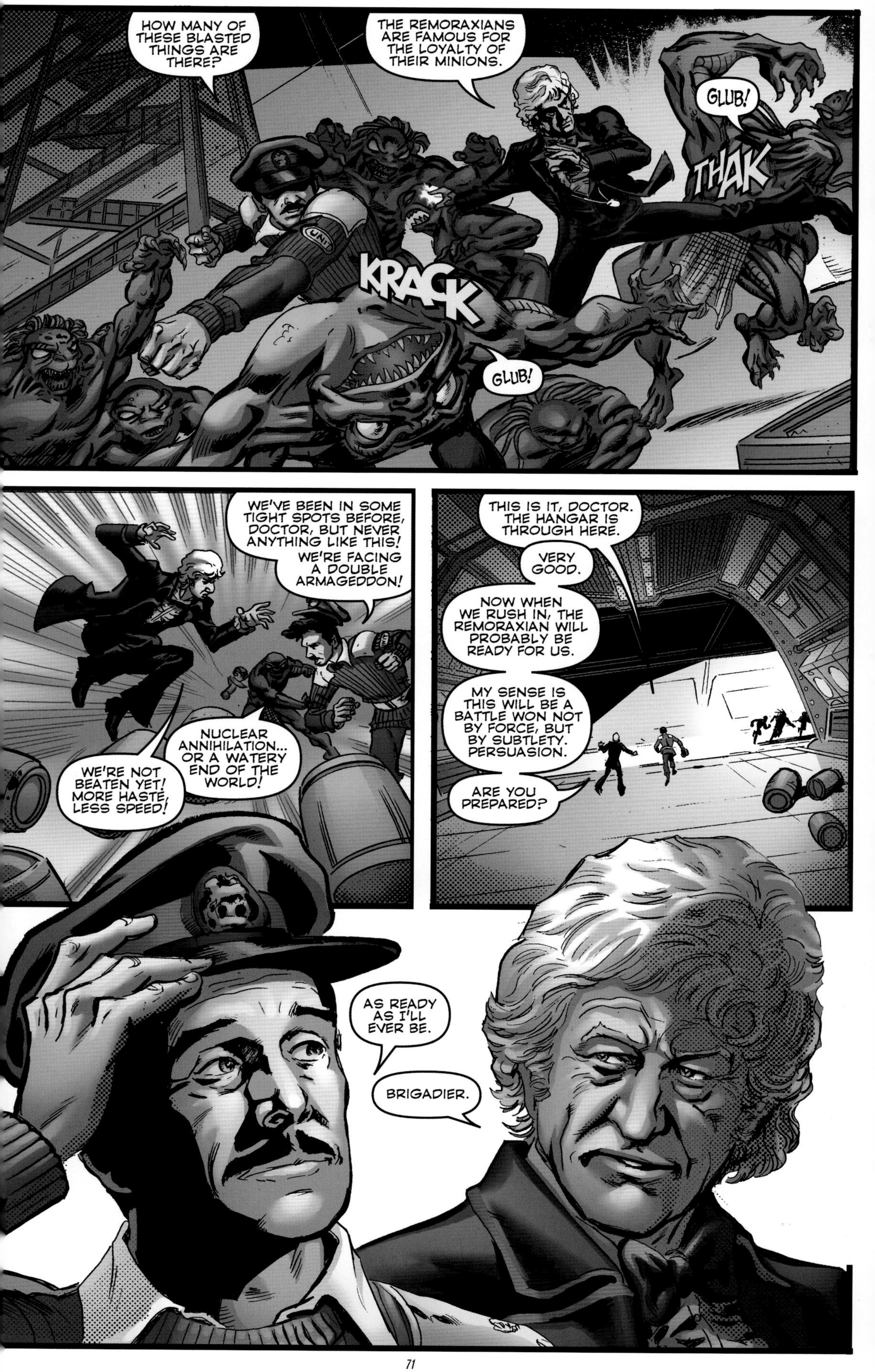
HOW MANY OF THESE BLASTED THINGS ARE THERE?
THE REMORAXIANS ARE FAMOUS FOR THE LOYALTY OF THEIR MINIONS.
GLUB!
THAK
KRACK
GLUB!
WE'VE BEEN IN SOME TIGHT SPOTS BEFORE, DOCTOR, BUT NEVER ANYTHING LIKE THIS!
WE'RE FACING A DOUBLE ARMAGEDDON!
NUCLEAR ANNIHILATION... OR A WATERY END OF THE WORLD!
WE'RE NOT BEATEN YET! MORE HASTE, LESS SPEED!
THIS IS IT, DOCTOR. THE HANGAR IS THROUGH HERE.
VERY GOOD.
NOW WHEN WE RUSH IN, THE REMORAXIAN WILL PROBABLY BE READY FOR US.
MY SENSE IS THIS WILL BE A BATTLE WON NOT BY FORCE, BUT BY SUBTLETY. PERSUASION.
ARE YOU PREPARED?
AS READY AS I'LL EVER BE.
BRIGADIER.

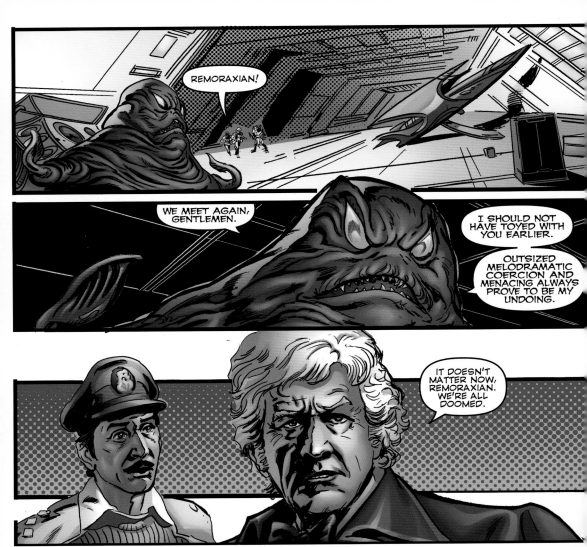

REMORAXIAN!

WE MEET AGAIN, GENTLEMEN.

I SHOULD NOT HAVE TOYED WITH YOU EARLIER.

OUTSIZED MELODRAMATIC COERCION AND MENACING ALWAYS PROVE TO BE MY UNDOING.

IT DOESN'T MATTER NOW, REMORAXIAN. WE'RE ALL DOOMED.

WILL THEY REALLY DO IT?

OBLITERATE THIS ENTIRE ISLAND, SACRIFICING THEIR PEOPLE?

HAVE NO DOUBT.

WE LIVE WITH THE THREAT OF MUTUALLY ASSURED DESTRUCTION EVERY DAY.

WE'RE USED TO IT.

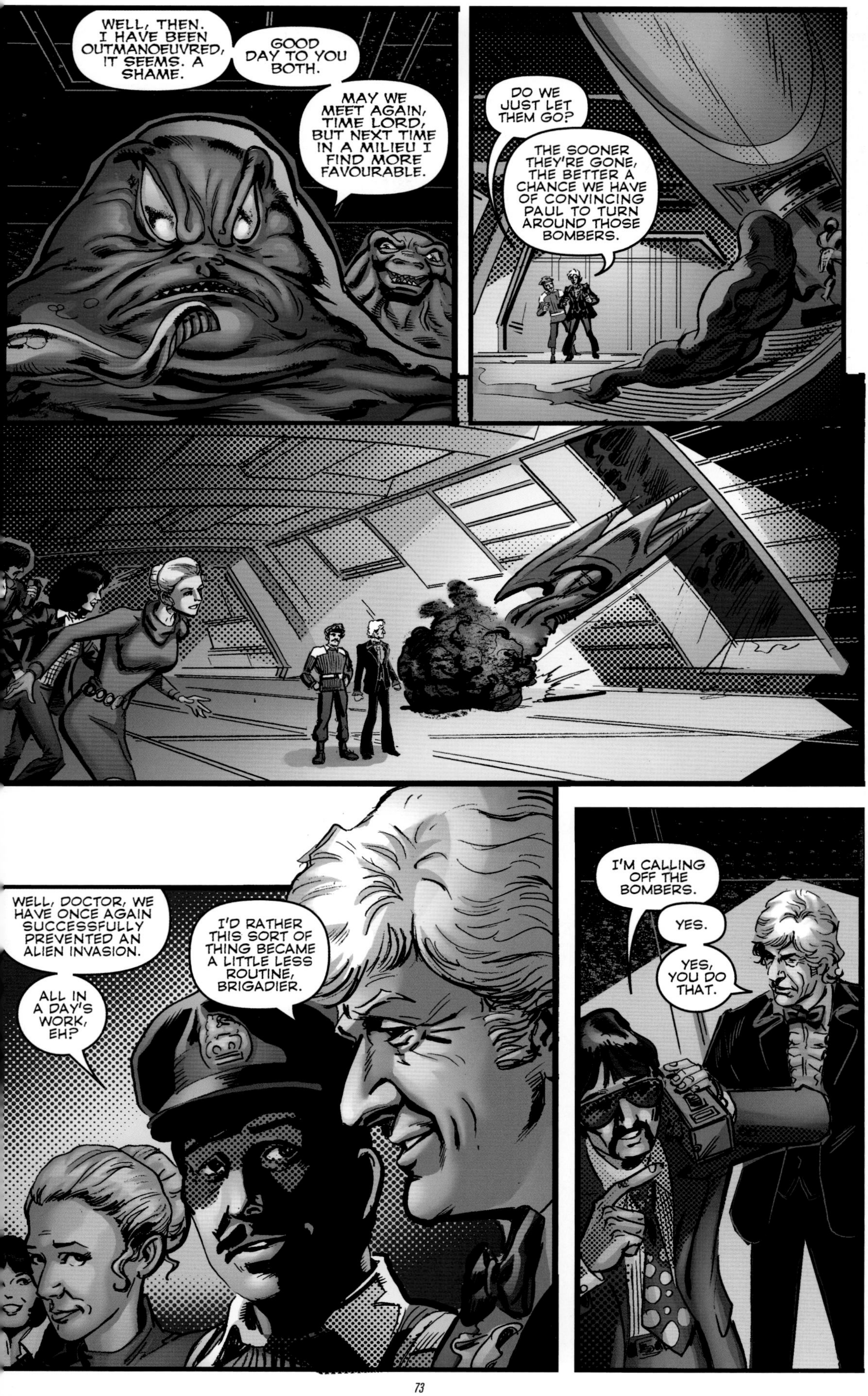

WELL, THEN. I HAVE BEEN OUTMANOEUVRED, IT SEEMS. A SHAME.
GOOD DAY TO YOU BOTH.
MAY WE MEET AGAIN, TIME LORD, BUT NEXT TIME IN A MILIEU I FIND MORE FAVOURABLE.
DO WE JUST LET THEM GO?
THE SOONER THEY'RE GONE, THE BETTER A CHANCE WE HAVE OF CONVINCING PAUL TO TURN AROUND THOSE BOMBERS.
WELL, DOCTOR, WE HAVE ONCE AGAIN SUCCESSFULLY PREVENTED AN ALIEN INVASION.
ALL IN A DAY'S WORK, EH?
I'D RATHER THIS SORT OF THING BECAME A LITTLE LESS ROUTINE, BRIGADIER.
I'M CALLING OFF THE BOMBERS.
YES.
YES, YOU DO THAT.

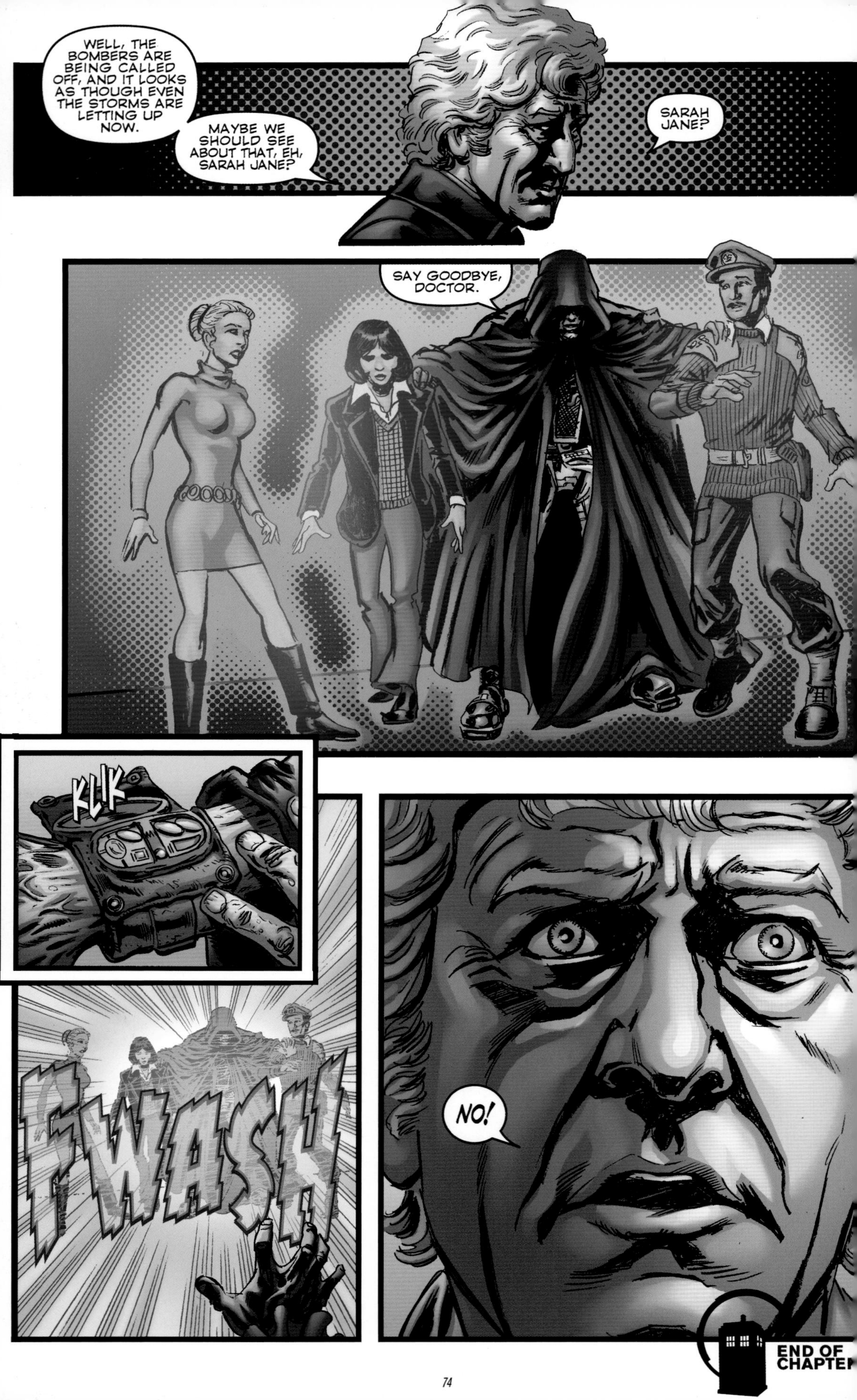
WELL, THE BOMBERS ARE BEING CALLED OFF, AND IT LOOKS AS THOUGH EVEN THE STORMS ARE LETTING UP NOW.
MAYBE WE SHOULD SEE ABOUT THAT, EH, SARAH JANE?
SARAH JANE?
SAY GOODBYE, DOCTOR.
KLIK
SWASH
NO!
END OF CHAPTER

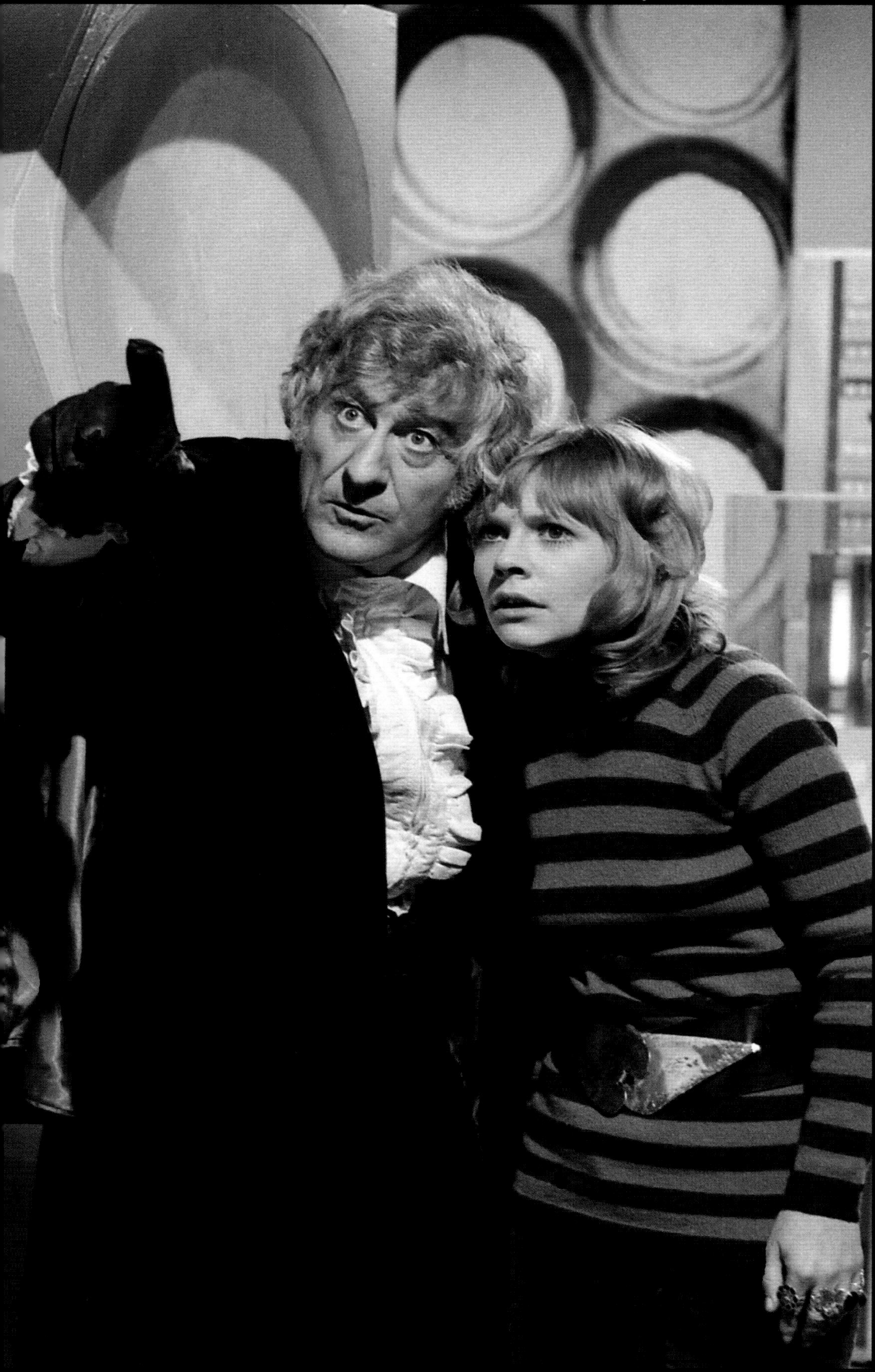

CHAPTER 4
"A Rare Gem"
Cover Art by Francesco Francavilla

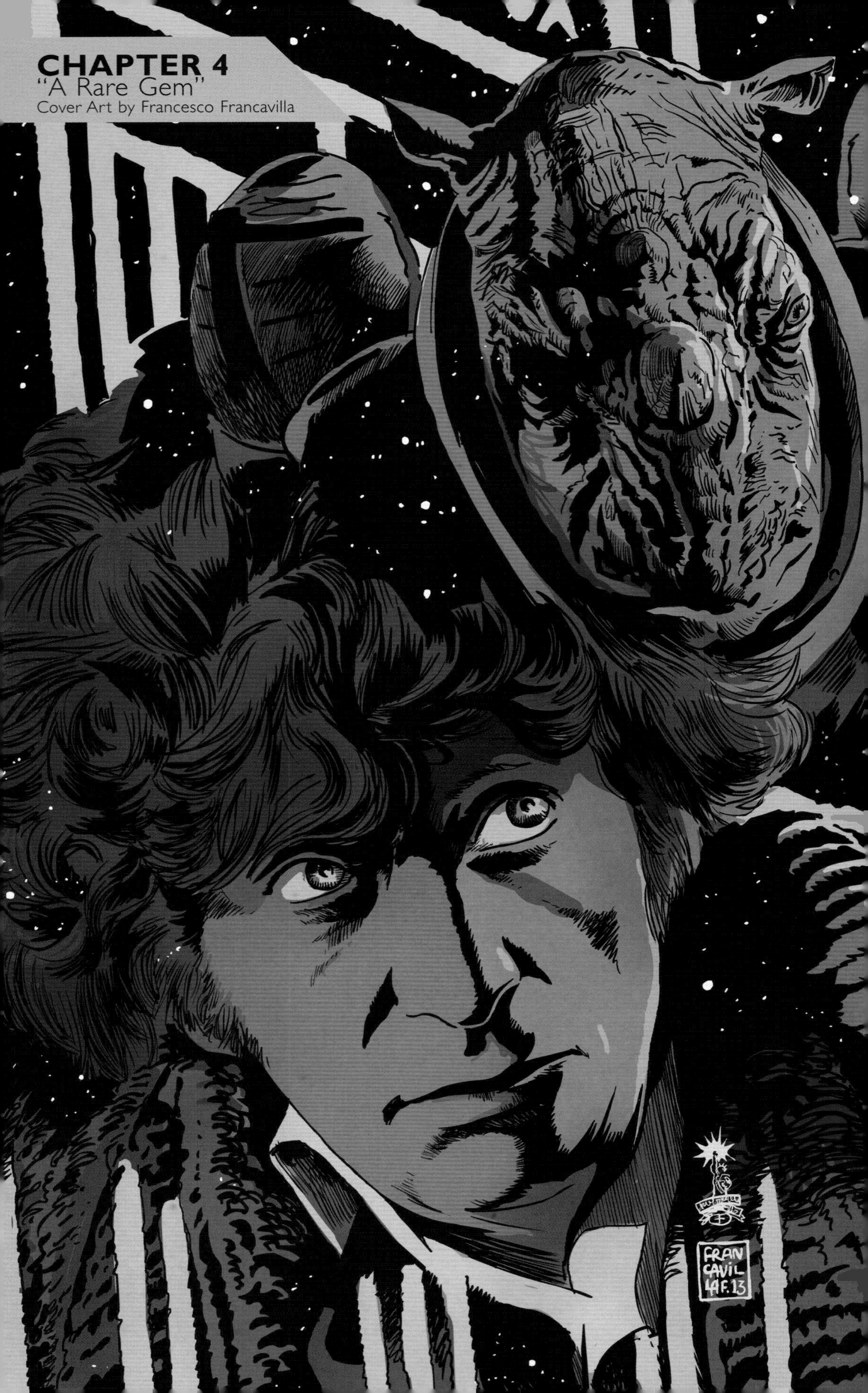
FRAN CAVIL LA F. 13

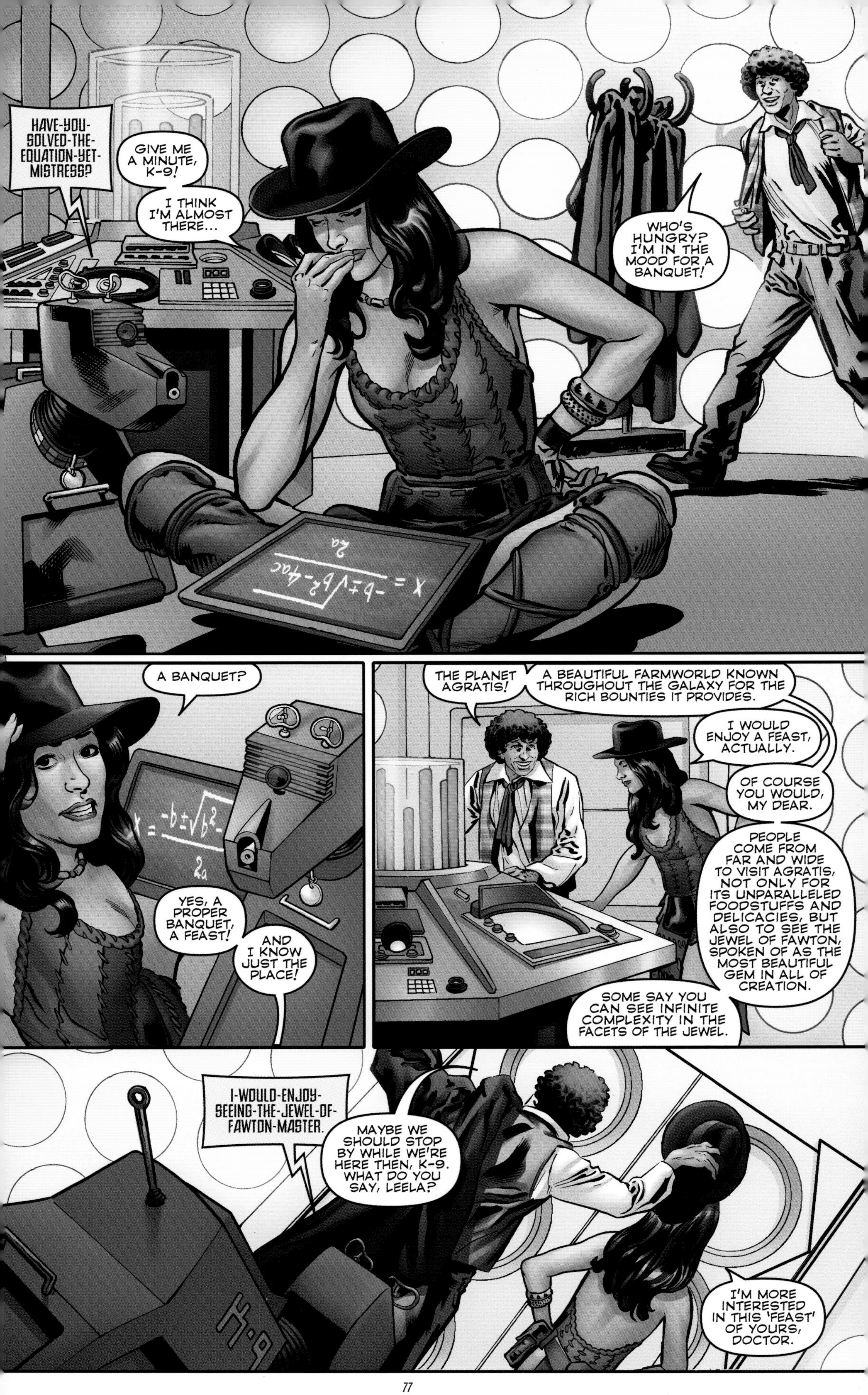
HAVE-YOU-SOLVED-THE-EQUATION-YET-MISTRESS?
GIVE ME A MINUTE, K-9!
I THINK I'M ALMOST THERE...
WHO'S HUNGRY? I'M IN THE MOOD FOR A BANQUET!
A BANQUET?
YES, A PROPER BANQUET, A FEAST!
AND I KNOW JUST THE PLACE!
THE PLANET AGRATIS!
A BEAUTIFUL FARMWORLD KNOWN THROUGHOUT THE GALAXY FOR THE RICH BOUNTIES IT PROVIDES.
I WOULD ENJOY A FEAST, ACTUALLY.
OF COURSE YOU WOULD, MY DEAR.
PEOPLE COME FROM FAR AND WIDE TO VISIT AGRATIS, NOT ONLY FOR ITS UNPARALLELED FOODSTUFFS AND DELICACIES, BUT ALSO TO SEE THE JEWEL OF FAWTON, SPOKEN OF AS THE MOST BEAUTIFUL GEM IN ALL OF CREATION.
SOME SAY YOU CAN SEE INFINITE COMPLEXITY IN THE FACETS OF THE JEWEL.
I-WOULD-ENJOY-SEEING-THE-JEWEL-OF-FAWTON-MASTER.
MAYBE WE SHOULD STOP BY WHILE WE'RE HERE THEN, K-9. WHAT DO YOU SAY, LEELA?
I'M MORE INTERESTED IN THIS 'FEAST' OF YOURS, DOCTOR.

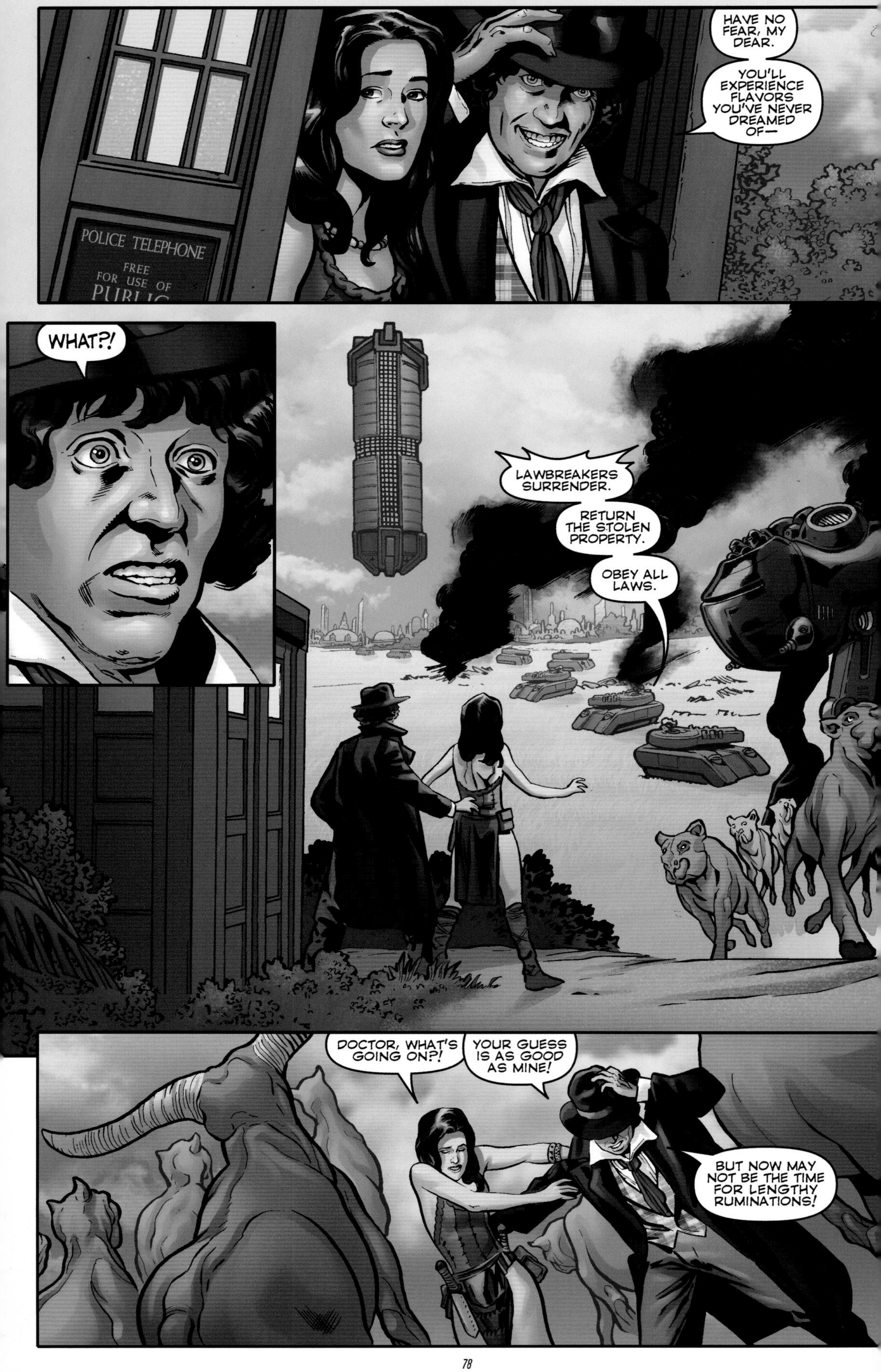
POLICE TELEPHONE
FREE
FOR USE OF
PUBLIC
HAVE NO FEAR, MY DEAR.
YOU'LL EXPERIENCE FLAVORS YOU'VE NEVER DREAMED OF—
WHAT?!
LAWBREAKERS SURRENDER.
RETURN THE STOLEN PROPERTY.
OBEY ALL LAWS.
DOCTOR, WHAT'S GOING ON?!
YOUR GUESS IS AS GOOD AS MINE!
BUT NOW MAY NOT BE THE TIME FOR LENGTHY RUMINATIONS!

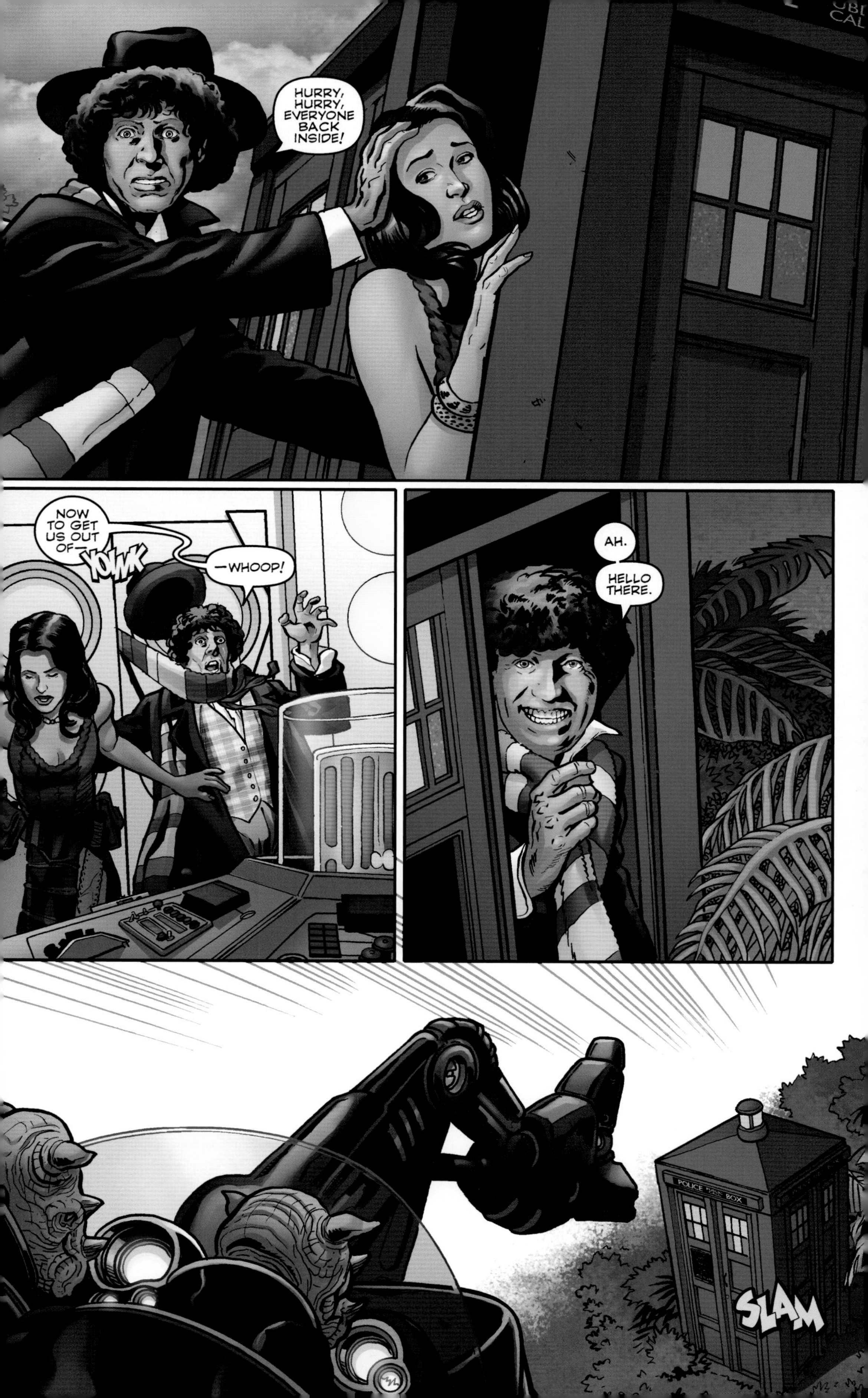
HURRY, HURRY, EVERYONE BACK INSIDE!
NOW TO GET US OUT OF—
YOWK
—WHOOP!
AH.
HELLO THERE.
POLICE BOX
SLAM

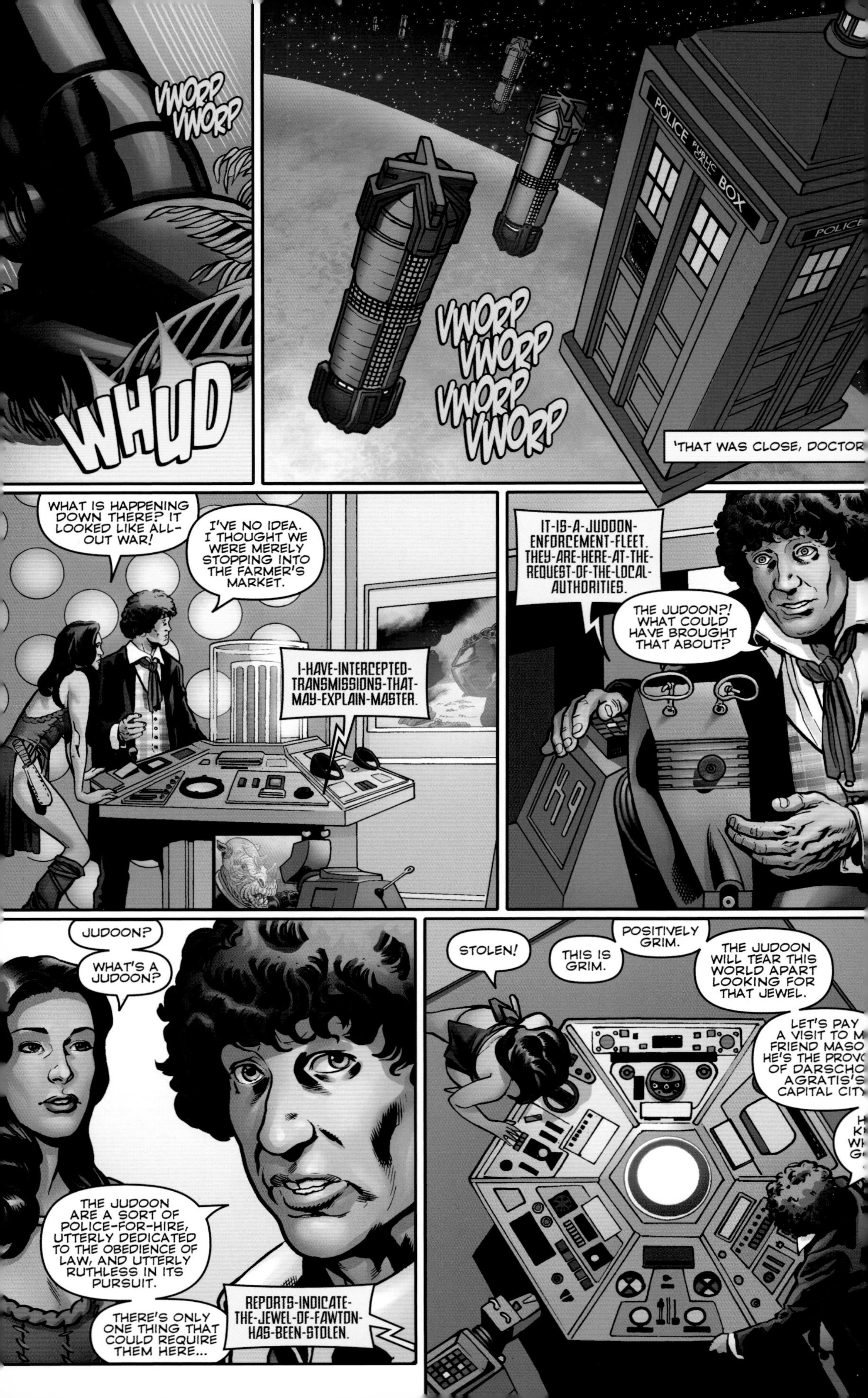
VWORP VWORP
WHUD
VWORP VWORP VWORP VWORP
POLICE PUBLIC CALL BOX
POLICE
'THAT WAS CLOSE, DOCTOR
WHAT IS HAPPENING DOWN THERE? IT LOOKED LIKE ALL-OUT WAR!
I'VE NO IDEA. I THOUGHT WE WERE MERELY STOPPING INTO THE FARMER'S MARKET.
I-HAVE-INTERCEPTED-TRANSMISSIONS-THAT-MAY-EXPLAIN-MASTER.
IT-IS-A-JUDOON-ENFORCEMENT-FLEET. THEY-ARE-HERE-AT-THE-REQUEST-OF-THE-LOCAL-AUTHORITIES.
THE JUDOON?! WHAT COULD HAVE BROUGHT THAT ABOUT?
JUDOON?
WHAT'S A JUDOON?
THE JUDOON ARE A SORT OF POLICE-FOR-HIRE, UTTERLY DEDICATED TO THE OBEDIENCE OF LAW, AND UTTERLY RUTHLESS IN ITS PURSUIT.
THERE'S ONLY ONE THING THAT COULD REQUIRE THEM HERE...
REPORTS-INDICATE-THE-JEWEL-OF-FAWTON-HAS-BEEN-STOLEN.
STOLEN!
THIS IS GRIM.
POSITIVELY GRIM.
THE JUDOON WILL TEAR THIS WORLD APART LOOKING FOR THAT JEWEL.
LET'S PAY A VISIT TO M FRIEND MASO HE'S THE PROVO OF DARSCHO AGRATIS'S CAPITAL CITY

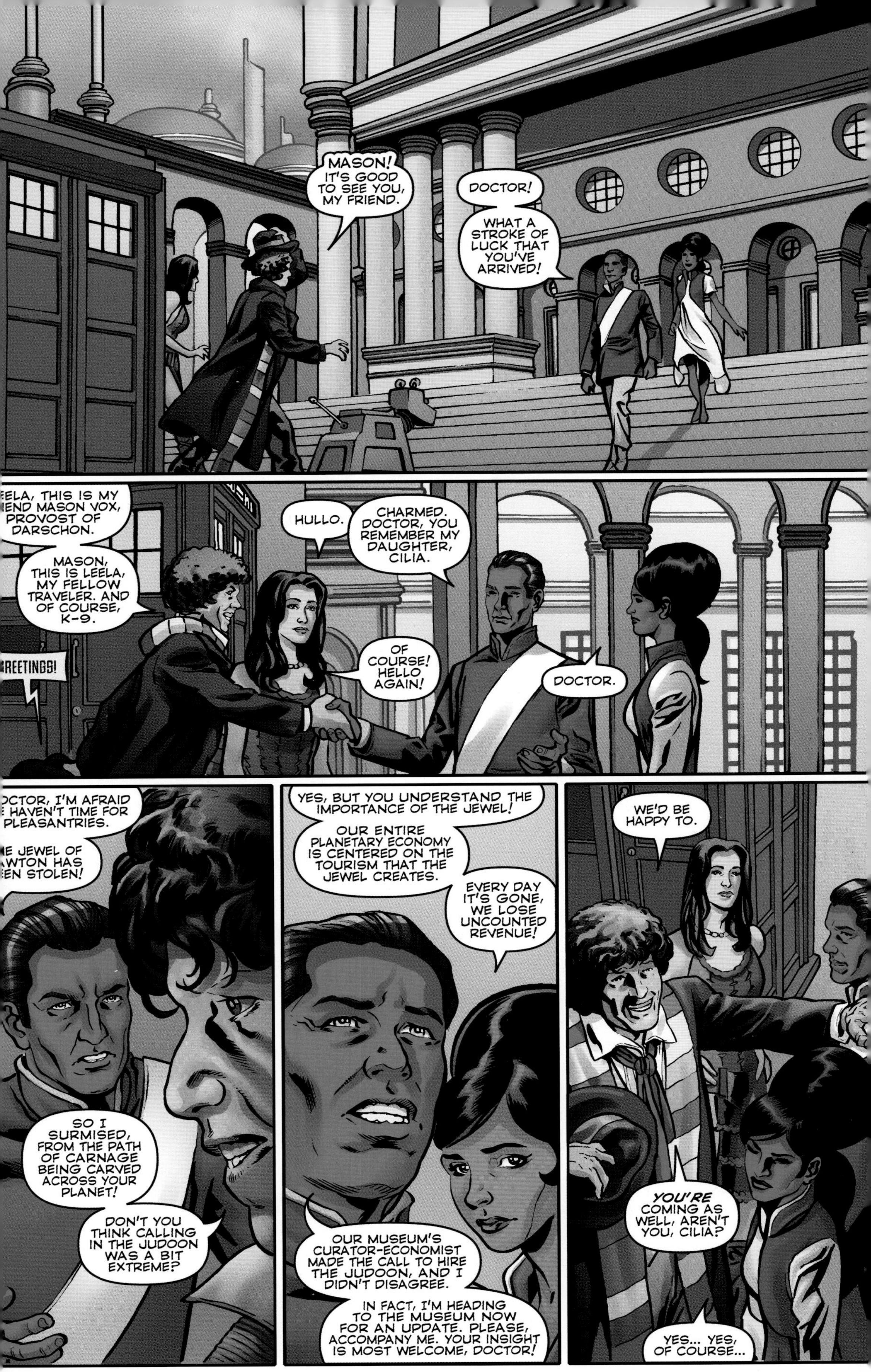
MASON! IT'S GOOD TO SEE YOU, MY FRIEND.
DOCTOR!
WHAT A STROKE OF LUCK THAT YOU'VE ARRIVED!
EELA, THIS IS MY IEND MASON VOX, PROVOST OF DARSCHON.
MASON, THIS IS LEELA, MY FELLOW TRAVELER. AND OF COURSE, K-9.
REETINGS!
HULLO.
CHARMED. DOCTOR, YOU REMEMBER MY DAUGHTER, CILIA.
OF COURSE! HELLO AGAIN!
DOCTOR.
OCTOR, I'M AFRAID E HAVEN'T TIME FOR PLEASANTRIES.
E JEWEL OF AWTON HAS EEN STOLEN!
SO I SURMISED, FROM THE PATH OF CARNAGE BEING CARVED ACROSS YOUR PLANET!
DON'T YOU THINK CALLING IN THE JUDOON WAS A BIT EXTREME?
YES, BUT YOU UNDERSTAND THE IMPORTANCE OF THE JEWEL!
OUR ENTIRE PLANETARY ECONOMY IS CENTERED ON THE TOURISM THAT THE JEWEL CREATES.
EVERY DAY IT'S GONE, WE LOSE UNCOUNTED REVENUE!
OUR MUSEUM'S CURATOR-ECONOMIST MADE THE CALL TO HIRE THE JUDOON, AND I DIDN'T DISAGREE.
IN FACT, I'M HEADING TO THE MUSEUM NOW FOR AN UPDATE. PLEASE, ACCOMPANY ME. YOUR INSIGHT IS MOST WELCOME, DOCTOR!
WE'D BE HAPPY TO.
YOU'RE COMING AS WELL, AREN'T YOU, CILIA?
YES... YES, OF COURSE...

FREZ! IS THERE ANY NEWS?

NONE, PROVOST VOX. THE JEWEL STILL REMAINS UNFOUND.

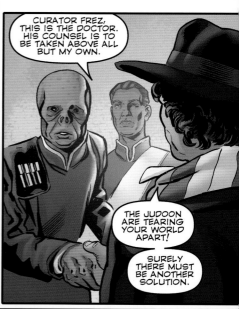

CURATOR FREZ, THIS IS THE DOCTOR. HIS COUNSEL IS TO BE TAKEN ABOVE ALL BUT MY OWN.

THE JUDOON ARE TEARING YOUR WORLD APART! SURELY THERE MUST BE ANOTHER SOLUTION.

I KNOW WHAT THEY'RE DOING! BUT WHAT'S THE ALTERNATIVE?! WE NEED THE JEWEL! WITHOUT IT, OUR ENTIRE SOCIETY IS MERELY DAYS FROM COLLAPSE!

ASK THE PROVOST! WHEN WE FIRST ARRIVED TO THIS WORLD, WE HAD NOTHING!

THE TOURISM AFTER OUR DISCOVERY OF THE JEWEL MADE ALL OUR ADVANCEMENTS POSSIBLE, ALLOWED US TO CULTIVATE AND DEVELOP THE FRUITS AND DELICACIES THAT BEINGS COME FROM LIGHT YEARS AWAY TO SAMPLE!

IT'S ALL BECAUSE OF THE JEWEL!

THIS IS MADNESS.

THIS IS LAW ENFORCEMENT? THESE ARE YOUR PROTECTORS?

SUCH AS THEY ARE, MY DEAR.

SUCH AS THEY ARE...

FATHER? I... HAVE SOMETHING TO TELL YOU.

I THINK ROGET MAY HAVE TAKEN THE JEWEL.

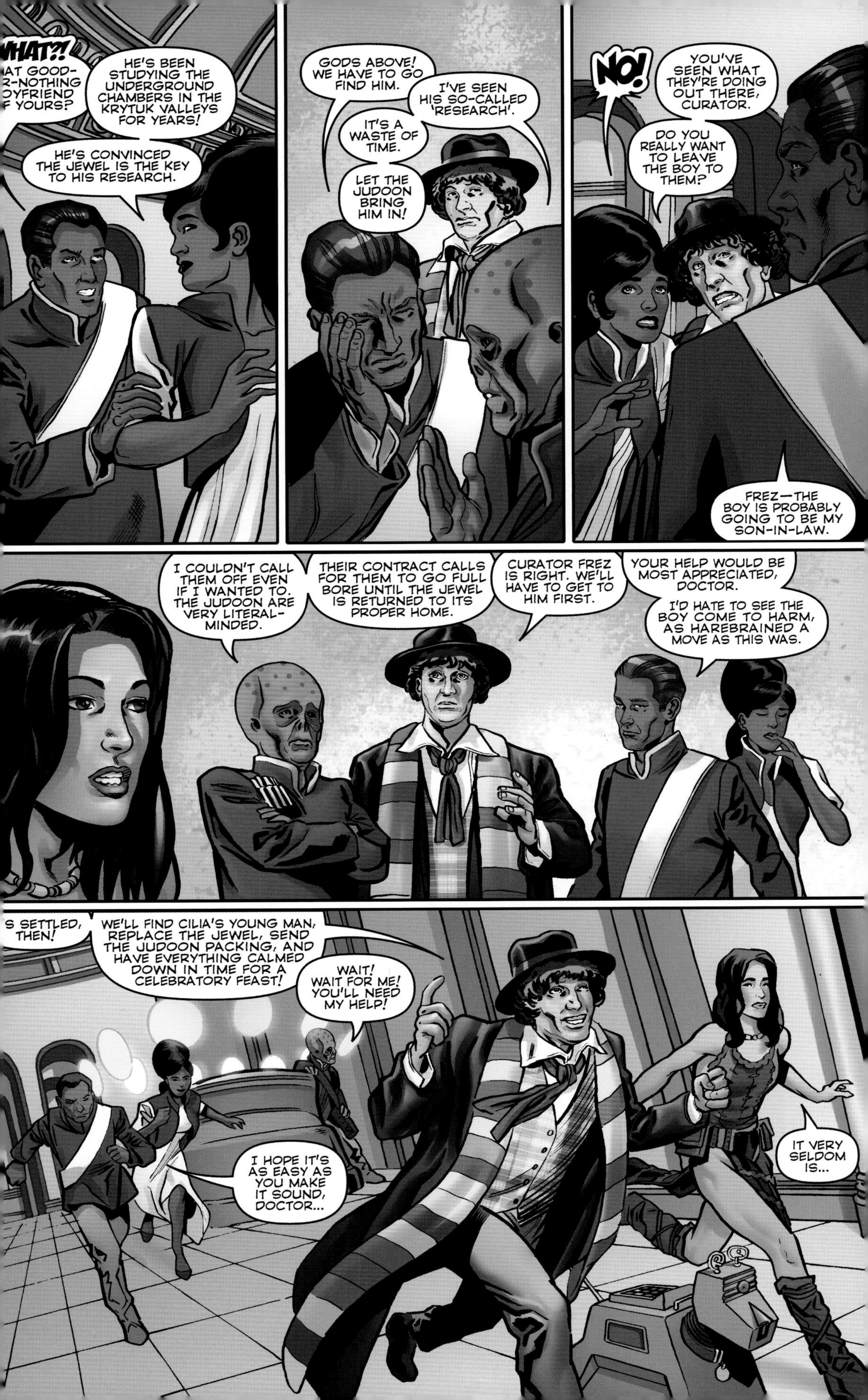
WHAT?!
AT GOOD-
R-NOTHING
OYFRIEND
F YOURS?
HE'S BEEN STUDYING THE UNDERGROUND CHAMBERS IN THE KRYTUK VALLEYS FOR YEARS!
HE'S CONVINCED THE JEWEL IS THE KEY TO HIS RESEARCH.
GODS ABOVE! WE HAVE TO GO FIND HIM.
I'VE SEEN HIS SO-CALLED 'RESEARCH'.
IT'S A WASTE OF TIME.
LET THE JUDOON BRING HIM IN!
NO!
YOU'VE SEEN WHAT THEY'RE DOING OUT THERE, CURATOR.
DO YOU REALLY WANT TO LEAVE THE BOY TO THEM?
FREZ—THE BOY IS PROBABLY GOING TO BE MY SON-IN-LAW.
I COULDN'T CALL THEM OFF EVEN IF I WANTED TO. THE JUDOON ARE VERY LITERAL-MINDED.
THEIR CONTRACT CALLS FOR THEM TO GO FULL BORE UNTIL THE JEWEL IS RETURNED TO ITS PROPER HOME.
CURATOR FREZ IS RIGHT. WE'LL HAVE TO GET TO HIM FIRST.
YOUR HELP WOULD BE MOST APPRECIATED, DOCTOR.
I'D HATE TO SEE THE BOY COME TO HARM, AS HAREBRAINED A MOVE AS THIS WAS.
S SETTLED, THEN!
WE'LL FIND CILIA'S YOUNG MAN, REPLACE THE JEWEL, SEND THE JUDOON PACKING, AND HAVE EVERYTHING CALMED DOWN IN TIME FOR A CELEBRATORY FEAST!
WAIT! WAIT FOR ME! YOU'LL NEED MY HELP!
I HOPE IT'S AS EASY AS YOU MAKE IT SOUND, DOCTOR...
IT VERY SELDOM IS...

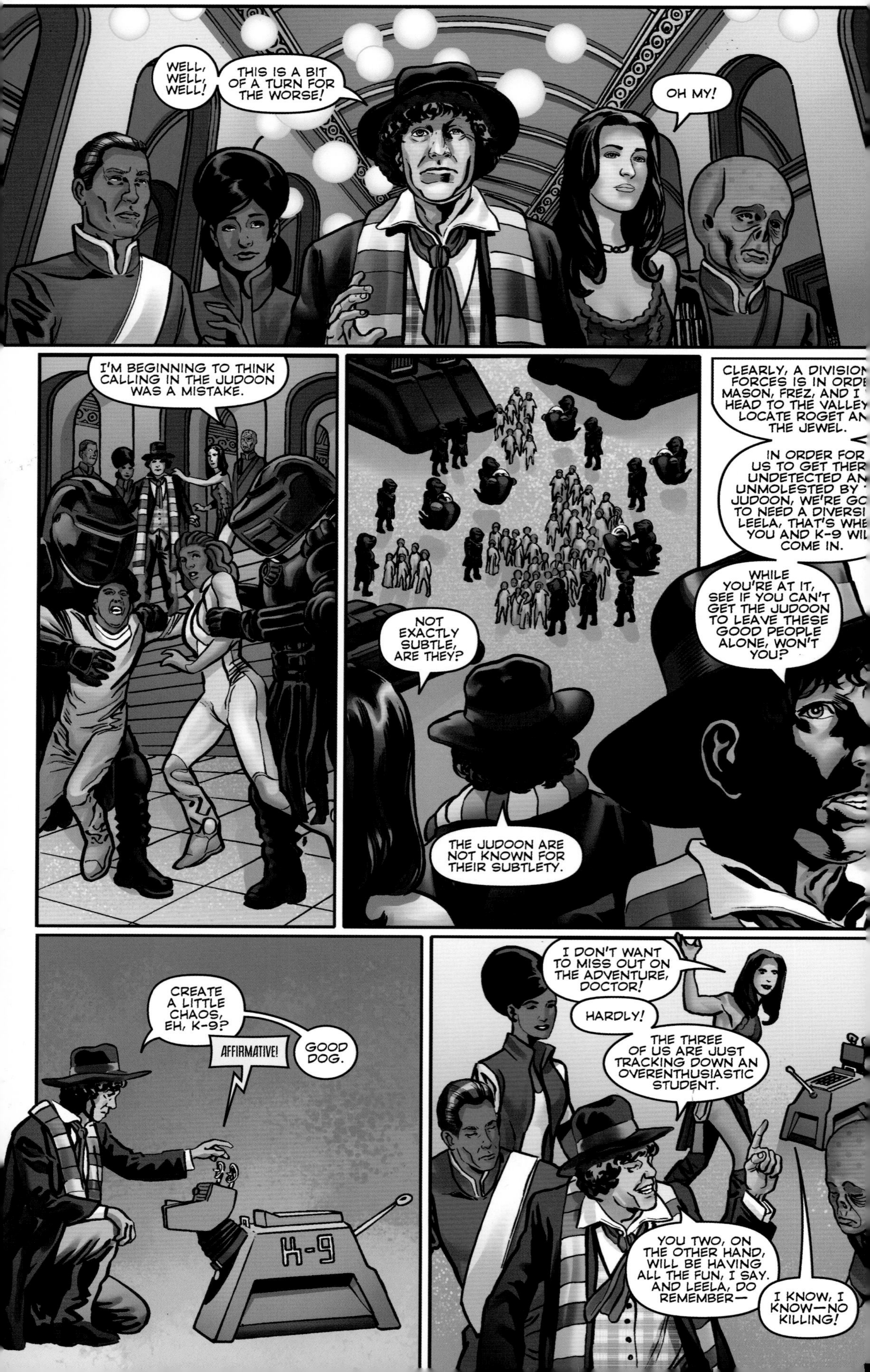
WELL, WELL, WELL!
THIS IS A BIT OF A TURN FOR THE WORSE!
OH MY!
I'M BEGINNING TO THINK CALLING IN THE JUDOON WAS A MISTAKE.
NOT EXACTLY SUBTLE, ARE THEY?
THE JUDOON ARE NOT KNOWN FOR THEIR SUBTLETY.
CLEARLY, A DIVISION
FORCES IS IN ORDE
MASON, FREZ, AND I
HEAD TO THE VALLEY
LOCATE ROGET AN
THE JEWEL.
IN ORDER FOR
US TO GET THER
UNDETECTED AN
UNMOLESTED BY
JUDOON, WE'RE GO
TO NEED A DIVERSI
LEELA, THAT'S WHE
YOU AND K-9 WIL
COME IN.
WHILE YOU'RE AT IT, SEE IF YOU CAN'T GET THE JUDOON TO LEAVE THESE GOOD PEOPLE ALONE, WON'T YOU?
CREATE A LITTLE CHAOS, EH, K-9?
AFFIRMATIVE!
GOOD DOG.
K-9
I DON'T WANT TO MISS OUT ON THE ADVENTURE, DOCTOR!
HARDLY!
THE THREE OF US ARE JUST TRACKING DOWN AN OVERENTHUSIASTIC STUDENT.
YOU TWO, ON THE OTHER HAND, WILL BE HAVING ALL THE FUN, I SAY. AND LEELA, DO REMEMBER—
I KNOW, I KNOW—NO KILLING!

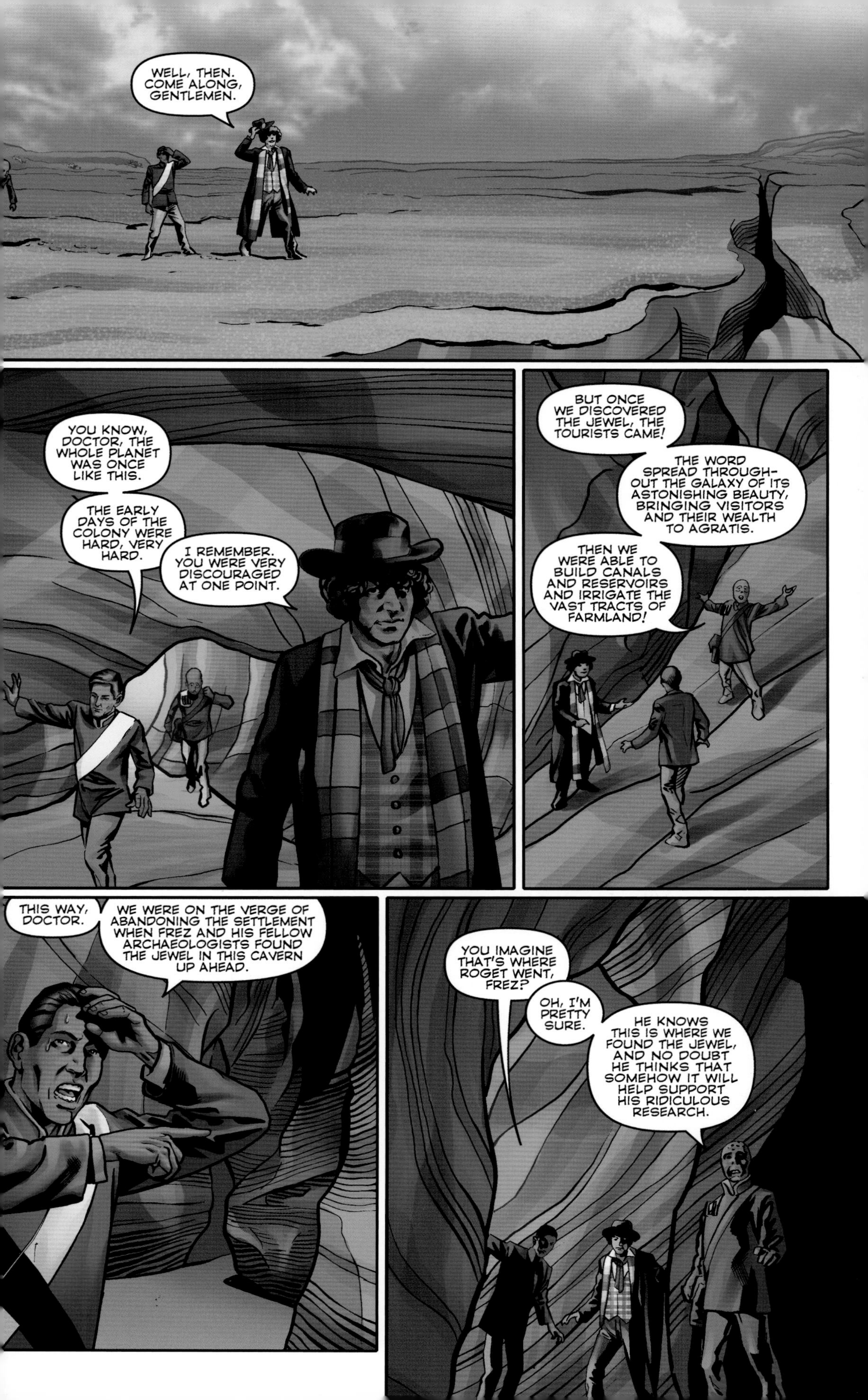
WELL, THEN. COME ALONG, GENTLEMEN.
YOU KNOW, DOCTOR, THE WHOLE PLANET WAS ONCE LIKE THIS.
THE EARLY DAYS OF THE COLONY WERE HARD, VERY HARD.
I REMEMBER. YOU WERE VERY DISCOURAGED AT ONE POINT.
BUT ONCE WE DISCOVERED THE JEWEL, THE TOURISTS CAME!
THE WORD SPREAD THROUGH-OUT THE GALAXY OF ITS ASTONISHING BEAUTY, BRINGING VISITORS AND THEIR WEALTH TO AGRATIS.
THEN WE WERE ABLE TO BUILD CANALS AND RESERVOIRS AND IRRIGATE THE VAST TRACTS OF FARMLAND!
THIS WAY, DOCTOR.
WE WERE ON THE VERGE OF ABANDONING THE SETTLEMENT WHEN FREZ AND HIS FELLOW ARCHAEOLOGISTS FOUND THE JEWEL IN THIS CAVERN UP AHEAD.
YOU IMAGINE THAT'S WHERE ROGET WENT, FREZ?
OH, I'M PRETTY SURE.
HE KNOWS THIS IS WHERE WE FOUND THE JEWEL, AND NO DOUBT HE THINKS THAT SOMEHOW IT WILL HELP SUPPORT HIS RIDICULOUS RESEARCH.

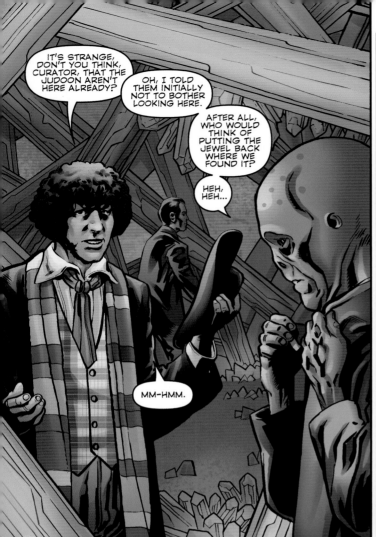

IT'S STRANGE, DON'T YOU THINK, CURATOR, THAT THE JUDOON AREN'T HERE ALREADY?

OH, I TOLD THEM INITIALLY NOT TO BOTHER LOOKING HERE.

AFTER ALL, WHO WOULD THINK OF PUTTING THE JEWEL BACK WHERE WE FOUND IT?

HEH, HEH...

MM-HMM.

WHAT A REMARKABLE CAVERN.

YES. IT'S FULL OF THESE CRYSTALLINE WALLS AND INTRICATE STRUCTURES. AT FIRST, WE THOUGHT MAYBE THIS PLACE WOULD BE A LUCRATIVE RESOURCE FOR MINING.

BUT THE MINERALS TURNED OUT TO BE NOT VERY VALUABLE.

NOTHING IN HERE SEEMED WORTHWHILE UNTIL WE FOUND THE JEWEL.

ROGET! ARE YOU IN HERE?

WHOOA-OA-OOOOA...

MASON!

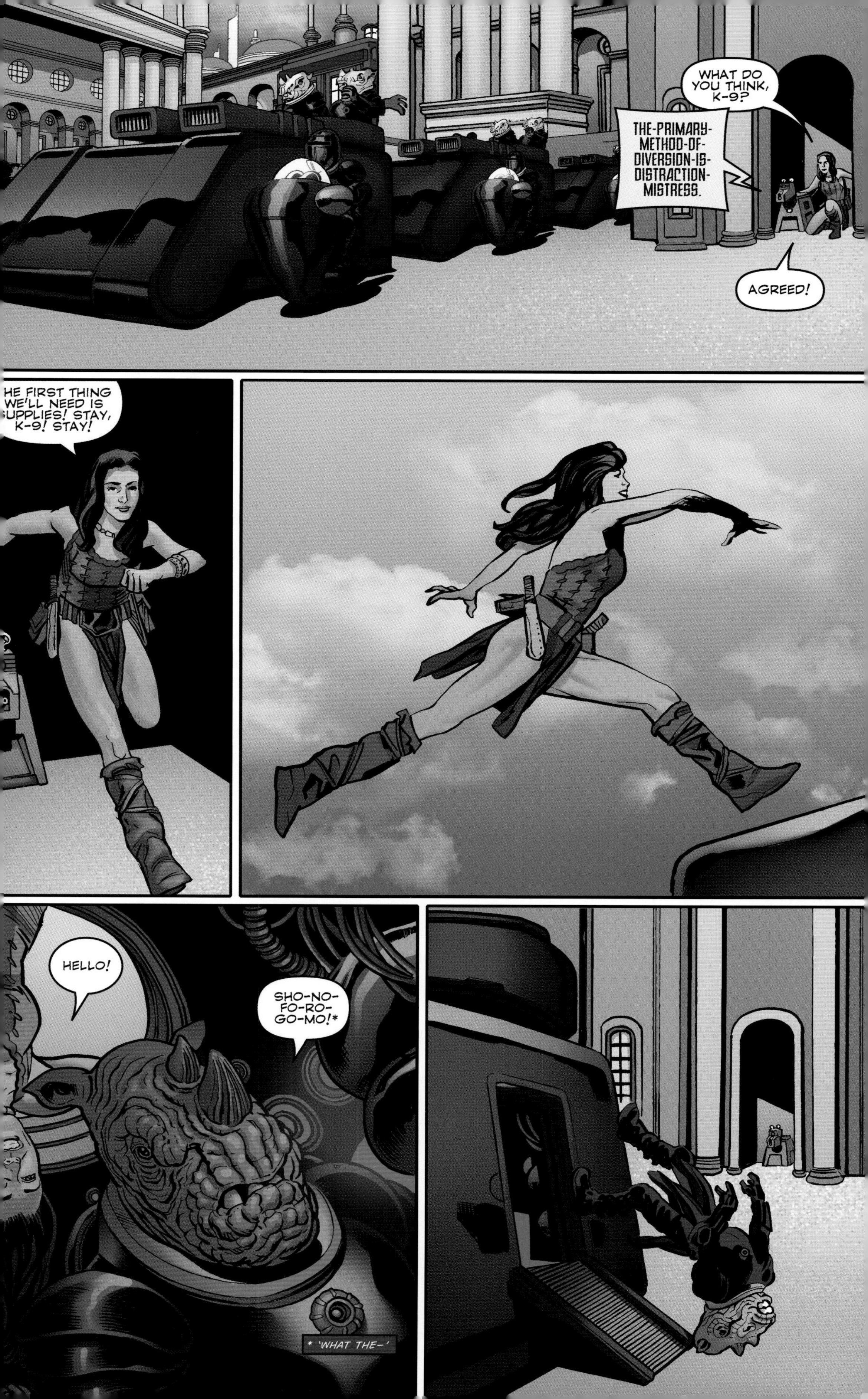
WHAT DO YOU THINK, K-9?
THE-PRIMARY-METHOD-OF-DIVERSION-IS-DISTRACTION-MISTRESS.
AGREED!
HE FIRST THING WE'LL NEED IS SUPPLIES! STAY, K-9! STAY!
HELLO!
SHO-NO-FO-RO-GO-MO!*
* 'WHAT THE–'

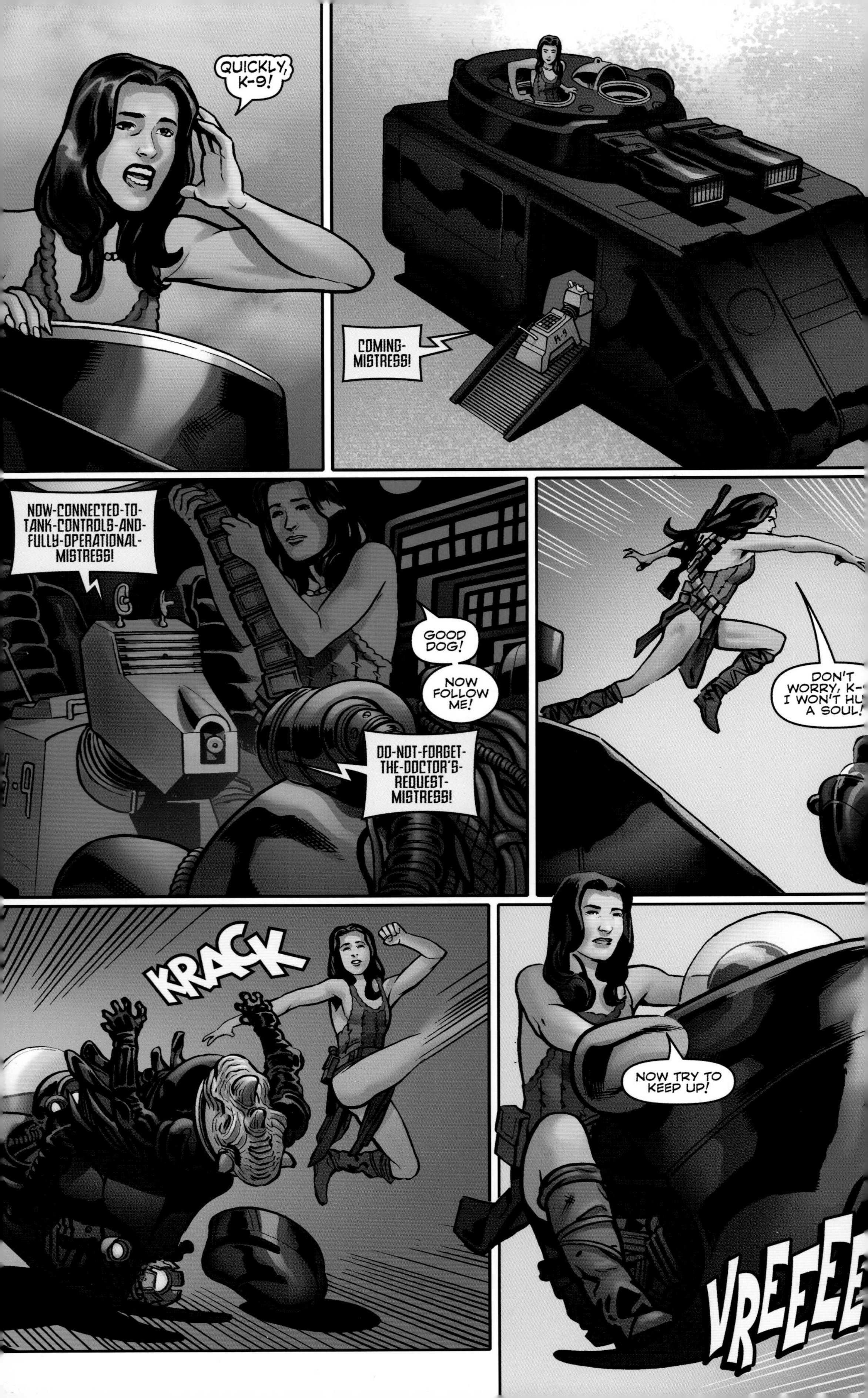
QUICKLY, K-9!
COMING-MISTRESS!
NOW-CONNECTED-TO-TANK-CONTROLS-AND-FULLY-OPERATIONAL-MISTRESS!
GOOD DOG!
NOW FOLLOW ME!
DO-NOT-FORGET-THE-DOCTOR'S-REQUEST-MISTRESS!
KRACK
NOW TRY TO KEEP UP!
VREEEE

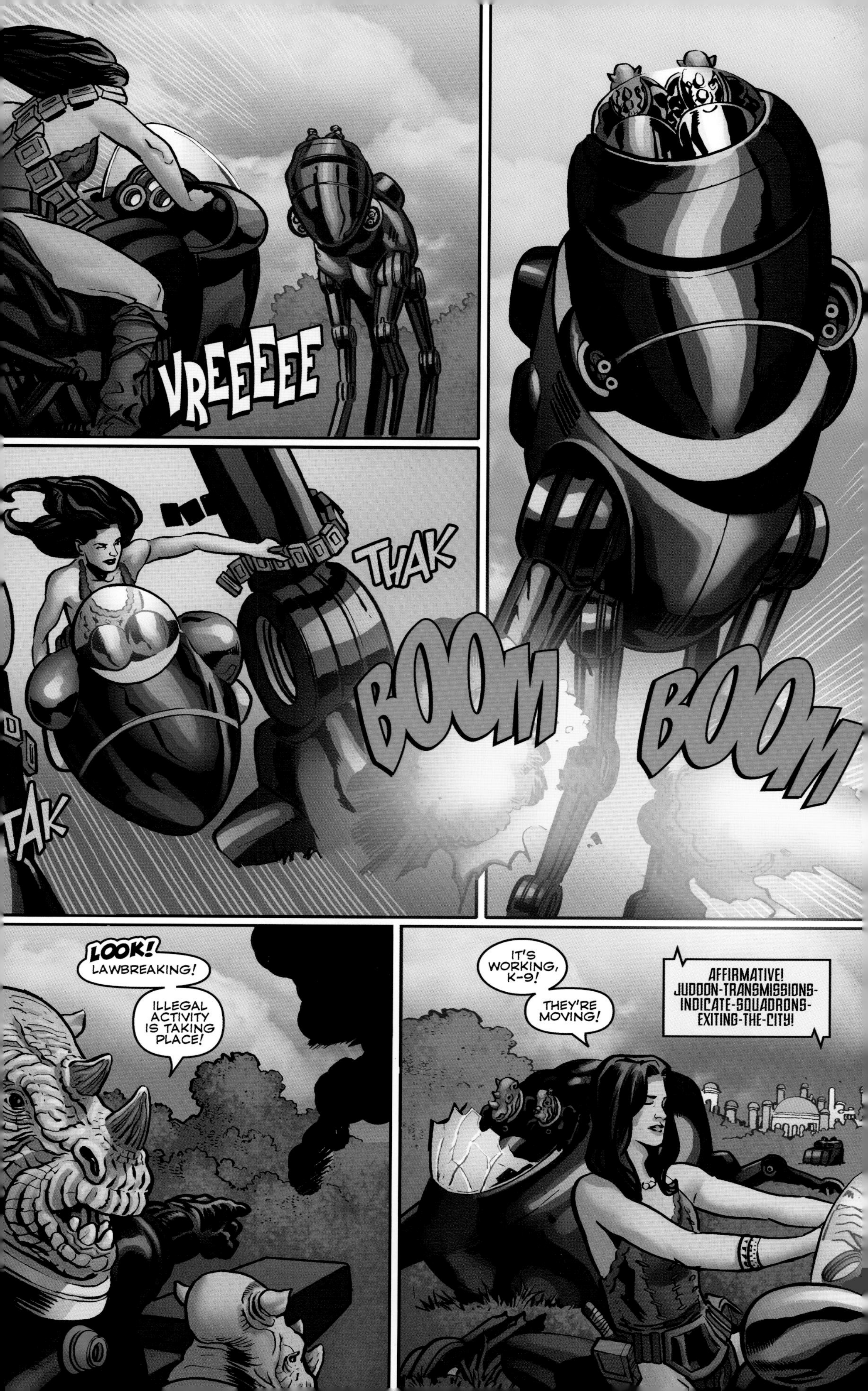

VREEEEEE
THAK
TAK
BOOM
BOOM
LOOK! LAWBREAKING!
ILLEGAL ACTIVITY IS TAKING PLACE!
IT'S WORKING, K-9!
THEY'RE MOVING!
AFFIRMATIVE! JUDOON-TRANSMISSIONS-INDICATE-SQUADRONS-EXITING-THE-CITY!

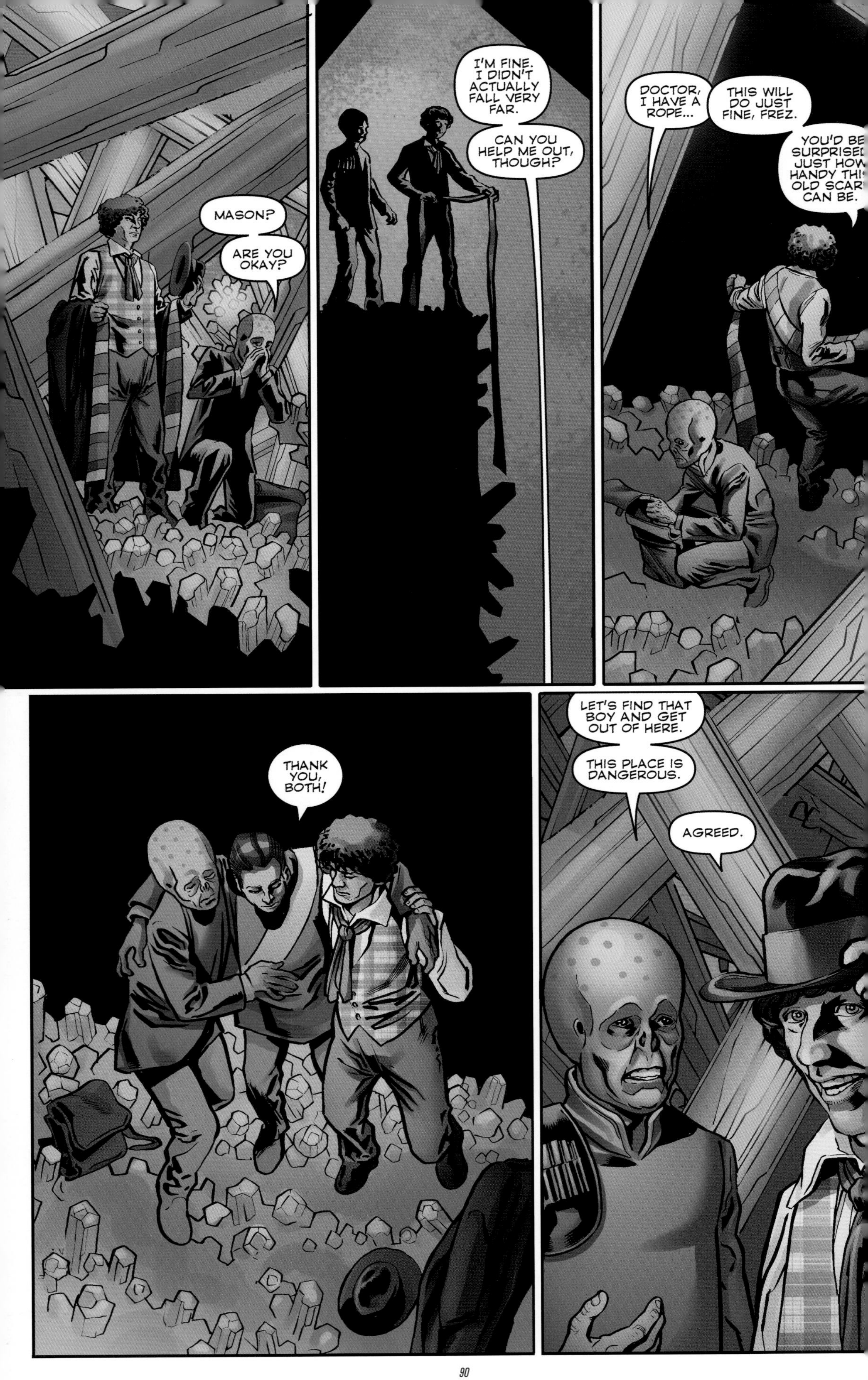
MASON?
ARE YOU OKAY?
I'M FINE. I DIDN'T ACTUALLY FALL VERY FAR.
CAN YOU HELP ME OUT, THOUGH?
DOCTOR, I HAVE A ROPE...
THIS WILL DO JUST FINE, FREZ.
YOU'D BE SURPRISED JUST HOW HANDY THIS OLD SCARF CAN BE.
THANK YOU, BOTH!
LET'S FIND THAT BOY AND GET OUT OF HERE.
THIS PLACE IS DANGEROUS.
AGREED.

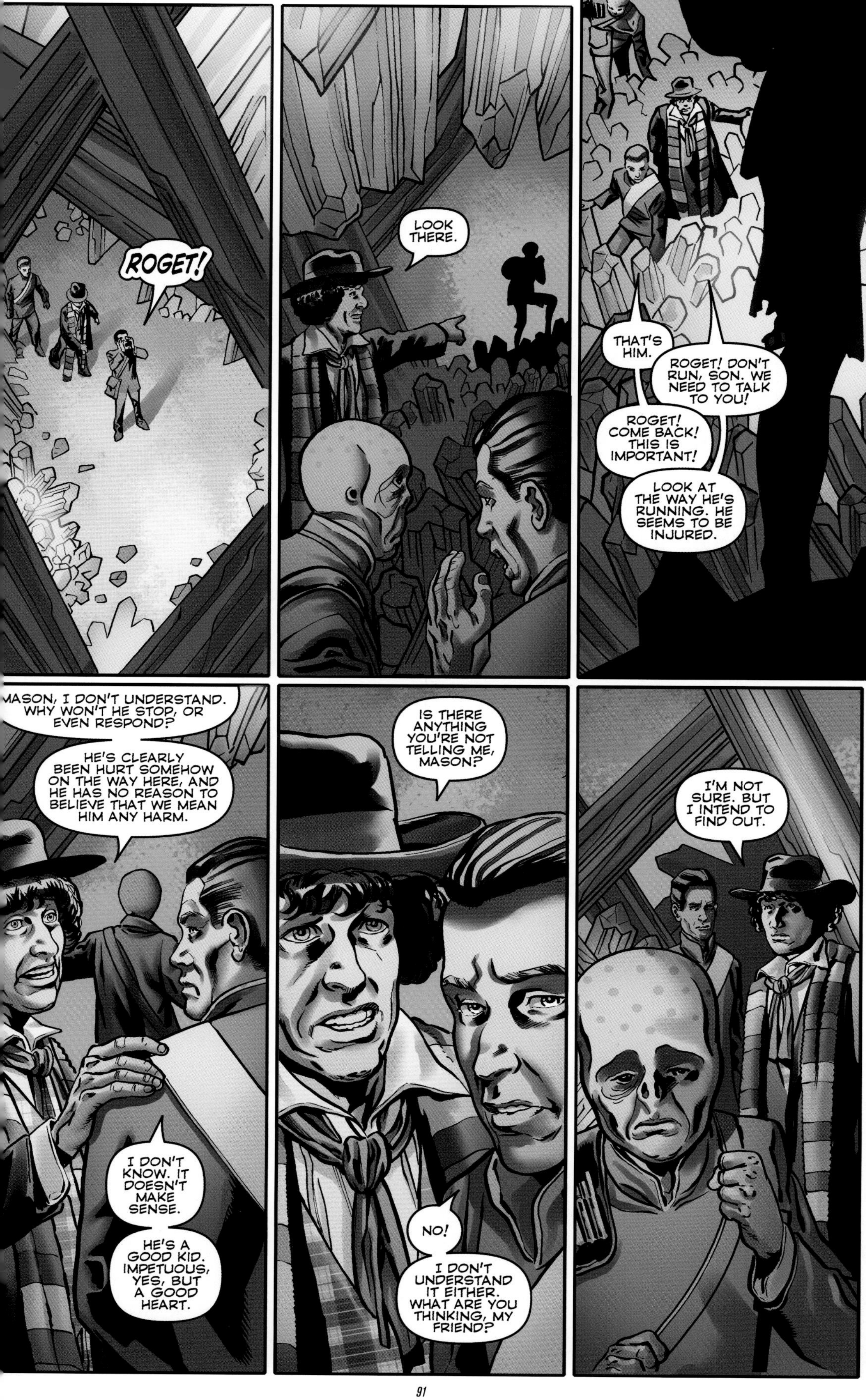
ROGET!
LOOK THERE.
THAT'S HIM.
ROGET! DON'T RUN, SON. WE NEED TO TALK TO YOU!
ROGET! COME BACK! THIS IS IMPORTANT!
LOOK AT THE WAY HE'S RUNNING. HE SEEMS TO BE INJURED.
MASON, I DON'T UNDERSTAND. WHY WON'T HE STOP, OR EVEN RESPOND?
HE'S CLEARLY BEEN HURT SOMEHOW ON THE WAY HERE, AND HE HAS NO REASON TO BELIEVE THAT WE MEAN HIM ANY HARM.
I DON'T KNOW. IT DOESN'T MAKE SENSE.
HE'S A GOOD KID. IMPETUOUS, YES, BUT A GOOD HEART.
IS THERE ANYTHING YOU'RE NOT TELLING ME, MASON?
NO!
I DON'T UNDERSTAND IT EITHER. WHAT ARE YOU THINKING, MY FRIEND?
I'M NOT SURE. BUT I INTEND TO FIND OUT.

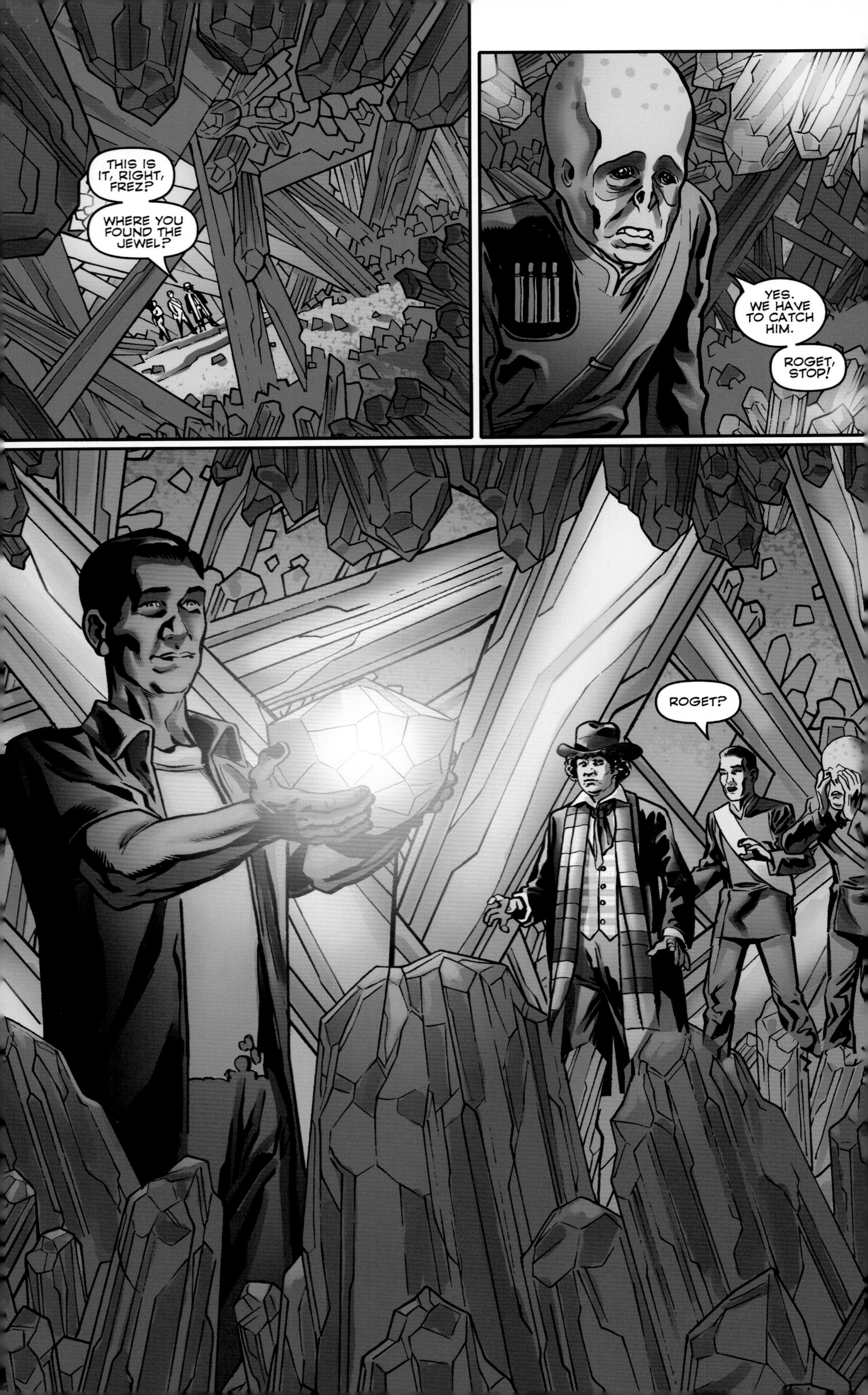
THIS IS IT, RIGHT, FREZ?
WHERE YOU FOUND THE JEWEL?
YES. WE HAVE TO CATCH HIM.
ROGET, STOP!
ROGET?

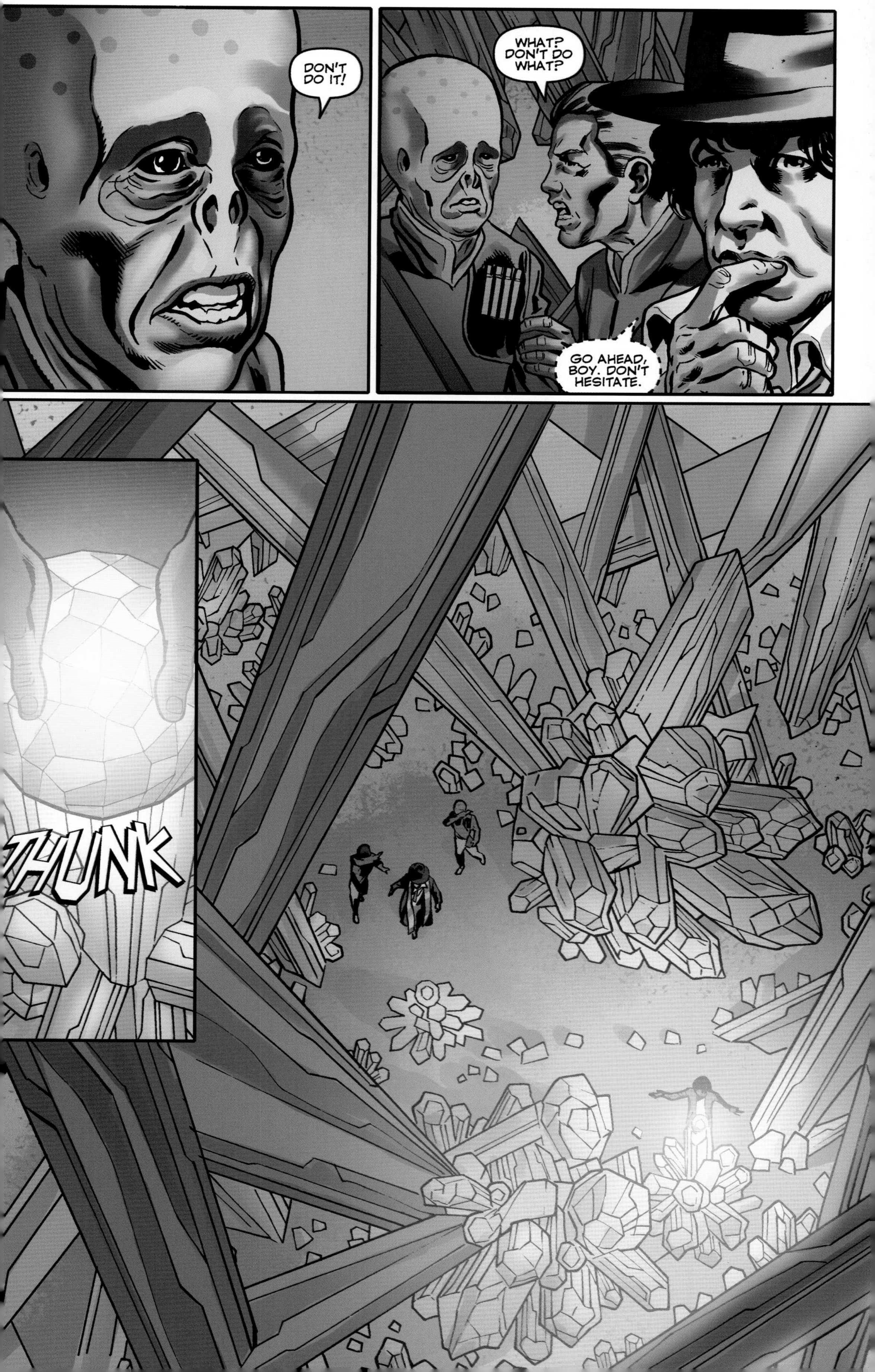
DON'T DO IT!
WHAT? DON'T DO WHAT?
GO AHEAD, BOY. DON'T HESITATE.
THUNK

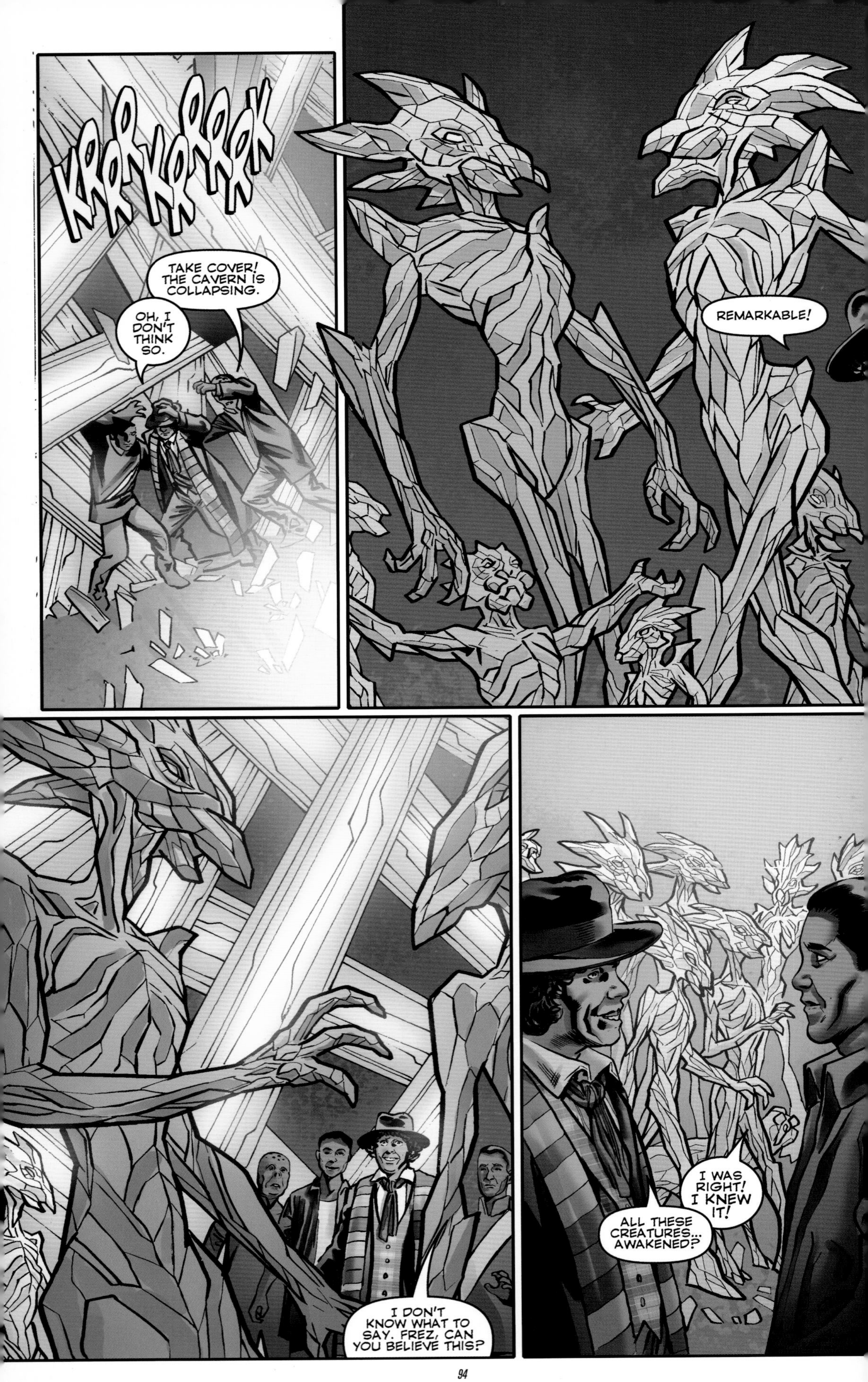
KRRKRRRRK
TAKE COVER! THE CAVERN IS COLLAPSING.
OH, I DON'T THINK SO.
REMARKABLE!
I DON'T KNOW WHAT TO SAY. FREZ, CAN YOU BELIEVE THIS?
ALL THESE CREATURES... AWAKENED?
I WAS RIGHT! I KNEW IT!

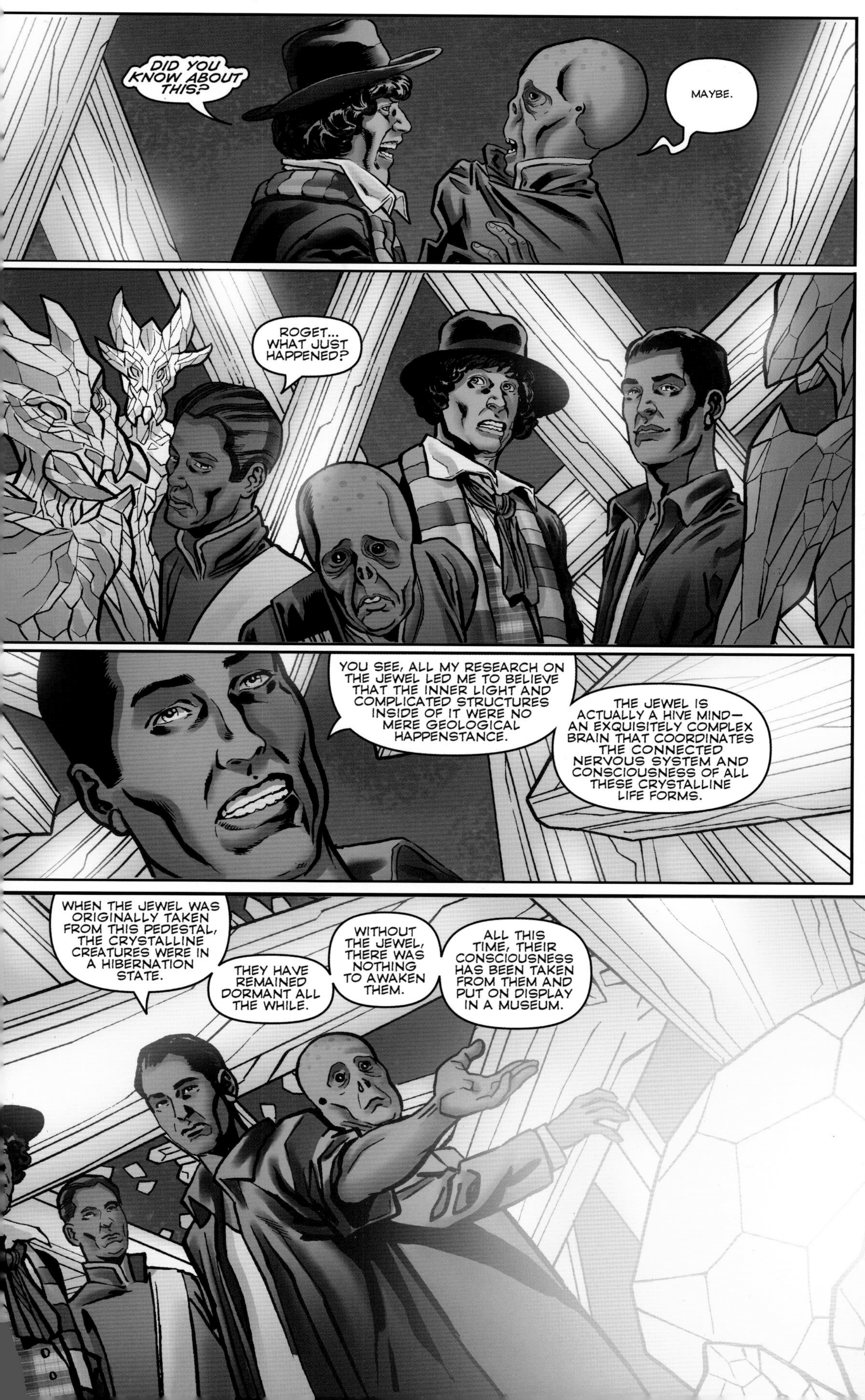
DID YOU KNOW ABOUT THIS?
MAYBE.
ROGET... WHAT JUST HAPPENED?
YOU SEE, ALL MY RESEARCH ON THE JEWEL LED ME TO BELIEVE THAT THE INNER LIGHT AND COMPLICATED STRUCTURES INSIDE OF IT WERE NO MERE GEOLOGICAL HAPPENSTANCE.
THE JEWEL IS ACTUALLY A HIVE MIND— AN EXQUISITELY COMPLEX BRAIN THAT COORDINATES THE CONNECTED NERVOUS SYSTEM AND CONSCIOUSNESS OF ALL THESE CRYSTALLINE LIFE FORMS.
WHEN THE JEWEL WAS ORIGINALLY TAKEN FROM THIS PEDESTAL, THE CRYSTALLINE CREATURES WERE IN A HIBERNATION STATE.
THEY HAVE REMAINED DORMANT ALL THE WHILE.
WITHOUT THE JEWEL, THERE WAS NOTHING TO AWAKEN THEM.
ALL THIS TIME, THEIR CONSCIOUSNESS HAS BEEN TAKEN FROM THEM AND PUT ON DISPLAY IN A MUSEUM.

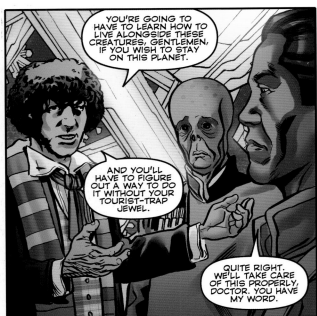

YOU'RE GOING TO HAVE TO LEARN HOW TO LIVE ALONGSIDE THESE CREATURES, GENTLEMEN, IF YOU WISH TO STAY ON THIS PLANET.

AND YOU'LL HAVE TO FIGURE OUT A WAY TO DO IT WITHOUT YOUR TOURIST-TRAP JEWEL.

QUITE RIGHT. WE'LL TAKE CARE OF THIS PROPERLY, DOCTOR. YOU HAVE MY WORD.

IT GOES WITHOUT SAYING THAT YOU NEED TO CALL OFF THE JUDOON, FREZ, RIGHT AWAY.

I THINK NOW THAT WE'VE FOUND THE JEWEL AND PLACED IT WITH ITS REAL, PROPER OWNERS, THAT SHOULD SATISFY THE LEGALISTIC RATIONALE OF THE JUDOON AND PROVIDE THEM WITH A CONTRACTUAL REASON TO STAND DOWN FROM THEIR SEARCH. WOULDN'T YOU SAY, CURATOR?

YES, OF COURSE.

FRZZZYRK. BRIZZL. MEK! MEK!

THEY CAN TALK?

SEEMS THAT WAY.

YOU'LL HAVE A LOT OF EXPLAINING TO DO ONCE ROGET THERE FIGURES OUT THEIR LANGUAGE.

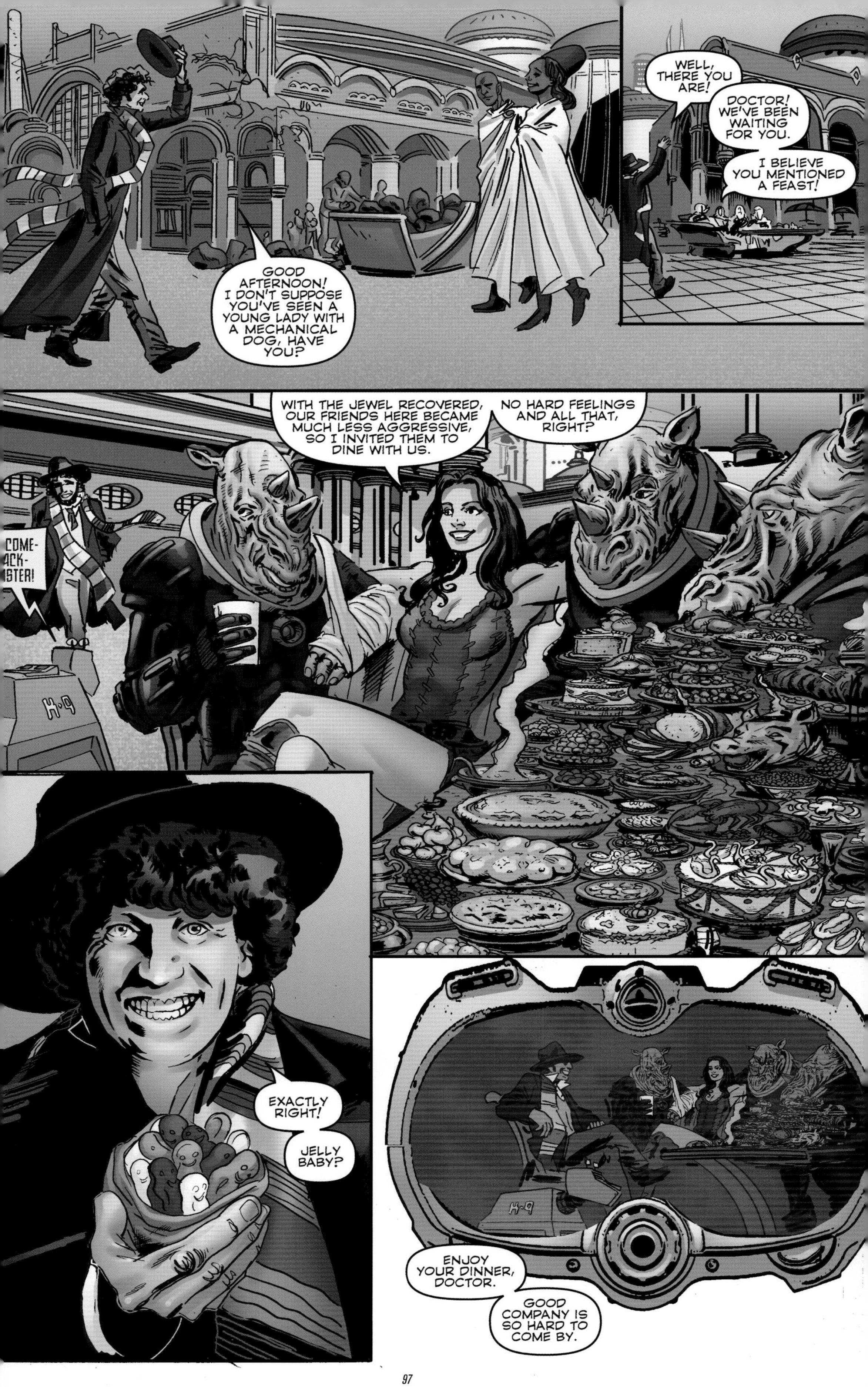
GOOD AFTERNOON! I DON'T SUPPOSE YOU'VE SEEN A YOUNG LADY WITH A MECHANICAL DOG, HAVE YOU?
WELL, THERE YOU ARE!
DOCTOR! WE'VE BEEN WAITING FOR YOU.
I BELIEVE YOU MENTIONED A FEAST!
COME- ACK- STER!
WITH THE JEWEL RECOVERED, OUR FRIENDS HERE BECAME MUCH LESS AGGRESSIVE, SO I INVITED THEM TO DINE WITH US.
NO HARD FEELINGS AND ALL THAT, RIGHT?
...
K-9
EXACTLY RIGHT!
JELLY BABY?
ENJOY YOUR DINNER, DOCTOR.
GOOD COMPANY IS SO HARD TO COME BY.

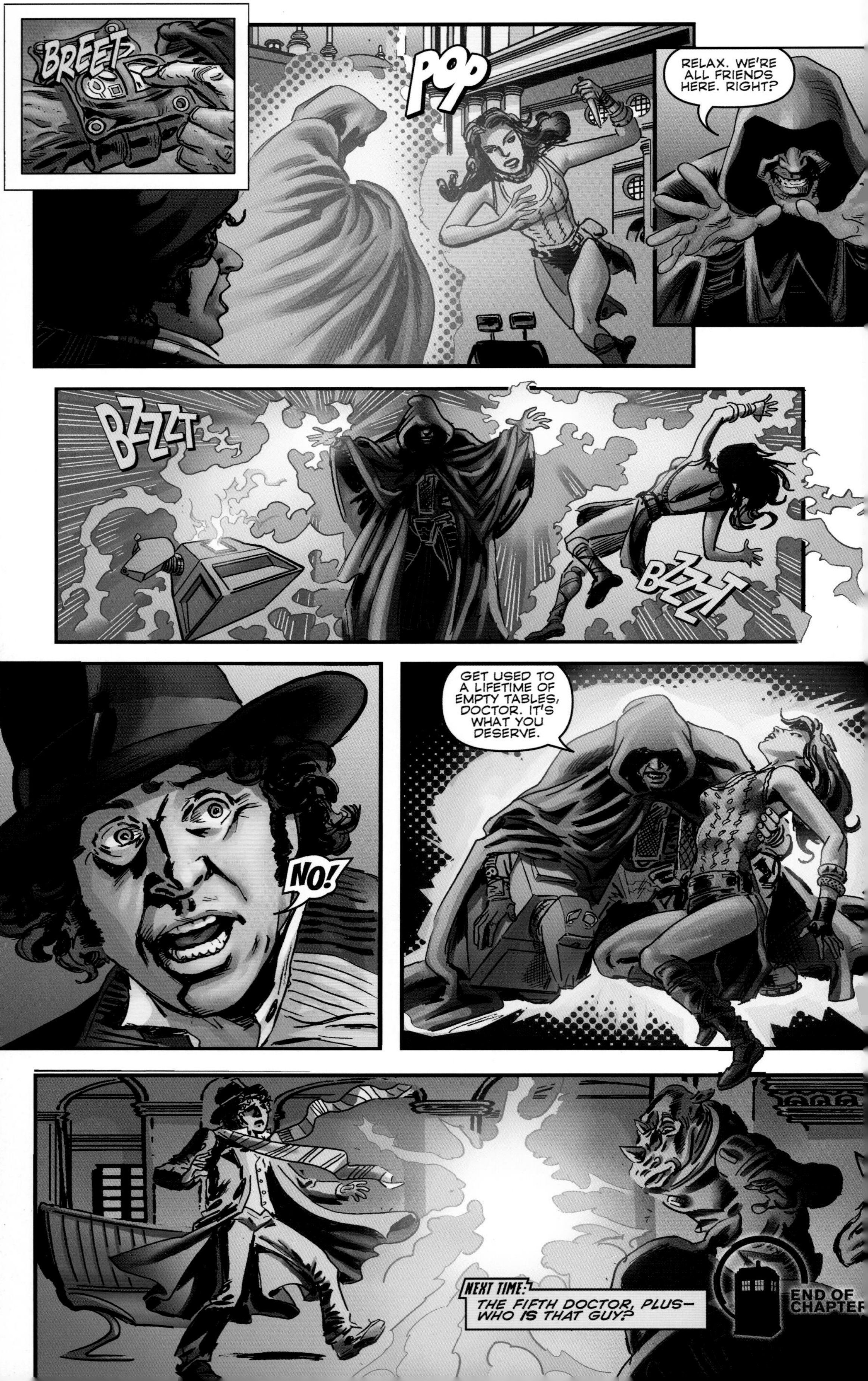
BREET
POP
RELAX. WE'RE ALL FRIENDS HERE. RIGHT?
BZZZT
BZZZT
NO!
GET USED TO A LIFETIME OF EMPTY TABLES, DOCTOR. IT'S WHAT YOU DESERVE.
NEXT TIME:
THE FIFTH DOCTOR, PLUS— WHO IS THAT GUY?
END OF CHAPTER

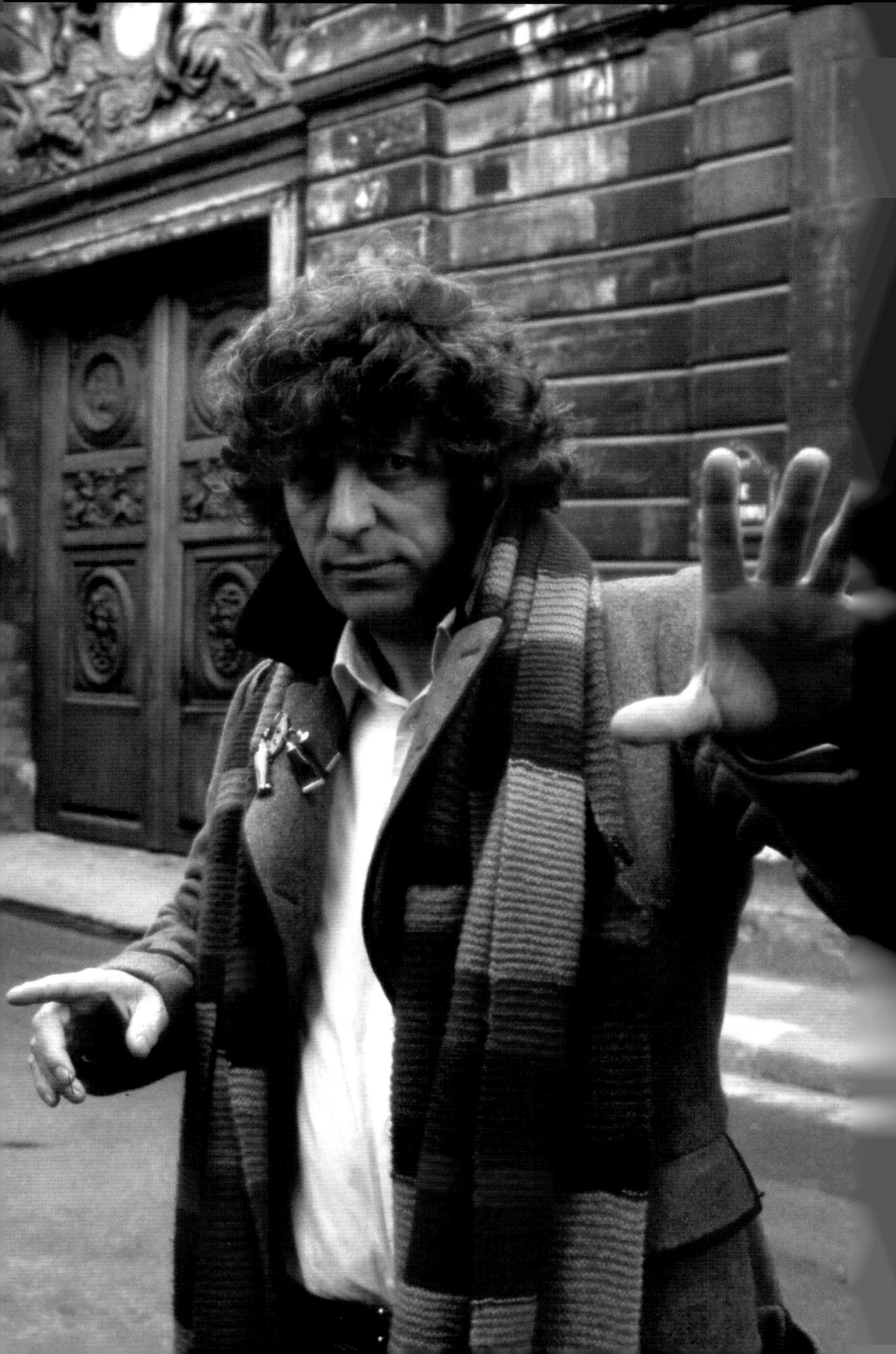

Art by Simon Fraser
Colors by Gary Caldwell

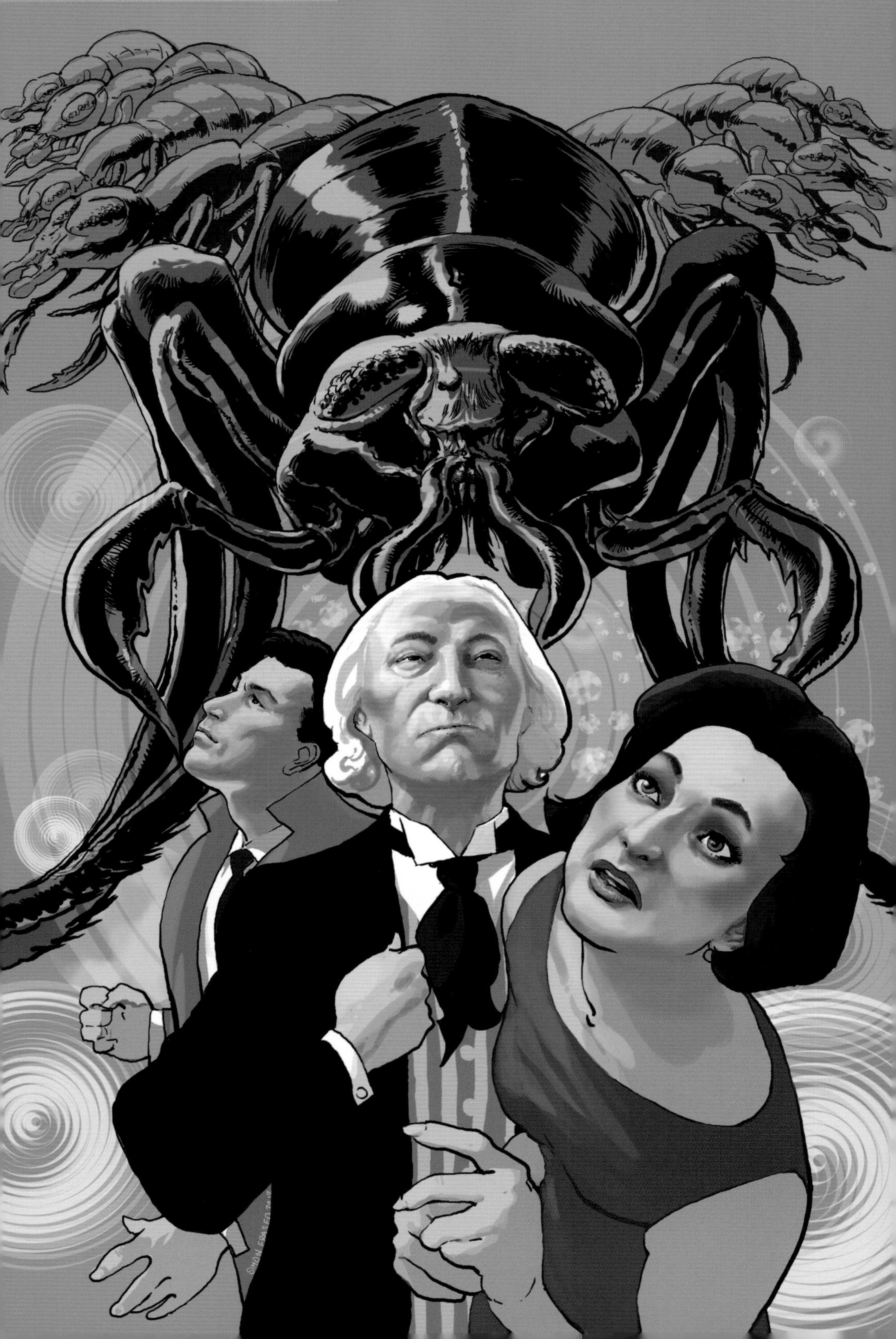

Art by Lee Sullivan
Colors by Phil Elliott

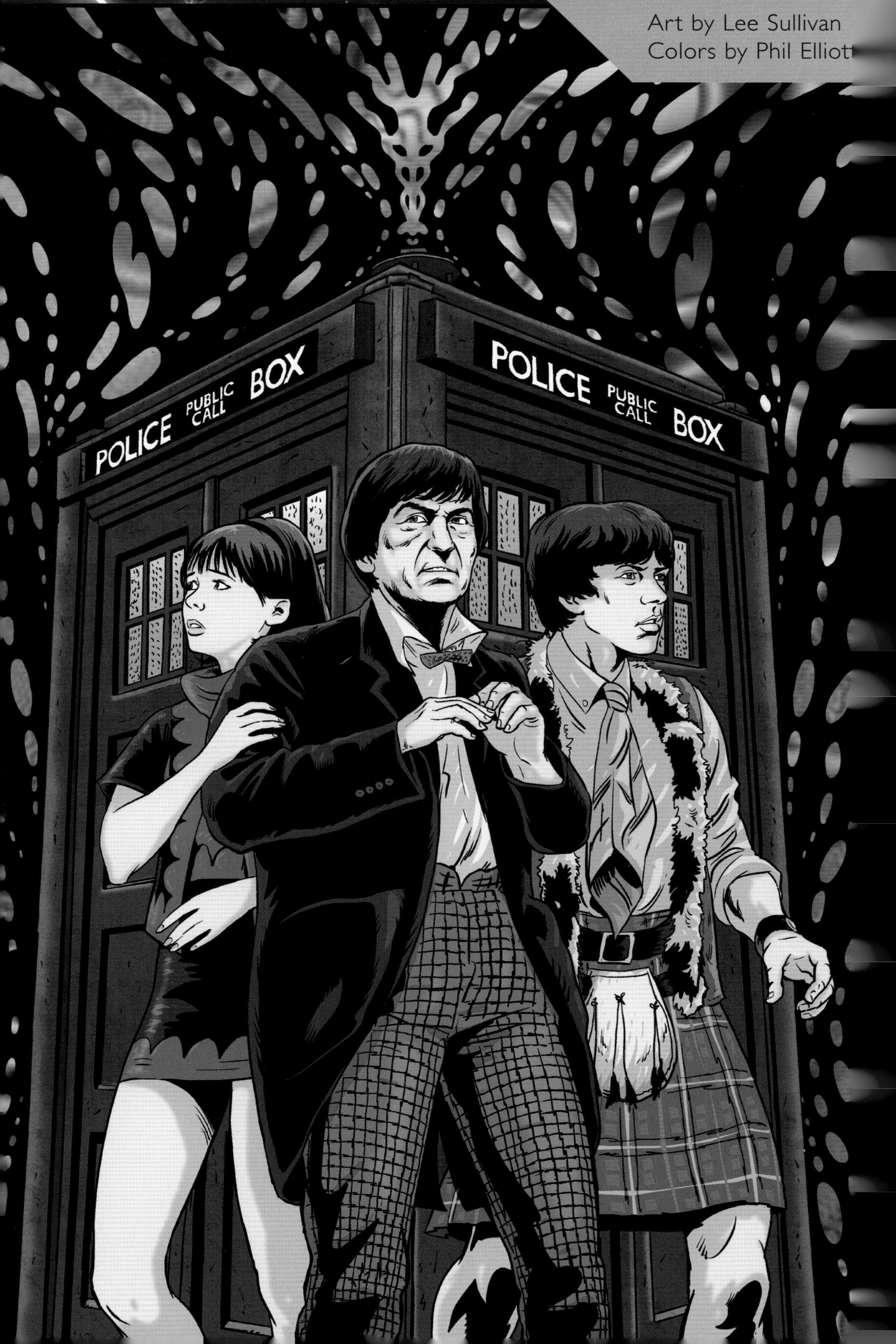
POLICE PUBLIC CALL BOX
POLICE PUBLIC CALL BOX

Art by by Mike Collins

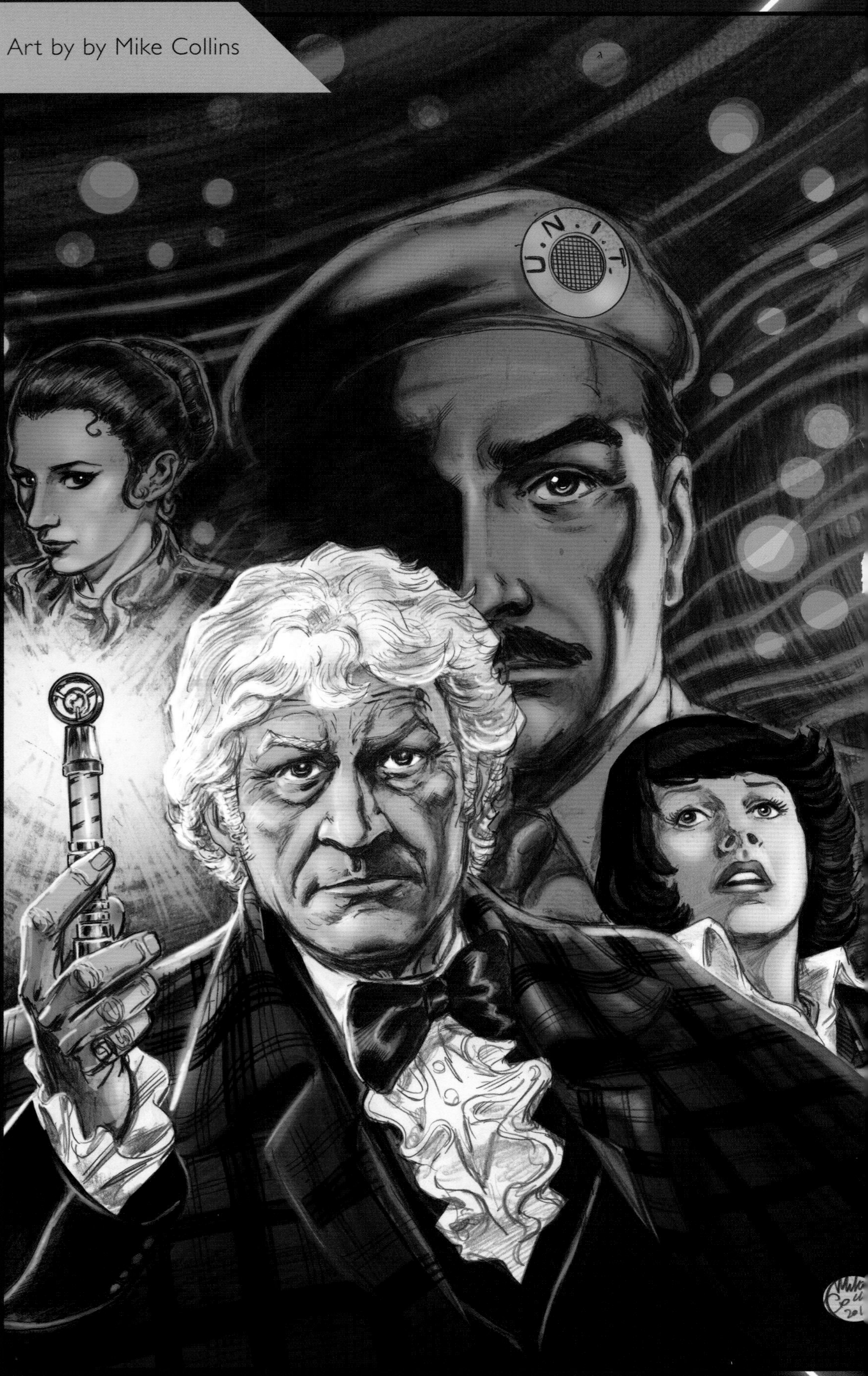
U.N.I.T.

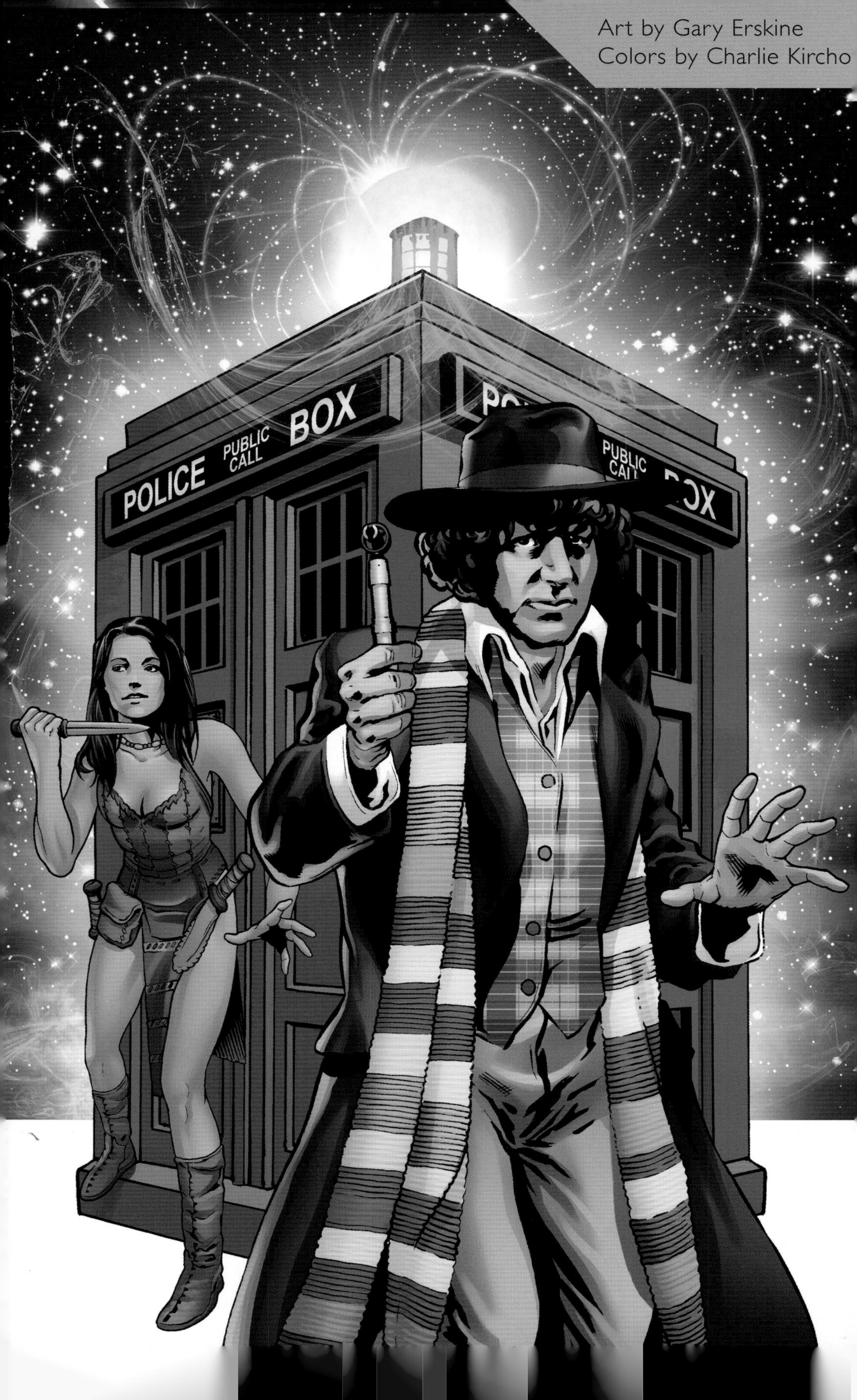
POLICE
PUBLIC CALL
BOX
PUBLIC CALL
BOX

Art by Gary Erskine
Colors by Charlie Kircho

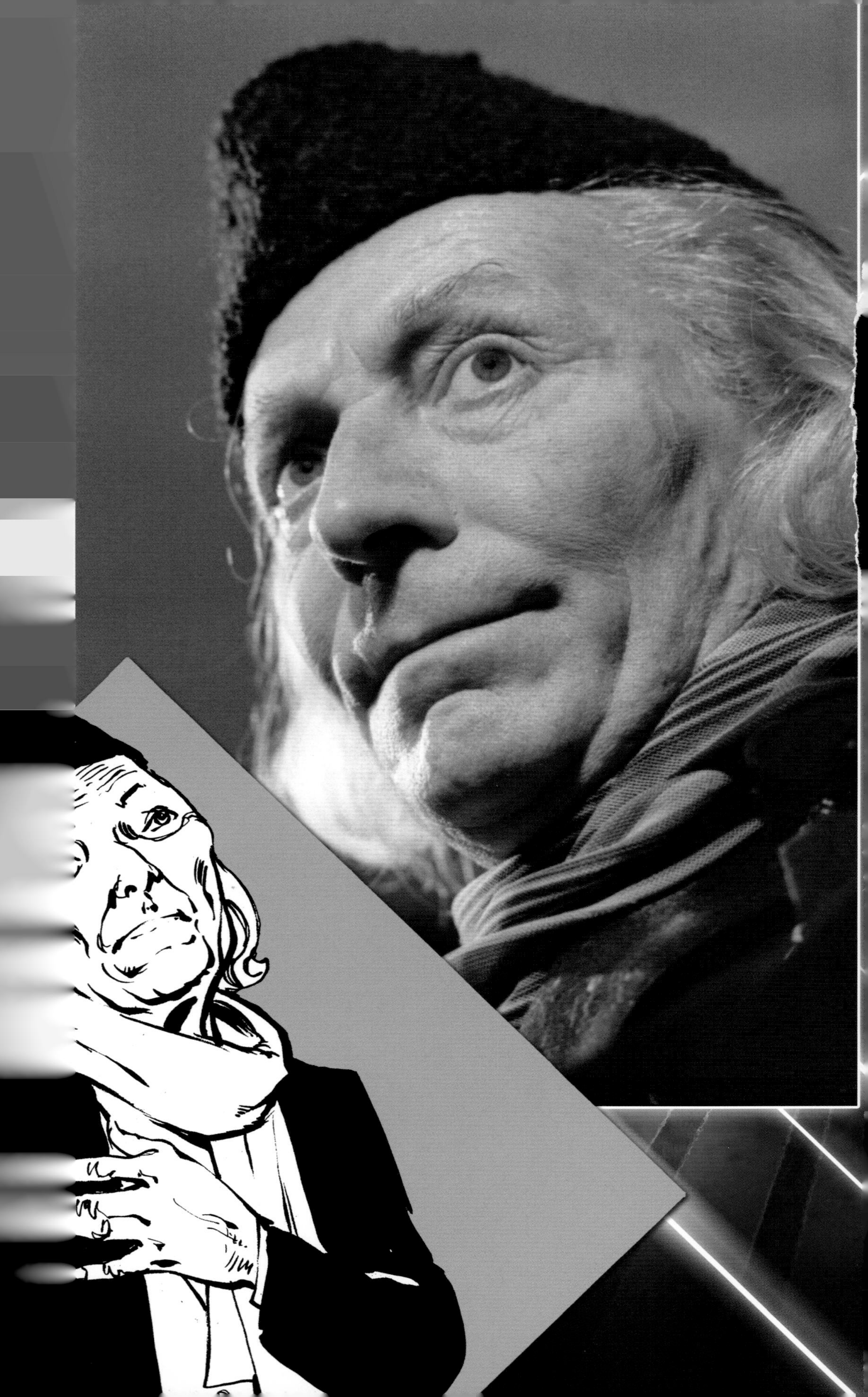

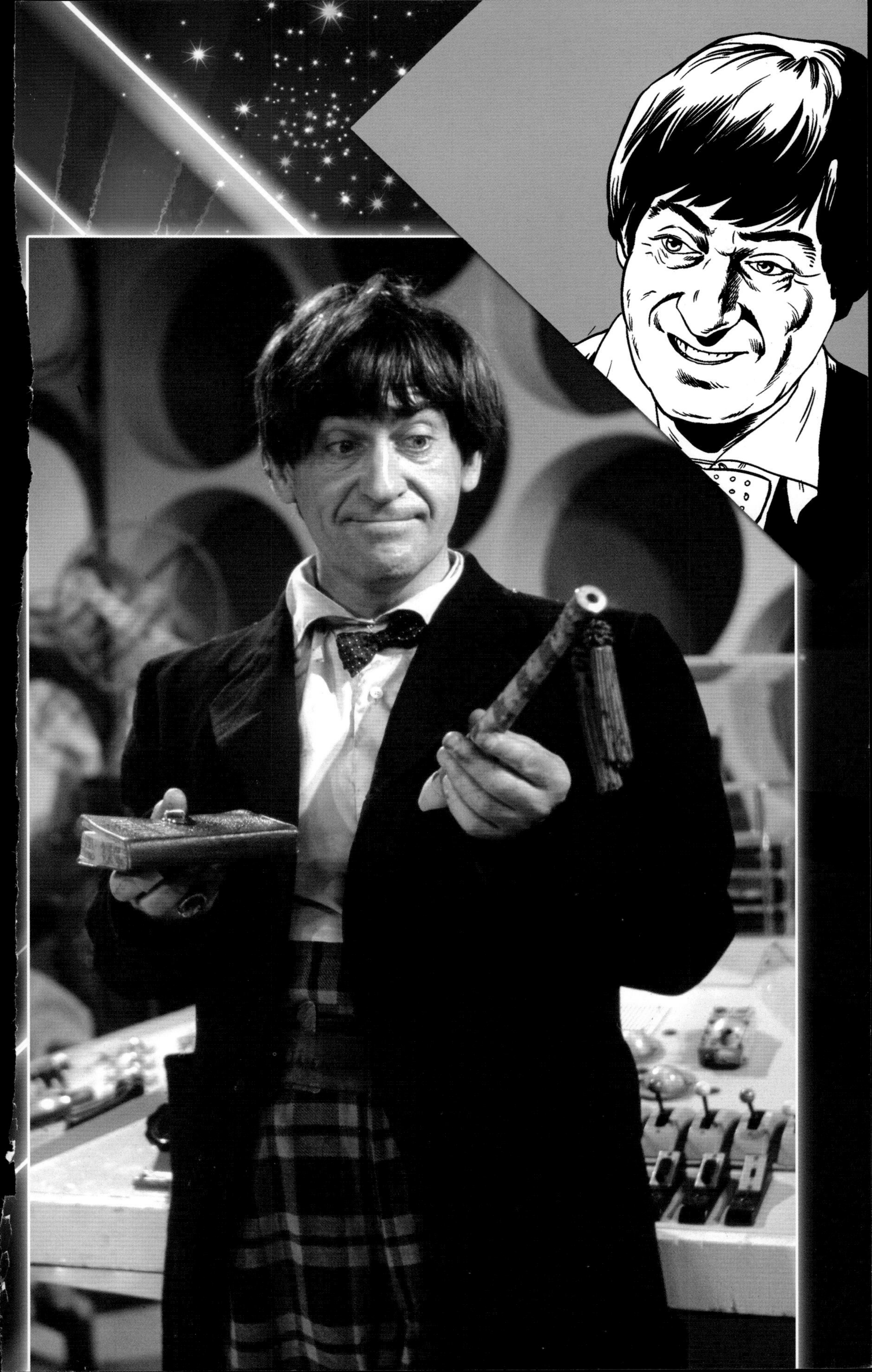

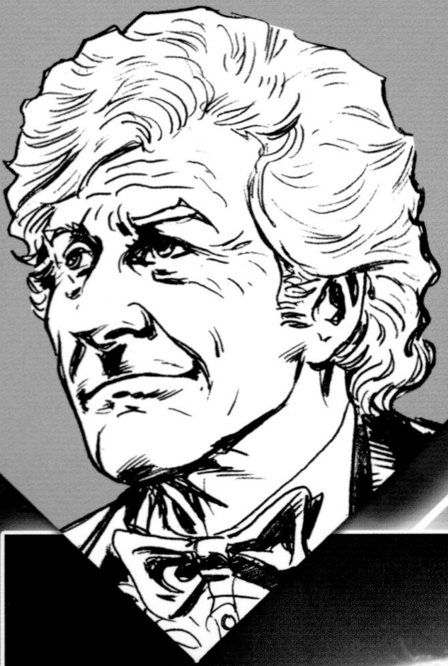

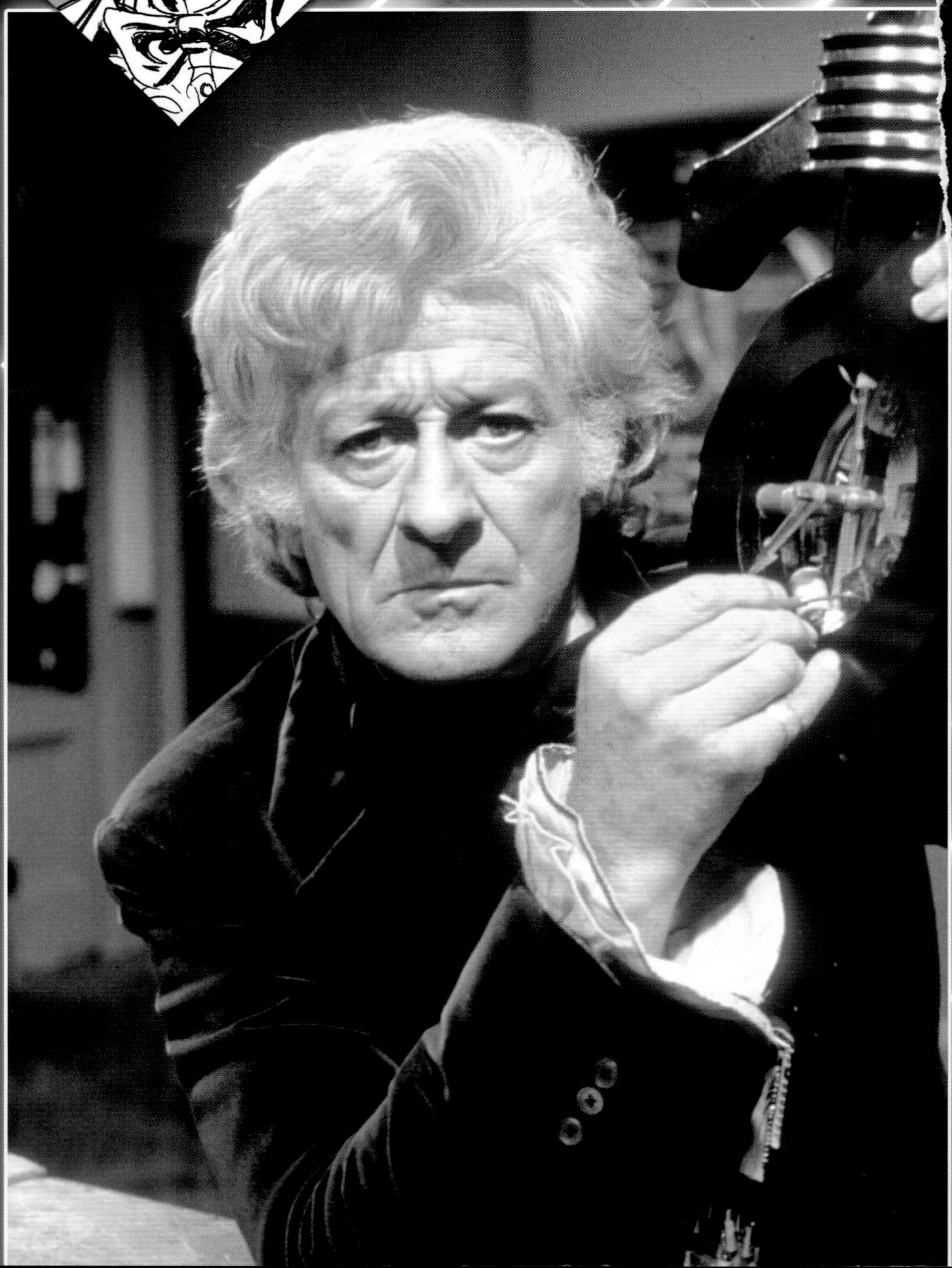

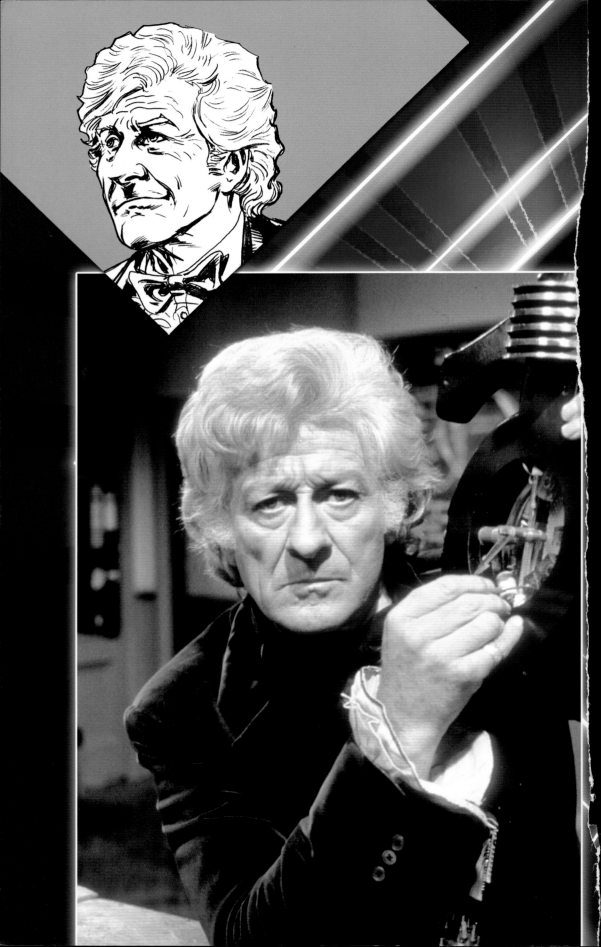

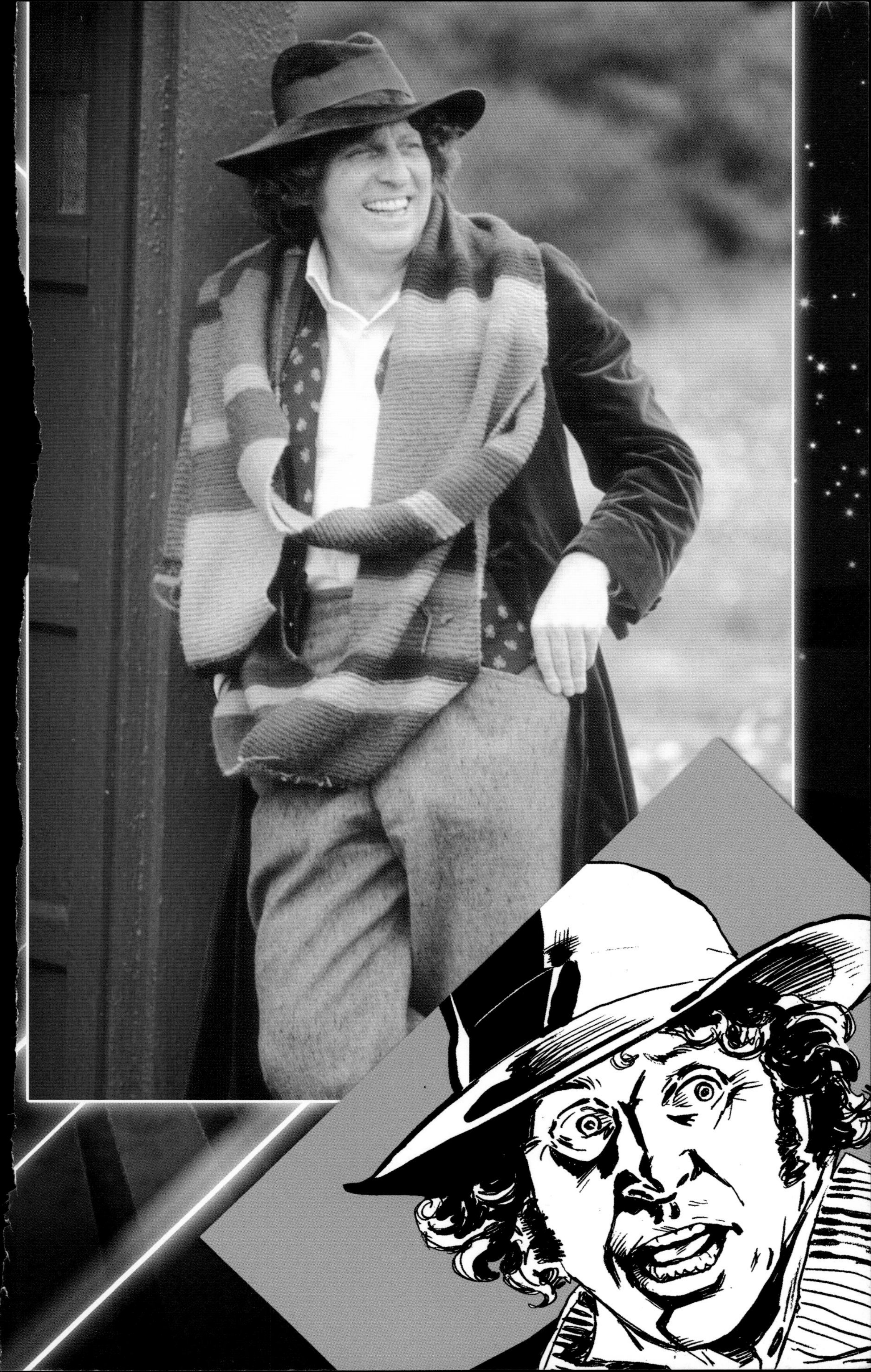

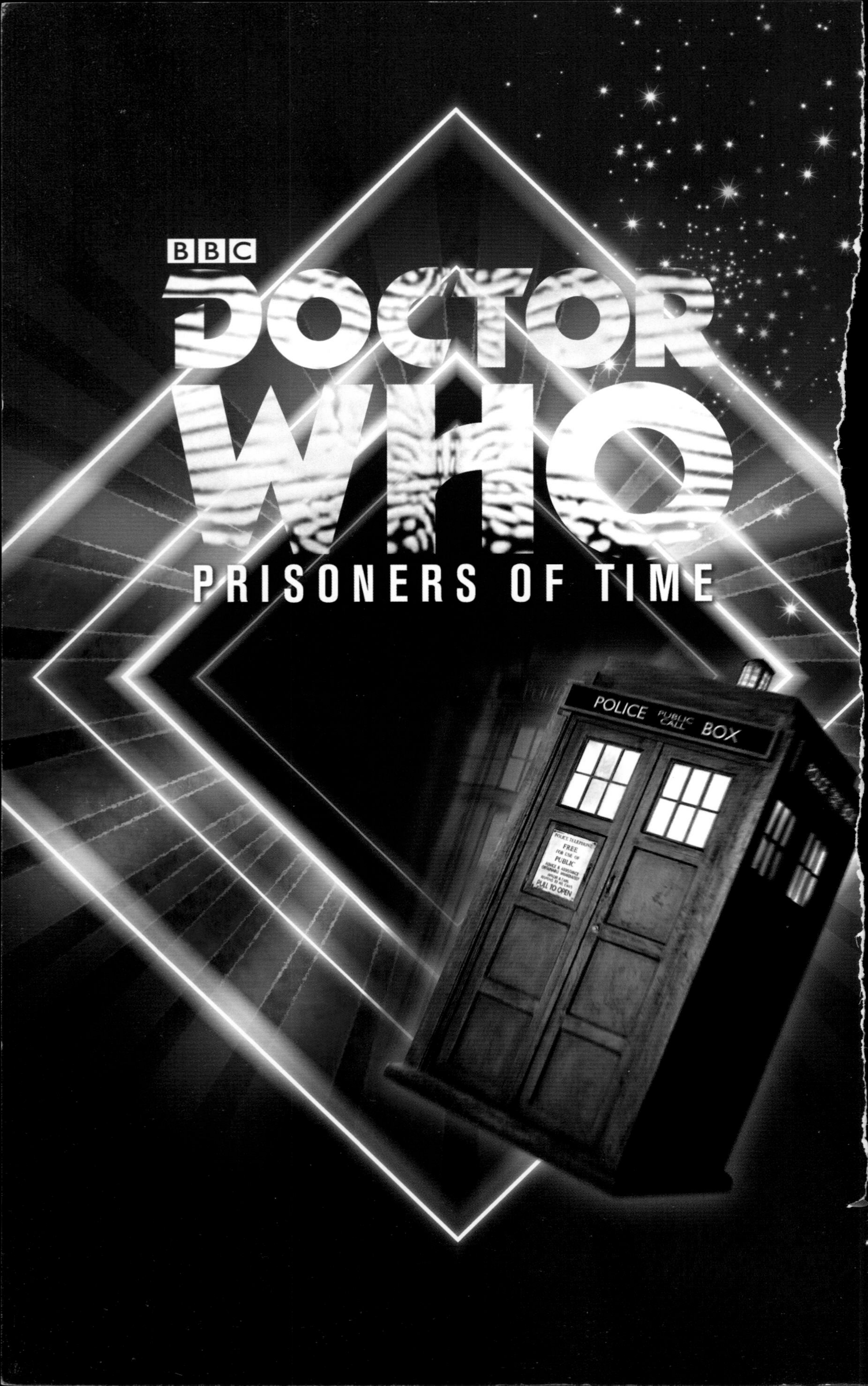
BBC
DOCTOR WHO
PRISONERS OF TIME
POLICE PUBLIC CALL BOX
PULL TO OPEN